RESEARCH GUIDE
TO AMERICAN LITERATURE

Romanticism and Transcendentalism 1820–1865

Research Guide
to American Literature

RESEARCH GUIDE
TO AMERICAN LITERATURE

Romanticism and Transcendentalism 1820–1865

Robert D. Habich
Ball State University
and
Robert C. Nowatzki
Ball State University

A BRUCCOLI CLARK LAYMAN BOOK

An imprint of Infobase Publishing

Research Guide to American Literature: Romanticism and Transcendentalism, 1820–1865
Copyright © 2010 by Robert D. Habich and Robert C. Nowatzki

Facts On File, Inc.
An imprint of Infobase Publishing
132 West 31st Street
New York NY 10001

Library of Congress Cataloging-in-Publication Data
Research guide to American literature. — New ed.
    p. cm.
"A Bruccoli Clark Layman book."
Includes bibliographical references and index.
ISBN 978-0-8160-7861-5 (v. 1 : acid-free paper)—ISBN 978-0-8160-7862-2 (v. 2 : acid-free paper)—ISBN 978-0-8160-7863-9 (v. 3 : acid-free paper)—ISBN 978-0-8160-7864-6 (v. 4 : acid-free paper)—ISBN 978-0-8160-7865-3 (v. 5 : acid-free paper)—ISBN 978-0-8160-7866-0 (v. 6 : acid-free paper)—ISBN 978-0-8160-7867-7 (v. 7 : acid-free paper) 1. American literature—Research—Methodology—Handbooks, manuals, etc. 2. American literature—History and criticism. 3. Canon (Literature) I. Franklin, Benjamin, 1939– II. Vietto, Angela III. Habich, Robert D., 1951– IV. Quirk, Tom, 1946– V. Scharnhorst, Gary. VI. Anderson, George Parker, 1957– VII. Cusatis, John. VIII. Moser, Linda Trinh, 1964– IX. West, Kathryn, 1962– X. Facts on File, Inc.
PS51.R47 2010
810.7'2—dc22

                                2009047815

Text design by Erika K. Arroyo
Composition by Bruccoli Clark Layman
Cover printed by Art Print, Taylor, PA
Book printed and bound by Maple Press, York, PA
Date printed: March 2010
Printed in the United States of America
10 9 8 7 6 5 4 3 2 1
This book is printed on acid-free paper.

Contents

Acknowledgments

The authors would like to thank Andrea Powell Wolfe for her thorough work as a research assistant and Brenda Yates Habich and Lauren Onkey for their patience, support, and advice.

Series Introduction

Research Guide to American Literature is a series of handbooks for students and teachers that recommends strategies for studying literary topics and frequently taught literary works and authors. The rationale for the series is that successful study is predicated on asking the right questions and then devising a logical strategy for addressing them. The process of responsible literary investigation begins with facts and usually ends with opinions. The value of those opinions depends on the ability of the reader to gather useful information, to consider it in context, to interpret it logically, and finally to decide what the interpretation means outside the confines of the literary work. Often the answers to questions a sophisticated reader asks about a literary topic are subjective, involving a reader's perception of an author's or a character's motive; always the search for the answer to a meaningful question involves a process of self-education and, in the best of circumstances, self-awareness.

RGAL is intended as a resource to assist readers in identifying questions to ask about literature. The seven volumes in this series are organized chronologically, corresponding to generally accepted literary periods. Each volume follows this general pattern:

Part I provides the social and historical context for a literary period, explaining its historical boundaries, describing the nature of the literary output of the time, placing the literature in its social and historical contexts, identifying literary influences, and tracing the evolution of critical approaches.

Part II comprises ten study guides on general themes or topics related to the period, organized alphabetically. Each guide first provides necessary background information, then suggests questions or research topics that might be fruitfully considered, with specific primary and secondary works that students will find useful. Each guide also includes an annotated checklist of recommended secondary works and capsule identifications of people mentioned.

Part III comprises some thirty study guides for particular literary works or authors, organized alphabetically by the author's name. Each guide begins with a brief overview of the author's career to provide context, and then suggests some half a dozen topics for discussion and research, with advice about how to begin investigating the topic. These topics are meant to facilitate classroom discussion as well as to suggest interesting ideas for research papers. Each guide includes an annotated checklist of recommended secondary works.

Part IV is an annotated general bibliography recommending the most useful general works of literary history, literary criticism, and literary reference pertinent to the period.

Part V is a glossary of terms used in the volume.

A keyword index is included in each volume.

The purpose of *RGAL* is not to tell students what literature means but to help them determine the meaning for themselves by asking significant questions and seeking answers diligently and thoughtfully. That is how learning that matters takes place. The method is as old as Socrates.

—*Richard Layman*

Part I
Overview

Boundaries of the Period

Walt Whitman, whose epic "Song of Myself" is arguably the quintessential Romantic text, wrote a brief poem in 1867 that begins, "One's-Self I sing—a simple, separate Person; / Yet utter the word Democratic, the word En-masse." A triumph of compression, repetition, and alliteration, the couplet celebrates the power of art to reconcile opposites: the self and the group, poetic singing and prosaic utterance, simplicity and separation expressed in the vernacular along with the foreign-sounding compound "en-masse." In its structure and its themes "One's-Self I Sing" is an inscription not just for Whitman's poems but for the Romantic movement itself, which was less a collection of ideas or positions than an attempt to dramatize and reconcile competing claims of the individual and the social world.

While few literary periods have definite beginnings and ends, Romanticism in America is usually defined as the era following the War of 1812 (1812–1815) and through the Civil War (1861–1865). Both conflicts had long-term consequences beyond the military ones. The reopening of sea routes after the War of 1812 thrust the United States into a world economy and created a global market for Southern cotton that ensured the continued vitality of the plantation system and the slave population required to serve it. Economic interdependence subjected the United States to boom-and-bust cycles that resulted in major financial crises roughly every two decades for the rest of the century (1819, 1837, 1857, 1873, and 1893). The victory over the British gave new impetus to expressions of American nationalism, reflected in expansionist policies and in renewed efforts to create a distinct national literature separate from the artistic traditions of Europe. Further, the economic split between Southern agriculture and Northern manufacturing contributed to a growing sectionalism that would eventuate in the Civil War. In many ways the presidency of Andrew Jackson from 1829 to 1837, often called "The Era of the Common Man," typified the disruptions and contradictions of the Romantic era. While Jackson stood for individual liberty and popular democracy, his presidency also saw the Indian Removal Act of 1830, the growth of slavery and unregulated industrial exploitation, a rise in nativism and anti-Catholic sentiment, the disastrous economic Panic of 1837, and the continued disenfranchisement of African Americans, immigrants, American Indians, women, and the poor. For many Americans the Jackson presidency legitimized a distrust of government and of social authority in general.

Individualism and antiauthoritarianism became defining motifs for writers and thinkers of the Romantic period, but so did communalism, respect for institutions (certainly among those who tried to improve them), economic prosperity, and social progress. Romantic thinkers and writers embraced both radical individualism and a total commitment to social reform, religious freethinking and the most conventional pieties, artistic experiment and self-conscious imitation. Ambivalence characterized Romantic attitudes toward nature—on the one hand a source of spiritual renewal, on the other the raw material of industrialization—and toward national expansionist policy, at once an expression of freedom and opportunity and an excuse for rapacious land-grabs. Native Americans were seen as "noble savages" but scorned as impediments to civilization. Literary nationalism was either a sign that "poetry will revive and lead in a new age," as Ralph Waldo Emerson put it in 1837 in his "American Scholar" address, or "the gross paradox of liking a stupid book the better, because, sure enough, its stupidity is American," as Edgar Allan Poe put it a year earlier, in a scathing review of the contemporary poet Joseph Rodman Drake.

It is often held that the American Civil War rang the death knell for Romanticism—variously because the Northern victory signaled a moral victory for anti-slavery reformers, or because the Southern defeat ended a culture of chivalry, or because the assassination of Abraham Lincoln destroyed Romantic optimism. All three explanations are oversimplifications; indeed, some historians have argued that the war represented the fruition of Romantic idealism, not its final unraveling. Literary movements do not begin on a military timetable, of course, or end with the cessation of hostilities. However, the ramp-up for the war effort created a lasting infrastructure of manufacturing, communication, and transportation that forever changed the agrarian character of the nation, and the triumph of union over secession forced Americans to change the way they conceived of their nationality. The Civil War undeniably redirected national and political priorities and prompted a new emphasis on social and economic realities that occupied writers after the war far more deeply than before it.

MOVEMENTS

Romanticism was not exclusively American, nor did it originate in the middle of the nineteenth century. In fact, the term "romance" dates to the 1300s, when it denoted both the vernacular of French as opposed to Latin and the verse narratives of chivalry, adventure, and legend written in the language of "the people" rather than the Church. (The medieval emphasis on adventure, exoticism, and love endures today in the modern "romance novel.") Romanticism had many literary influences, discussed elsewhere in this volume. Its European roots were in German and especially English literature, formulated by such poets as William Wordsworth and Samuel Taylor Coleridge, who promoted the transforming power of nature and the nobility of the individual. Its political background may be traced to the eighteenth-century republican revolutions in America and France that lasted well into the nineteenth century in France, Germany, and Italy. In art, philosophy, music, and architecture, Romanticism was a worldwide phenomenon in the nineteenth century.

One factor that separated American Romanticism from the global movement was the expectation—often self-promoted—of American exceptionalism. According to this theory, the United States during the Romantic era occupied a unique historical moment. In the formulation of R. W. B. Lewis in *The American Adam* (1955), the mythic personality to emerge from the still-new nation was an Adamic figure prior to the Fall, "standing alone, self-reliant and self-propelling, ready to confront whatever awaited him with the aid of his own unique and inherent resources." The challenges to this national narrative are many, from its gender specificity and Judeo-Christian imagery to its valorization of separation and defiance as the essential American values. Yet, it is hard not to see the expression of that personality in James Fenimore Cooper's Leather-Stocking, Herman Melville's Ahab, and Nathaniel Hawthorne's Hester Prynne, while at the same time recognizing that each of these quintessentially Romantic characters was destined for tragedy. The Romantic temper struggled to reconcile faith in the individual with the legitimacy of outside authority.

Such contradictions were in fact a hallmark of a transitional age still working out the promise of the American Revolution. "Do I contradict myself?" Whitman's narrator famously asks in "Song of Myself." "Very well then I contradict myself, / (I am large, I contain multitudes.)" The largeness of Romantic multitudes cautions against assuming too easily a simple or consistent set of themes or positions. It is more productive to see the Romantic writers and thinkers asking questions such as these:

What is the proper relation of the individual to the social and natural worlds?
How can we know that relationship with some degree of confidence?
To what extent does the world represent some larger scheme of things?

These ontological, epistemological, and theological questions animated a varied group of literary artists who—with true Romantic individualism—did not agree on the answers.

Transcendentalism was an extreme expression of Romanticism. As discussed at greater length elsewhere in this volume, though the Transcendentalists generally accepted such Romantic ideas as the divinity of the individual and of nature and the primacy of intuition over logic and observation, adherence to any dogmatic "ism" is fundamentally inimical to the premise of "transcending" the boundaries of received wisdom or conventional truth. In their work the Transcendentalists tended to blur the distinctions between literary and other intellectual activities; though Emerson reserves the highest praise for the poet, for instance, he conflates the roles of "saying" and "seeing," the artist and the visionary, the poet and the priest. Perhaps because many of the male Transcendentalists were trained as ministers, Transcendentalism framed Romantic questions in religious or at least spiritual ways. But the traditional view of the group as impractical dreamers is belied by their courageous activism in religious and social reform, particularly in their critique of conventional religion and their participation in the anti-slavery, educational reform, and women's movements. Like other Romantics, the Transcendentalists felt profoundly the disruptions and contradictions of their world. Economic turmoil and commercialism raised questions about their vocation for Emerson, Henry David Thoreau, and Margaret Fuller. Expanding roles for women challenged their expectations about family, marriage, child rearing, and education. The ironies and excesses of Jacksonian democracy prompted them to reconsider the value of "common-ness" in a society that permitted slavery, the decimation of Native American tribes, and the legal and social restriction of women.

Dominant Genres and Literary Forms

The lyric poem, long associated with musicality, emotionalism, and personal expression, is the signature literary genre of western Romanticism. That said, the American Romantic era saw the rise of other genres prompted by the conditions of literary professionalism, increased readership and availability of print materials, and the evolution of critical opinion.

Among the most significant developments in long narratives was the distinction between the novel and the romance. Despite popular demand for entertaining stories, proscriptions against novel reading persisted in the nineteenth century (as they did, even more successfully, against attending plays). Reading fiction was thought to be a waste of time and a distraction from moral pursuits, and even such important Romantic writers as Emerson took little pleasure in reading novels. As a result, Romantic fiction writers thought especially carefully about their craft. Hawthorne called the romance the place "where the Actual and the Imaginary may meet" and expanded on the distinction in his preface to *The House of the Seven Gables* (1851). Generally, the novel was associated with verisimilitude, middle-class values, and social issues, while the romance was marked by mystery, extremism in emotions and plot, intrusions of the supernatural, nature as a powerful and sympathetic force, and hyperbolic characters. But works as different as Susan Warner's *The Wide, Wide World* (1851), Melville's *Moby-Dick* (1851), and Harriet Beecher Stowe's *Uncle Tom's Cabin* (1852) reveal the difficulty of separating the two forms, for all three show romanticized protagonists operating in very real social and commercial contexts. Also notable is the popularity of novels of seduction and crime. As David S. Reynolds has shown, Romantic artists routinely borrowed and transformed the themes of these subgenres. Integral to the Romantic movement were less canonized writers, such as George Lippard, whose best-selling *The Quaker City; or, the Monks of Monk-Hall: A Romance of Philadelphia Life, Mystery, and Crime* (1845) was a sensationalist treatment of a real case of seduction and murder, or Maria Susanna Cummins, whose novel *The Lamplighter* (1854) told the story of a young girl's triumph over the brutality of city life.

Related closely to the growth of the romance was the increasing popularity of the tale and the short story, whose proliferation can be attributed at least in part to commercial demand by magazines and newspapers. (Though the terms "sketch," "tale," and "short story" were often used interchangeably, they are not identical. The sketch is usually brief and descriptive, focused more on scene and event than on character; the tale derived from an oral tradition that emphasized narration and plot; the short story tended to develop one or two characters, usually at a single climactic event in their lives.) Many scholars trace the development of the nineteenth-century short story to Washington Irving, whose *Sketch Book of Geoffrey Crayon, Gent.* (1820) included such famous tales as "The Legend of Sleepy Hollow" and "Rip Van Winkle." Edgar Allan Poe is notable for his carefully constructed tales; other particularly successful practitioners during the Romantic era were Hawthorne, Melville, Stowe, Rebecca Harding Davis, and the Southwestern humorists, all discussed elsewhere in this volume.

The anthologist movement, the expansion of the literary marketplace during the Romantic era, and the lingering belief that literature must be "delightful instruction" resulted in an increased appreciation for moral and didactic poetry. The Fireside Poets enjoyed great popularity, as did regional poets such as Connecticut's Lydia Huntley Sigourney, known as the "Sweet Singer of Hartford," and the sisters Alice and Phoebe Cary of Cincinnati. Often sentimental, moralistic, and ideologically conservative, such poetry provides a valuable window into the emotional lives of women at a time when other outlets were closed to them.

Perhaps the most striking new literary genre of the period was the slave narrative, which numbered dozens of full-length titles and hundreds of brief narratives printed in magazines and newspapers, often sponsored by antislavery societies. Firmly political in their purpose but written with the appeal of sentimental novels, adventure stories, and tales of seduction, slave narratives reached artistic peaks with the work of Frederick Douglass and Harriet Jacobs.

THE LEGACY OF ROMANTICISM

One value in reading Romantic writers today is to see the similarities between their world and ours. The Romantics struggled to accommodate the demands of a multicultural and globalized society, to figure out new ways to make a living and communicate with each other, and to balance the preservation of a threatened environment with the demands of an industrial economy. Another reason to read the Romantics is to find comfort and inspiration in their responses to such challenges—hyperbole, boldness, innovation, and principle. While some sought moral and artistic certainties, ambivalence and disruption did not make Romantics timid. The defining Romantic stance was what Thoreau calls at the end of *Walden* (1854) "extra-vagance"—the desire to write and think without boundaries. Nonconformity and individualism were courageous and dangerous intellectual positions in the Romantic era, and they remain so today.

In conventional literary history, the era following the Civil War is usually called the Age of Realism. Just as the Romantics consciously reacted against the limitations of the rationalist past, so Realism defined itself in response to Romanticism's excesses. Even when vilified, though, the Romantic writers endured, sometimes as iconic figures like Emerson or Stowe, other times as convenient reminders of a quaint if mythic past, like Cooper or the Fireside Poets. The *spirit* of Romanticism was even more robust. Realism's most accomplished scoffer, Mark Twain, called the Leather-Stocking tales "destitute of every detail that goes to the making of a work of art" because of their Romantic improbabilities. Yet, Twain himself published in 1884 a classic story of antiauthoritarianism and self-reliance, told by a young Romantic rebel named Huckleberry Finn.

Faced with a world of contradictions, Romantic writers struck out, like the sailors in *Moby-Dick*, for the "deep waters" of artistic expression. We can see their legacy in the stories of quixotic dreamers, such as F. Scott Fitzgerald's Jay Gatsby and Arthur Miller's Willy Loman, who reenact the Romantic struggle of the self against an unsympathetic society; in the unconventionalities of the Beat and confessional poets, who push the limits of poetic materials and evidence their debt to the "barbaric yawp" of Walt Whitman; and in the work of contemporary novelists from N. Scott Momaday to Sandra Cisneros to Toni Morrison, whose work redefines the heroic and the American in ethnic and racial terms. In the themes, techniques, and artistic individualism of the Romantic era lay the roots of modern American literature.

Historical and Social Context

All literary texts may be seen as productions and reflections of their social context, even when their writers deny those connections and try to produce "art for art's sake." In mid-nineteenth-century America many authors were highly conscious of their social context and wrote about their world, often in an attempt to improve it. Thus, it is important to understand what American authors responded to in their world and how they tried to intervene in it through their works.

The 1820s began with a fierce debate in Congress over the expansion of slavery into Missouri, and by extension, other new southwestern states and territories. In 1820 there were eleven Northern free states and eleven Southern states. Thus, the Senate was evenly divided between the two regions, and while the South feared a loss of power in Congress if more free states than slave states were admitted, the North feared the opposite scenario. Senator Henry Clay of Kentucky proposed a compromise that would allow Missouri into the Union with a constitution that legalized slavery, and would allow Maine to join the Union as a free state. In addition, slavery would be prohibited in all territory west of Missouri north of the 36° 30' latitude line. The so-called Missouri Compromise managed to satisfy both North and South regarding the expansion of slavery for three decades.

The 1828 election to the presidency of Andrew Jackson, who had come to national attention as a major general in the U.S. Army by defeating the British in the Battle of New Orleans during the War of 1812, signaled the rise of the "common man" in American politics. Jackson, a backwoods Democrat from Tennessee, was the first U.S. president who was not born in one of the original thirteen states, and his election made it seem possible for any white man of any social class (though not women or non-white men) to gain political power. In literature, the celebration of the "common man" surfaced in the rough-speaking rural male characters of Southwestern humor as well as Transcendentalist texts such as Ralph Waldo Emerson's "American Scholar" address (1837).

While lower-class white men benefited from Jackson's brand of democracy, American Indians did not. Jackson's military actions against the Seminoles in Florida in 1818 earned him the nickname "Indian Killer," and in 1830 he signed the Indian Removal Act, which allowed him to grant land west of the Mississippi to Indians who gave up their homelands. This much-abused legislation gave federal sanction to states who responded to their growing and westward-moving white populations by pushing native peoples out by force and treaty. In 1838 some sixteen thousand members of the Cherokee nation were forced to evacuate from their homelands in Georgia, Tennessee, Alabama, and North Carolina over the infamous Trail of Tears to Indian territory in Oklahoma, a journey that caused the deaths of more than a quarter of them. Indian removal was tied to the theme of the vanishing Indian in Catharine Maria Sedgwick's novel *Hope Leslie* (1827). This trend of enforced displacement of native people also elicited protest from the Cherokee writer Elias Boudinot in his *An Address to the Whites* (1829).

As American Indians were being pushed westward, the white population was growing. In 1820 the U.S. population stood at just under ten million, and in 1865 it was over thirty-five million. One reason for this startling increase was the huge influx of immigrants from Ireland, Germany, Scandinavia, and other European nations. These immigrants, along with the increasing number of native-born Americans, often moved to the growing cities of the eastern seaboard and the new towns further west, but many also sought land along the frontier to build homesteads. This migration is dramatized in Caroline Kirkland's novel *A New Home—Who'll Follow?* (1839). Still others sought work building railroads or looked for gold in California

Beginning in the 1840s, Manifest Destiny, the belief that it was God's will to have white Americans expand the nation to the Pacific Ocean, regardless of whether other people had claims to those lands, gained currency, both in the popular mind and in federal policy. In early 1820 there were twenty-two states admitted into the Union; by 1865 there were thirty-six. Some Americans also looked to Mexico, Canada, and Cuba for potential territorial additions to the growing nation. Manifest Destiny was endorsed by the *U.S. Magazine and Democratic Review*, edited by John L. O'Sullivan. This geographical expansion and the doctrine of Manifest Destiny played a major role in the Mexican War of 1846–1848. Formerly part of Mexico, Texas declared itself an independent republic in 1836 and was annexed as a state by the United States in 1845. Many Texans were dissatisfied with their southern boundary. The Mexican government already resented the loss of Texas and refused to give in to Texans' demands for more land. As a result of the standoff, President James K. Polk ordered an army to take the disputed territory away from Mexican control. By the fall of 1847 Mexico surrendered to American forces, and the Treaty of Guadalupe Hidalgo, signed early in the following year, granted California and New Mexico to the United States and marked the end of the war.

Polk and other Democrats were opposed by the Whigs, who did not share the strong expansionist and proslavery stances of their rivals. The abolitionist Liberty Party was formed in 1840, but it was not a significant factor in federal elections. The Free Soil Party, a coalition of abolitionists and negrophobes who opposed the extension of slavery into new territories and states, formed in 1848. The Free Soil newspaper, *The National Era*, serially published Harriet Beecher Stowe's novel *Uncle Tom's Cabin* in 1851–1852 and became a national sensation. Former members of the Whig, Liberty, and Free Soil parties formed the Republican Party in 1854. Like the Liberty Party, the Republican Party opposed the expansion of slavery and appealed to abolitionists.

While the thirteen years following the end of the Mexican War were mostly peaceful in military terms, the nation became increasingly divided during the 1850s over the issue of slavery, a split that in many ways fell along geographic lines. Most Southern political leaders supported both the continuation of slavery and its expansion into the Southwest, and many Northern leaders opposed the latter and in some cases the former. Many Southerners feared that antislavery forces in the North would eventually eradicate the institution of slavery by restricting its growth, and they saw this trend as a threat to the doctrine of state sovereignty. These bitter regional conflicts were played out in Congress and were not quelled by the four presidents who served during the 1850s, Zachary Taylor, Millard Fillmore, Franklin Pierce, and James Buchanan.

The Compromise of 1850 allowed California to enter the Union as a free state, but to placate proslavery congressmen it also brought passage of the Fugitive Slave Law. This legislation made it easier for slaveholders and slave catchers to capture runaway slaves in free states by making it illegal to harbor fugitives or to refuse to aid in capturing them. In reaction many Northerners became even more opposed to slavery than they were before, and some antislavery writers protested against it, including Henry David Thoreau in his essay "Slavery in Massachusetts" (1854) and Harriet Jacobs in her narrative *Incidents in the Life of a Slave Girl* (1861). This conflict took a violent turn in the mid 1850s during the settlement of the Kansas-Nebraska territory, where supporters of slavery and Free Soilers often fought each other in what was later described as a dress rehearsal for the Civil War. The violent decade closed with an attack on the federal arsenal at Harpers Ferry in October 1859 by a small army led by the abolitionist John Brown, who had fought with the Free Soil militia forces in "Bleeding Kansas," as the territory was called. Brown and his supporters were executed later that year. He was eulogized in Thoreau's essay "A Plea for Captain John Brown" (1860) for taking a stand against a morally corrupt government.

Abraham Lincoln became the first Republican to be elected president in 1860, an event that alarmed many Southerners. As a result, South Carolina seceded from the Union in December 1860; soon ten other Southern states followed, forming the Confederate States of America. Four other slaveholding states—Missouri, Kentucky, Maryland, and Delaware—opposed secession and remained with the Union. The attack by South Carolina's military forces on Fort Sumter on 12 April 1861 sparked the Civil War. In response to this event, Walt Whitman wrote the poem "Beat! Beat! Drums!" (1861) as a rallying cry for Union troops.

During the first year of the Civil War, Confederate forces won several decisive battles. However, the Confederacy's superiority in military leadership over the Union was eventually overcome by the North's industrial might and the Union army's advantage in the sheer number of soldiers. Many Union soldiers were newly arrived immigrants from Ireland, Germany, and Scandinavia. In July 1862, partly as a result of pressure by African American abolitionist Frederick Douglass, the first African Americans were recruited by the Union army. On 1 January 1863, Lincoln issued the Emancipation Proclamation, declaring that all slaves in the Confederate states were free. Many saw this as an attempt to weaken the Confederacy, both economically, by depriving Southern slaveholders of their property, and militarily, by adding the liberated male slaves to the Union army. Throughout the four-year war, both sides suffered unprecedented casualties, the Southern economy was ruined, and the scars left on the nation's collective psyche lingered for decades. The war inspired several literary works, including the collection of poems *In War Time* (1864) by the abolitionist John Greenleaf Whittier and *Drum-Taps* (1865) by Walt Whitman. One of the best-known Southern works from this period dealing with the war is Mary Boykin Chesnut's diary.

Union forces finally declared victory with the surrender of Confederate General Robert E. Lee on 9 April 1865. The nation had lost over six hundred thousand lives (not counting innumerable civilian deaths). The relief felt by Northerners after Lee's surrender was shattered in less than a week by the assassination of Lincoln, who was shot on April 14 and died the next morning. Whitman wrote the poem "O Captain! My Captain!" (1865) in response to this event, and his poem "When Lilacs Last in the Dooryard Bloom'd" (1865) is the most famous elegy written about Lincoln's death.

ECONOMICS, INDUSTRY, AND TECHNOLOGY

At the dawn of the nineteenth century, it was virtually unimaginable to travel overland from New York City to San Francisco. By 1870, however, it was possible to make that journey by train in a matter of days. Two developments that had a huge impact on long-distance travel during this period were the inventions of the steamboat and the locomotive. These inventions were followed by the building of canals and railroads. The digging of the Erie Canal that joined New York's Hudson River to Lake Erie between 1817 and 1825 was the largest transportation project of its time and made it possible to travel from New York into the northwestern territories. The first major railroad appeared in the late 1820s, and throughout the next four decades, the number and length of railroads grew exponentially. These changes stimulated the industrial economy by allowing goods to be shipped between the eastern seaboard and the western interior and also accelerated westward migration, resulting in the rapid growth of cities that in turn became major industrial centers.

While the economy grew quickly in terms of industrial production and transportation, the changes facing workers in many ways worsened conditions during this period. The growing power of factory owners enabled them to squeeze more work from their employees for less money, especially in places that attracted native-born migrants as well as immigrants. Many independent artisans were pushed out of work, unless they agreed to take low-paying factory jobs. Factories were unregulated by government, and many laborers worked fourteen hours per day for six days a week. Children were also exploited in the workplace. Workers were hard hit by two major economic depressions—in 1837 and in 1857. The hardships faced by industrial workers were dramatized most notably in Herman Melville's story "The Paradise of Bachelors and Tartarus of the Maids" (1855) and Rebecca Harding Davis's story "Life in the Iron Mills" (1861).

SOCIAL REFORM MOVEMENTS

A dramatic increase in social reform in American history occurred in the mid nineteenth century. Many Americans believed that it was their duty to work toward improving their society, either for their own benefit or for the welfare of others less fortunate. The most significant movements of the period were abolitionism, temperance, and the women's movement. Both abolitionism and temperance often overlapped with evangelical Protestantism, and while opponents of the women's movement often quoted scripture to defend the status quo, many early feminists argued that women needed to be given more power in order to perform their Christian duties effectively. Countless pamphlets, speeches, poems, and fictional texts emerged from the abolitionist and women's movements, and the former produced hundreds of slave narratives; readers can find more information about this literature in study guides focusing on these movements in sections II and III of this volume. Other reform movements worked toward helping the poor, improving working conditions for industrial laborers, reforming prisons and mental asylums, and improving elementary education.

Many reformers formed or joined local organizations to work toward their goals, but others felt the need to begin new communities in their search for utopia. Such intellectual communities as Robert Owen's in New Harmony, Indiana, and Brook Farm, the Transcendentalist community in Massachusetts founded by George Ripley, were secular in orientation. Nathaniel Hawthorne's novel *The Blithedale Romance* (1852) is the best-known fictional work about Brook Farm. Other communities, such as the Shaker communities and John Humphrey Noyes's perfectionist Oneida community in upstate New York, were religious in nature. Unlike other social reformers of the time, many communitarians may have been more interested in surrounding themselves with like-minded people and self-improvement than in trying to improve society at large. Both groups, however, shared a sense of idealism about the improvability of humans at the individual and societal level along with a belief that such improvement was necessary.

WRITING, PUBLISHING, AND THE LITERARY PROFESSION

The literature of mid-nineteenth-century America was shaped not only by reform movements or politics but also by the literary marketplace itself. The increasing literacy rate, combined with the concentration of the nation's population in cities and the greater potential for distributing literature across large regions, offered publishers and writers a growing market for literature. However, the lack of an international copyright law made it difficult for most writers to live off their literary work, because readers were tempted to buy the cheaper pirated works of British authors. Nevertheless, America enjoyed an unprecedented literary output during this period. The growing number of newspapers, as well as magazines such as *Putnam's* and *Harper's*, offered venues for poets and short-story writers; many novels of the time, such as Stowe's *Uncle Tom's Cabin*, were also published serially instead of or in addition to being published as bound volumes. Much of this literature advocated social reform, such as women's rights or abolition, and was published in periodicals devoted to those movements.

Literary Influences

Neither Romanticism nor Transcendentalism originated in the United States, though for a variety of reasons each movement took root in America. While most Romantic authors wrote during a period of literary nationalism, most show the influence of trends in literary, philosophical, and scientific changes that define the movement worldwide.

INTERNATIONAL INFLUENCES

Often ambivalent about their relationship to an English-language heritage, the American Romantics readily found inspiration in the literature of other European cultures, particularly Germany, which had undergone a revolution in literary taste a generation before most of the American Romantic writers were born. Chief among the German literary influences was Johann Wolfgang von Goethe, scientist, philosopher, dramatist, poet, and novelist. Ralph Waldo Emerson said of him in 1851, "Goethe is the pivotal man of the old & new times with us. He shuts up the old, he opens the new." Goethe wrote two novels that particularly influenced American writers: *The Sorrows of Young Werther* (1774; revised 1787) and *Wilhelm Meister's Apprenticeship* (1795–1796), both of which trace the journeys of young men in search of self-understanding. Goethe's writing was part of the Sturm und Drang ("storm and stress") movement in German literature, which emphasized emotionalism over rationalism, a key component of Romanticism worldwide. Also influential among German writers was Friedrich von Schiller, particularly for his drama *Wilhelm Tell* (1804), the story of the Austrian champion of individualism. The poet Samuel Taylor Coleridge and the Scottish essayist Thomas Carlyle were instrumental in translating and promoting German literature in the English-speaking world, and by the late 1830s "Germanism" reached its height in American colleges, particularly in New England. Emerson and Margaret Fuller taught themselves German to better appreciate this important literary heritage. The Romantics generally found that the German emphasis on individualism and emotionalism confirmed their own aesthetics.

Also originating in Germany was a new approach to biblical exegesis called "Higher Criticism" that had an enormous influence on the Transcendentalists. Higher Criticism opened the Bible to individual interpretation by placing its stories and doctrine in historical contexts rather than treating them as absolutes. The Higher Critics legitimized once again the personal apprehension of the divine that was a staple of Transcendentalism. Debates over the nature and historicity of the Bible reached public expression in the so-called "Transcendental Controversy" surrounding Emerson's "Divinity School Address" in 1838.

Another non-English tradition that shaped American Romanticism was literature of the Orient. By the late 1830s writers such as Henry David Thoreau found in Eastern scripture a confirmation that God and nature could be approached in mystical, nonrational ways. The Hindu holy book *The Bhagavad Gita* ("Song of God") provided Romantics with non-Western teachings leading to personal enlightenment, for example. Also influential was the medieval Persian poet Sa'adi; his lyric verse and the anecdotal, aphoristic perceptions of life in collections like the *Gulistan* (The Rose Garden, circa 1256) offered a model for the combination of poetry and philosophy.

Despite nationalistic calls for a literature independent of English traditions, the British influence on American Romantics remained strong, with contemporary English writers serving as models for American achievement. Writers such as James Fenimore Cooper and William Gilmore Simms found inspiration in the success of historical romances by the English novelist Sir Walter Scott, and Charles Dickens's celebrated reading tours of the United States in 1842 and 1867 were dramatic evidence of the new celebrity of authorship. American writers traveling abroad routinely made pilgrimages to see writers such as Carlyle, Coleridge, William Wordsworth, Alfred Lord Tennyson, and Matthew Arnold.

There was, for American poets especially, a significant awareness of contemporary or near-contemporary British counterparts. Percy Bysshe Shelley carried the social stigma of atheism and was therefore not widely admired until late in the Romantic period, but John Keats was revered for his lyricism, and his early death fit the sentimental myth of the tragic Romantic artist. But the most direct line of influence is undoubtedly the pioneering work of Coleridge and Wordsworth, in their poetry and especially in their critical manifestos. In the preface to the second edition of *Lyrical Ballads* (1800), Wordsworth laid out a new Romantic aesthetic, privileging the affective response to nature, the broadening of poetic language and subject matter, the conviction that the miraculous resides in the everyday event, and the distinction between Understanding (conscious rationality) and Reason (a higher, intuitive faculty) that undergirded the new Romantic epistemology. Coleridge in his *Biographia Literaria* (1817) transformed Romantic thinking about the province and theory of poetry. He distinguished the lower talent of *fancy* from the transforming power of *imagination*, and he separated poetry from the rational and prosaic with his requirement that readers approach it with a "willing suspension of disbelief."

NATIVE INFLUENCES

The promotion of literary nationalism that reached its peak during the Romantic era was in fact part of the worldwide phenomenon of Romanticism. In the United States, the desire for a separate but artistically equal literary accomplishment dates back at least to the 1780s, when Noah Webster wrote in his widely used *Grammatical Institute, of the English Language* (1783), "This country must in some future time, be as distinguished by the superiority of her literary improvements, as she is already by the liberality of her civil and ecclesiastical constitutions." American writers were stung by the charge of English critics like Sidney Smith, who sneered in the *Edinburgh Review* in 1820, "In the four corners of the globe, who reads an American book?" Romantics may have seen some glimmerings of hope in the accomplishments during the early national period of poets like the so-called Connecticut Wits, who strove to incorporate American settings and characters into such classical forms as the pastoral or the mock epic, or the achievements of Charles Brockden Brown, whose Gothic novels *Wieland* (1798) and *Edgar Huntly* (1799) enabled him, albeit briefly, to earn a living as a writer of fiction. Washington Irving was revered for his genteel travel sketches, and the American polemicist and poet Philip Freneau achieved some success with his political poems during the American Revolution and later with poetry that anticipated Romantic views of nature and the imagination, such as "Wild Honey Suckle" (1786) and "The Indian Burying Ground" (1788). While the American Romantics and Transcendentalists were aware of these forebears, however, they were more interested in artistic independence than in following the lead of others. Instead, they sought the subject matter, myths, geography, characters, and national traits that critics often refer to as a "usable past" for literature.

More influential than individual writers was a continuity in genres that nineteenth-century Romantics could appropriate and transform into personal statements. A rich tradition of political oratory and topical essays that defined the Revolutionary Era—Thomas Paine's pamphlet *Common Sense* (1776), for instance—created a precedent for Thoreau, who could transform his individualistic protest into a national imperative in "Resistance to Civil Government," with its revolutionary opener: "I heartily accept the motto, 'That government is best which governs least.'" The tall-tale tradition had been deeply engrained in American folk literature since the age of exploration; it would find new expression in the tales of the Southwestern Humorists and struck a chord with the Transcendentalists. (Thoreau admired the "strong and healthy but reckless, hit or miss style" of the seventeenth-century scientist and travel writer John Josselyn, who recorded such bizarre wonders as the "mere-man" spotted off the coast of Maine and the New England chimney swift, which supposedly tossed one of its chicks into settlers' fireplaces as a token of gratitude to its human hosts.) Eighteenth-century captivity narratives like the one by Mary Rowlandson in 1682, which chronicled the Christian resistance and escape of colonists captured by Native Americans, found Romantic expression in the narratives of African American slaves, which often emphasized the narrator's endurance, morality, and escape from brutal captors. And the spiritual autobiography of purification and regeneration, long a staple of New England Puritan divines, resurfaced in such Romantic explorations of the self as Thoreau's *Walden* (1854). The aesthetic movements of sentimentalism and Gothicism, discussed elsewhere in this volume, were also important contexts for Romantic writing.

HISTORICAL CONTINUITIES AND DISCONTINUITIES

Philosophically considered, Romanticism may be seen as an expression of idealism—not in the commonplace sense of optimism or hopefulness but in the philosophical reference to realities beyond the senses. Literary historians such as René Wellek see Romantic idealism as a reaction against the rationalism of the eighteenth century, known as the Age of Reason; but it is also possible to view Romanticism as a continuation of the past.

One important source of Romantic continuity was the philosophical debate between sensationalism and idealism that played out over the course of the eighteenth century and reached something of a peak during the first part of the nineteenth. While the discussion is far too complex to be easily summarized, the extreme positions can be seen in the epistemologies of John Locke and Immanuel Kant. In his *Essay Concerning Human Understanding* (1690) Locke posited that knowledge derived, with few exceptions, from our senses; that we entered the world (in his famous phrase) with a mind like a blank slate, and that our experience in the world inscribed knowledge onto us. Locke's emphasis on sensation, observation, and experience legitimized the empirical inquiry that marks the Age of Reason; but to the Romantics it seemed to restrict access to truth only to those whose broad experience allowed them to apprehend it, and limited truth only to confirmable and sensible facts. The Lockean premise that all knowledge was sensation led to the skepticism of, for instance, David Hume, who denied any confidence in such basic principles as cause and effect. An alternative psychology was proposed toward the end of the eighteenth century by Kant. While not denying the reality of sensory knowledge, in his *Critique of Pure Reason* (1781, revised 1787) Kant argued in favor of *a priori* knowledge that could be accessed intuitively; built-in concepts, or categories as Kant called them, allow us to make sense of the world we experience. In a Neo-Platonic view of the world, Kant distinguished between the matter of a thing, which we sense, and the form or essence of it, which we intuit.

For the American Romantics, Kant's metaphysics confirmed their fascination with the transforming power of the individual mind. Some were steadfast in their belief in psychological self-reliance, like Emerson, who championed introspection and intuition; others, including Edgar Allan Poe and Herman Melville, worried that a mind responsible only to itself for forming knowledge ran the risk of self-deception, solipsism, and madness. The Romantics generally were eclectic in their appropriation of philosophy, though the Transcendental group certainly were more uniform in valuing Kantian intuition. For Romantics, the debate went beyond a merely academic disagreement—it had implications for political thought, psychology, social policy, and art. Idealism legitimized a democratic access to knowledge and therefore to power, supporting the republican revolutions founded on principles of political equality and liberty. It surfaced in debates over the historicity of the Bible that resulted in the so-called Transcendental (or Miracles) Controversy of the late 1830s: the Transcendentalists, who accepted that the miraculous lay all around us, found little need to confirm the validity of Christianity with the "proof" of long-ago biblical miracles. Idealism confirmed for the Romantics that Reason (that is, intuition) was a higher faculty than Understanding (that is, sensationalism) for apprehending truth, thereby making enlightenment and emotionalism more important literary qualities than logic or education. And idealism located moral issues not in civil law or religious scripture but in the individual conscience, a key concept for Romantic writers that had profound implications for developments in religion, education, and social reform during the period.

For the Transcendentalists, rejection and appropriation of the religious past was a particularly complicated matter. They found religious relevance, certainly, in the idealistic view of intuitive access to the divine, and many Transcendentalists read Neo-Platonic philosophers for their religious implications. The mystic

Emanuel Swedenborg (1688–1772), for instance, was valued for his theory of the correspondence between the material and the spiritual worlds. In the beliefs of the American Society of Friends ("Quakers"), the Transcendentalists found the congenial idea of an "inner light" that permitted individuals to access God and morality directly. But in religious history Transcendentalism's most immediate and fruitful context lay in the development of Protestant Congregationalism into Unitarianism. Unitarianism emerged in the later eighteenth century as a liberalizing of Calvinist doctrines, and by the 1820s Unitarian thinking had become the religious preference of the educated and powerful in New England. Though the issues separating them are too complicated to summarize completely, in general Unitarians differed from their Calvinist forebears in accepting that a) human nature was not inherently sinful but held a "spark of Divinity"; b) human powers were not weakened by sin but enabled by reason; and c) God was compassionate, not vengeful, and Jesus was exemplary, not redemptive—a model and inspiration for human behavior, not the savior of it. As Unitarianism extended Calvinist doctrine, so the Transcendentalists extended Unitarian doctrine, seeing equations between the divine and the human that even liberal Unitarians found hard to accept and granting to individual intuition a kind of integrity that mainstream Unitarians thought socially dangerous and theologically heretical. Andrews Norton, a leading Unitarian polemicist, referred to Emerson's "Divinity School Address" and the arguments in support of it as irresponsible and arrogant, "the latest form of infidelity." For his part, Emerson pronounced his own denomination "corpse-cold" and overly rational. Transcendentalism may be seen as both denying its Unitarian roots and pushing Unitarian doctrines to their logical extremes.

Rejecting the strictly empiricist psychology of the Age of Reason, the Romantics also rebelled against the aesthetics of the eighteenth century and its critical standards. "True wit," the neoclassical poet Alexander Pope had written in his *Essay on Criticism* (1711), derived from "what oft was Thought, but ne'er so well Exprest." For the Romantics, concerned as they were with moving the hearts of their readers as well as their minds, literature was defined by originality of thought *and* of expression. Certainly, many of the earlier Romantics adhered in their poetry to conventions of meter and rhyme in ways that acknowledged the traditions of the century before, a tradition that continued to influence the Fireside Poets and much popular verse of the era. However, artistic experimenters like Walt Whitman and Emily Dickinson consciously flouted poetic conventions in subject matter, form, and diction. If neoclassical taste privileged education, balance, and decorum, the Romantic aesthetic encouraged inspiration, organicism, and spontaneity, while not denying the need for artistic discipline and form. In its literary precepts, as in its religious and philosophical views, Romanticism in America was both evolutionary and revolutionary.

Evolution of Critical Opinion

Although literary criticism is often seen as secondary to literature itself, this perception undervalues the importance of criticism in shaping not only the reading tastes and experiences of the reading public but also literature itself. Even when authors neglect or scorn critics and their notions of what constitutes good literature, their own literary tastes and principles are often informed by the literary theories and judgments of critics. The relationship between literature and criticism is also strengthened by the fact that many critics are also authors, as was the case with William Cullen Bryant, Margaret Fuller, Edgar Allan Poe, William Gilmore Simms, and several other American authors of this period. These author/critics exerted their influence through quarterly and monthly literary magazines and journals that emerged during the mid nineteenth century, most of which were based in Boston, New York, and Philadelphia.

In his 1961 study, *The Origins of American Critical Thought 1810–1835*, William Charvat points out that early American literary critics viewed themselves as guides who educated the masses on literary taste and protected them from immoral and poorly written texts. Charvat also observes that most critics during this time were either lawyers or clergymen; as a result, they often adopted a judicial or moralistic tone and perspective in their reviews and focused on the social aspects of literature. Furthermore, as members of the dominant social class, they were more likely to condemn any threat to existing social relations or prevailing ideologies. They shared the nation's sense of optimism and preferred literature that conveyed that attitude; in contrast, Gothic literature as well as gloomy Romantic texts were seen as a menace to the social order and found little favor among American critics. Such attitudes help to explain the critical hostility toward such radical texts as Herman Melville's *Moby-Dick* (1851). It also enables an understanding of the prevalence of didacticism (that is, moral instruction) in much American literature of this period.

American literary critics were also slow to appreciate the novel, a relatively new literary genre that was often denounced on moral grounds. In particular, they feared that novels would corrupt the virtue of young women, who made up a significant portion of the novel-reading public. In response, early American novelists often included apologetic prefaces to their work and tried to defuse charges of immorality by explicitly promoting virtue in their works, as can be seen in two of the earliest American novels, Susanna Haswell Rowson's *Charlotte: A Tale of Truth* (1794; republished as *Charlotte Temple*) and Hannah Webster Foster's *The Coquette; or, The History of Eliza Wharton* (1797), both cautionary tales about "fallen women." Although such moralistic novels continued to appear well into the mid nineteenth century, critics often ignored novels altogether, resulting in a dearth of criticism about the genre during the early nineteenth century. However, the decline of Puritanical prejudice against novels among critics, combined with the gravitation of many of the nation's most talented authors toward long fiction, led to more positive critical attitudes toward the genre.

American literary criticism was shaped not only by the conservative social attitudes of the nation's intelligensia but also by its British counterpart. In particular, Charvat demonstrates, it often followed the lead of Scottish "common sense" rhetoric and philosophy that emerged during the late eighteenth century, which was central to American college education. These philosophers argued that external objects exist and can be directly perceived by human minds, and they rejected philosophical idealism's claim that no world exists outside of human consciousness. American literary critics influenced by this philosophy preferred literary texts that could be understood by common people, not just theorists, and favored simplicity, plausibility, and intelligibility over obscurity, supernaturalism, and mysticism. Such beliefs were well suited to a proudly democratic nation. In another sense, however, these principles were conservative in that they discouraged innovation and rejected Romantic literature that celebrated the uniqueness of the individual, focused on the obscure and improbable, and questioned Christian dogma, though increasingly critics made exceptions for William Wordsworth and Samuel Taylor Coleridge.

American literary criticism's debt to Scottish rhetoricians and philosophers was paralleled by the imitation of British and European literature by early American authors. Despite their emulation of Scottish criticism, many American critics during the years following the War of 1812 pushed authors to reject British models and be more original and "American." While the United States defeated Britain in its war for independence and established a democratic government during the 1780s, American authors struggled to create a distinctive national literature for several decades afterward. This disjunction between America's political independence from British rule and its authors' imitation of British literature was discussed by Ralph Waldo Emerson in his famous 1837 address to the Phi Beta Kappa society at Harvard College (later titled "The American Scholar"): "Our day of dependence, our long apprenticeship to the learning of other lands, draws to a close." Seven years later, in his essay "The Poet," Emerson admitted, "We have yet had no genius in America, with tyrannous eye, which knew the value of our incomparable materials." Emerson was not alone in his desire for a uniquely American literary tradition or his frustration with its absence; we can also see these ideas expressed in the essays of Melville, Fuller, and Theodore Parker. These attitudes were linked to literary nationalism, one of the most dominant trends in American literary criticism of this period. Literary nationalism may be defined as any celebration of the literature of one's nation (particularly by celebrating its difference from the literature of other nations) or the deliberate creation of a uniquely national literature. American literary nationalism was often defensive in tone, and its proponents were often anxious to disprove the claims by British critics that American literature was both thin and derivative. The American literature produced during this period contradicted such judgments, but there was not always a clear consensus about what separated this national literature from its British ancestors and contemporaries. American literature was heavily influenced by such European genres and movements as Romanticism, Gothicism, the Enlightenment, sentimental novels, and domestic fiction. While American authors incorporated new themes into their texts, it was up to critics to argue how these elements set American literature apart from the works of British and European authors. The desires of literary nationalists were eventually fulfilled by the outpouring of literature in the United States during this period, which later critics termed the American Renaissance. Inspired by the popularity of the Scottish author Sir Walter Scott, many American novelists such as Lydia Maria Child, Catharine Maria Sedgwick, James Fenimore Cooper, and Simms adopted the European genre of the historical romance as a vehicle for literary nationalism by romanticizing both European settlers and the Native Americans they encountered, or by dramatizing the heroic exploits of rebels fighting the British army during the Revolutionary War.

Several American critics joined Emerson in promoting the development of such a national literature. One such critic was Margaret Fuller, who discusses this issue in her 1846 essay "American Literature: Its Position in the Present Time, and Prospects for the Future." Like Emerson, she laments the lack of originality in American literature: "Books which imitate or represent the thoughts and life of Europe do not constitute an American literature. Before such can exist, an original idea must animate this nation and fresh currents of life must call into life fresh thoughts along its shores." The essay reprints a review of Henry Wadsworth Longfellow's 1845 volume *Poems*, which denounces the poems' derivative nature. Fuller's warning against such imitation in American literature echoes the language and sentiments of Emerson's "The Poet":

> What suits Great Britain ... does not suit a mixed race, continually enriched with new blood from other stocks the most unlike that of our first descent, with ample field and verge enough to range in and leave every impulse free, and abundant opportunity to develop a genius, wide and full as our rivers, flowery, luxuriant and impassioned as our vast prairies, rooted in strength as the rocks on which the Puritan fathers landed.

Fuller sees hope in America's ethnic diversity as the foundation for the future development of the nation's literary genius.

One author whose critical reception was largely shaped by literary nationalism is Nathaniel Hawthorne. "Hawthorne and His Mosses," Melville's 1850 review of Hawthorne's *Mosses from an Old Manse* (1846), is one of the best-known expressions of literary nationalism. Melville rejects the notion that Shakespeare is "unapproachable," and declares, "Shakespeares are this day being born on the banks of the Ohio." Although Melville admits that American literature has not yet equaled its English counterpart, he urges American authors to be original rather than imitate the English classics, even if such original works are inferior to those classics. Melville also advises future American writers to transcend their nationality: "it is not meant that all American writers should studiously cleave to nationality in their writings; only this, no American writer should write like an Englishman, or a Frenchman; let him write like a man, for then he will be sure to write like an American." A more famous critic of the day, Edgar Allan Poe, shared none of Melville's literary nationalism, but praised Hawthorne's tales for other reasons, especially their "unity of effect," or their ability to stimulate the reader's soul in a work that can be read in one sitting.

While both Melville and Poe commended Hawthorne's tales, these works were praised for other reasons, and critical acclaim for his fiction offers a glimpse into the prevailing and shifting notions of literary taste at the time. Jane Tompkins has examined Hawthorne's critical reception from the 1830s into the late twentieth century, and points out that critics during Hawthorne's time were less interested in what are now seen as his best short stories such as "Young Goodman Brown" and "The Minister's Black Veil" and instead preferred his lighter sketches such as "Little Annie's Ramble," which they praised for "the transparency of his style." The interest in Hawthorne's symbolic complexity and moral ambiguity was largely absent in his early critical reception. Tompkins also observes that these early works featured domestic settings and were rather typical of stories found in gift books and popular magazines such as *Godey's Lady's Book* and the *Southern Literary Messenger.*

Hawthorne's early sketches may be read as domestic fiction, one of the most popular literary genres of the day. Domestic fiction was sentimental and moralistic, often depicted young women facing and overcoming obstacles, and was written primarily for young female readers. Many authors of such fiction were women, and their popularity led Hawthorne to complain about the "damn'd mob of scribbling women" whose works outsold his own. One of the most popular novels of the period, Susan Warner's *The Wide, Wide World*, exemplifies this genre, and the most famous novel of the period, Harriet Beecher Stowe's *Uncle Tom's Cabin*, often relied on its conventions. Later generations of critics often rejected the heavy-handed didacticism of domestic fiction and preferred the complexities of *The Scarlet Letter* (1850) and *Moby-Dick*, but during the mid nineteenth century critics did not look down upon didacticism; in fact, they often praised literature that explicitly encouraged readers to live good, Christian lives.

Not all American critics valued didacticism in literature, however. One of the best-known and notorious literary critics, Poe, avoided didacticism in his creative work altogether, and denounced the "heresy of Didacticism" in his lecture "The Poetic Principle" (posthumously published in 1850) and in several reviews. For instance, in a review of a volume of poetry by his literary foe Longfellow, published in *Graham's Magazine* in 1842, Poe condemns didacticism: "that this mode of procedure will find stern defenders should never excite surprise, so long as the world is full to overflowing with cant and conventicles. There are men who will scramble on all fours through the muddiest sloughs of vice to pick up a single apple of virtue."

Poe argued that the worth of a text could be found not in truth but in beauty. In this lecture and in his famous essay "The Philosophy of Composition" (1846), he argues that the most important element of a poem is its aesthetic value, which Poe defines as the effect it produces for the reader. He then contends that the most poetical effect is beauty and that the most poetical tone is melancholy. From these statements he concludes that the most poetical subject is the death of a beautiful woman who is mourned by her lover. Indeed, that is the theme in many of Poe's poems as well as short stories, and while his conclusion seems morbid to many readers today, it was not far removed from the melancholy strains of Romanticism that prevailed in American literature as well as the fascination with death that permeated much of American society in Poe's day. Poe also argues that because a poem's effect was of prime importance, it should be short enough to be read in one sitting in order to produce the most powerful effect. Poe repeated this assertion more forcefully in his lecture "The Poetic Principle" and also applied it to fiction. Indeed, all of his poems and most of his fictional works can be read in one sitting, and his emphasis on brevity in this essay, along with the dozens of short stories he wrote, aided the development of the short story as a distinctive literary genre at the time.

Aside from his general judgments about literature and his development of the short story, Poe also influenced American literary taste through his reviews of specific works. Poe's voice as a critic was engaging and dogmatic, and he enjoyed mocking movements such as Transcendentalism, which he satirized in "How to Write a Blackwood Article" (1850). Additionally, Poe refused to praise second-rate works by American authors simply because of their nationality, and in an 1841 review for *Graham's Magazine*, he condemned the practice of "puffery" among American critics who lauded inferior American works. In his 1842 review of *Twice-Told Tales* for *Graham's Magazine* that helped Hawthorne establish his literary reputation, he laments: "With rare exception ... we have had no American tales of high merit. We have had no skilful compositions—nothing which could bear examination as works of art. Of twattle called tale-writing we have had, perhaps, more than enough." However, Poe praised Hawthorne's fiction as one of those rare exceptions, and declared, "As Americans, we feel proud of the book."

Despite his critical prowess, Poe was out of step with American critics' celebration of a distinctly American literature. Although American literary criticism was originally derived from Scottish common-sense philosophy, American critics were crucial in promoting the development of a uniquely American literary tradition, and their accomplishments should not be underestimated.

While later generations of critics were also interested in the evolution of a distinctly American literature, other interests shaped their analysis of this literary period. For instance, around 1920, Melville's fiction, which had fallen into neglect during his lifetime, began to attract the attention of scholars who were fascinated with his psychological insights and literary experimentation, which resembled much of the literature produced by modernist authors during the early twentieth century. The next generation of critics, led by F. O. Matthiessen, defined mid-nineteenth-century American literature as the American Renaissance and gave special attention to Hawthorne, Melville, Emerson, Thoreau, Whitman, and to a lesser extent Poe. Around this time, New Criticism, a critical movement interested in symbolism, irony, ambiguity, and complexity in literature, devoted much attention to the works Hawthorne and Melville.

Beginning in the 1960s, many scholars of mid-nineteenth-century American literature believed that the previous generation had focused too narrowly on a handful of authors and masterpieces, and they became interested in the works of female, African American, and Native American authors whose works had often been neglected and devalued. Critics like Tompkins began to examine *Uncle Tom's Cabin* and other domestic fiction by women authors and argued for their significance, while scholars such as Henry Louis Gates Jr., William L. Andrews, and Jean Fagan Yellin recovered many texts by African American authors that had fallen into oblivion, and argued that the importance of slave narratives and other works by non-white authors were central to the American Renaissance. The efforts of these critics has revealed that mid-nineteenth-century American literature is much more diverse than previous critics have acknowledged.

Part II
Study Guides
on General Topics

Antebellum African American Novelists

The turbulent decade of the 1850s witnessed the birth of African American fiction. This emergence was largely an outgrowth of the abolitionist movement and the popularity of slave narratives. Like slave narratives, the first novels written by African Americans depicted the horrors of slavery and the humanity and courage of its victims. These authors were inspired by the success of Harriet Beecher Stowe's antislavery best seller *Uncle Tom's Cabin*. This essay provides an overview of four African American novels written during the 1850s and 1860s. Other fictional works by African Americans during this period include Frederick Douglass's novella *The Heroic Slave* (1853), serialized in his newspaper *The North Star* and published in Julia Griffiths's *Autographs for Freedom;* Hannah Crafts's unpublished novel *The Bondwoman's Narrative* (circa 1857); Frances Ellen Watkins Harper's short story "The Two Offers" (1859); and Julia C. Collins's unfinished novel *The Curse of Caste; or the Slave Bride* (1865), serialized in *The Christian Recorder.*

William Wells Brown was born a slave in Kentucky in 1815 and was later sold to a slave trader in Missouri who made him help prepare slaves for market. He escaped in 1834 at age nineteen and later became active in the antislavery and temperance movements. Brown was perhaps the most prolific African American writer of his time—in addition to his 1847 narrative, he wrote two plays, three historical works, a travel narrative, and an autobiography; he also compiled *The Antislavery Harp* (1848), an anthology of abolitionist literature.

Brown's novel *Clotel; or, The President's Daughter* (1853), first published in London, was the first novel written by an African American. Brown's subtitle refers to the rumors regarding Thomas Jefferson's affair with his slave Sally Hemings, which resulted in a number of children. The novel suggests the nation's hypocrisy in condoning the enslavement of the descendants of one of its founding fathers. Brown shortened the novel for its publication in 1864 in abolitionist James Redpath's Campfire Series, which was sold to Union soldiers; it bore the title *Clotel: A Tale of the Southern States.* The American version removed any reference to Jefferson's biracial progeny, which was probably too controversial for an American audience.

The title character is a beautiful, virtuous biracial woman whose love for a white man leads to disaster because of the ban on interracial marriage. In this respect, Clotel is an example of the "tragic mulatta" stock character that often appears in literature dealing with miscegenation and slavery. Like many authors who portrayed this character, Brown may have used Clotel's light skin and beauty to appeal to white readers. *Clotel* also uses another staple of abolitionist literature, the auction scene in which slave families are separated. Clotel's white lover Horatio Green betrays her by marrying a white woman after Clotel gives birth to Horatio's child. While she later gets away by dressing as a white man, she is eventually arrested; and when her escape attempt fails, she commits suicide. Other characters are more fortunate—her daughter Mary escapes to Canada with a light-skinned slave named George (similar to George Harris in *Uncle Tom's*

Cabin), and her sister Althesa marries a white man despite the ban on interracial marriage.

Relatively little is known about Frank J. Webb. Several scholars believe that he was born in Philadelphia in 1828. In 1845 he married his wife Mary, who earned fame for her dramatic readings of Shakespeare and the works of other major poets. They visited London in 1856, where they were introduced to aristocratic abolitionists like the Duchess of Sutherland and the Earl of Shaftsbury. The Webbs moved to Jamaica in 1858 after Mary became ill. She died there within months and Webb eventually remarried. In 1869 he moved to Washington, D.C., where he contributed frequently to *The New Era: A Colored American National Journal*. Webb relocated to Galveston, Texas, by 1872, and he died there in 1894.

The Garies and Their Friends (1857) was published in London during the Webbs' sojourn there. Set in Philadelphia, *The Garies* is the first novel to provide an extended description of the lives of Northern urban blacks. Unlike most literary works by African Americans of the time, Webb's novel focuses more on Northern racism than slavery, and its description of a white mob's attack on the interracial Garie family makes it the first novel to depict a race riot in the North. These facts, along with the novel's unapologetic presentation of miscegenation and passing, may have contributed to the book's cool reception among Northern whites. On the other hand, the novel's focus on the black Ellis family and the interracial Garie family placed its characters in familiar domestic settings that encouraged white readers to identify with them.

Harriet E. Wilson's *Our Nig; or, Sketches from the Life of a Free Black, in a Two-Story White House, North* (1859) is the first novel by an African American to be published in the United States. It is also regarded by some scholars as the first novel written by an African American woman, although William Andrews and Mitch Kachun argue that it is an autobiography rather than a novel and that Julia Collins's novel *The Curse of Caste* (which they edited and published as a book) deserves this distinction. *Our Nig* was ignored by critics when it was published and languished in obscurity until it was rediscovered by Henry Louis Gates Jr. in 1982. Its author was born in Milford, New Hampshire, in 1825 to a black father, Joshua Green, and an Irish mother, Margaret Adams. Shortly after her father's death, the six-year-old Harriet was abandoned by her mother at the home of Nehemiah Hayward Jr. in Milford. Like Frado, the protagonist of *Our Nig*, Wilson was an indentured servant in the Hayward home and regularly suffered physical and emotional abuse. In 1851 Harriet married Thomas Wilson, who fraudulently claimed to be a fugitive slave. Wilson abandoned her and subsequently died, and in 1859 Wilson moved to Boston to look for work to support herself and her son. There she wrote her only novel, *Our Nig*, which was published by George C. Rand and Avery, a local printing shop. Wilson paid for its publication in an attempt to raise money from its sales and gain sympathy from its readers. Unfortunately, the novel failed in both respects, and her seven-year-old son George died the following year. In 1867 Wilson became involved in the Spiritualist movement, in which she worked as a lecturer for three decades. She died in Quincy, Massachusetts, in 1900.

Our Nig differs from abolitionist literature because it focuses on forced servitude in the North rather than Southern slavery, and its damning depictions of Northern racism and indentured servitude held little appeal to white Northerners. The novel was also controversial because it portrays the interracial marriage between Frado's parents without condemning or justifying it.

Martin Delany is considered to be one of America's first black nationalists. His commitment to racial uplift and his tireless energy led him into various careers in literature, journalism, medicine, exploration, government, real estate, and the military. He was born in Charles Town, Virginia, in 1912 and moved with his family to Pennsylvania ten years later. He began co-editing Frederick Douglass's newspaper *The North Star* in 1847, but Delany resigned because Douglass found him to be too radical on the slavery issue. His anger regarding American racism led him to advocate black emigration, most notably in his 1852 book *The Condition, Elevation, Emigration, and Destiny of the Colored People of the United States.* He later moved with his family to Ontario, Canada, and in 1859 he traveled to Liberia and other parts of West Africa in an attempt to buy land for African American settlement. During this time, an incomplete version of his novel *Blake* was published serially in the *Anglo-African Magazine;* a more complete version appeared in the same periodical (then named the *Weekly Anglo-African*) in 1861–1862, though the final chapters were not published. During the Civil War, Delany recruited black soldiers in the Union army and became the first black commissioned major in U.S. history. After the war, he worked for the Freedman's Bureau and made an unsuccessful bid for the lieutenant governorship of South Carolina. He died in Xenia, Ohio, in 1885.

Delany's criticism of Stowe's emphasis on black passivity in *Uncle Tom's Cabin* was one factor that led him to write *Blake*, his only literary work. Its protagonist, Henrico Blacus (a.k.a. Henry Blake), is a Cuban who sails to the United States, is enslaved there, escapes to Canada, and returns to the American South to look for his wife. During his search he visits various slave communities and tries to incite a nationwide slave revolt. He later finds his wife in Cuba and joins an insurrectionary group that is planning a transnational slave revolution. The novel is unusual for its time in its advocacy of black nationalism—an issue discussed by Katy Chiles—and its argument that eradicating slavery may require violence. One potential topic for research would be later black nationalist movements and their connections to Delany's writings. *Blake* is also significant for its attacks on Christianity, its realistic depictions of the living conditions of American slaves, and its transnational focus.

TOPICS FOR DISCUSSION AND RESEARCH

1. Consider how Brown and Wilson use the "tragic mulatta" character in their novels. In each text, what seems to be the author's purpose in depicting this character? How does this character allow the author to comment on racial categorization or on the connections between slavery and miscegenation? Several scholars, including M. Giulia Fabi, Angelyn Mitchell, and Eve Allegra Raimon, have discussed Brown's and Wilson's deployment and revision of

the "tragic mulatta" stereotype in Brown's depictions of black women in *Clotel*. Alternately, either novel could be compared to similar characters in Stowe's *Uncle Tom's Cabin* or Jacobs's *Incidents in the Life of a Slave Girl*. Another approach would be to compare the "tragic mulatto" Clarence Garie Jr. in *The Garies and Their Friends* to his female counterparts in Brown's and Wilson's novels.

2. Consider how black mothers are portrayed in these novels. Anna Mae Duane's essay is helpful in understanding Webb's depictions of black mothers. To what extent do these black maternal characters conform to dominant ideologies about femininity and maternity at the time? To what extent do they fail to meet these expectations or offer alternative models of maternity? It might be useful to compare these black maternal characters to black or white mothers in *Incidents in the Life of a Slave Girl*, *Uncle Tom's Cabin*, or Sojourner Truth's "Ar'n't I a Woman?" speech.

3. Both *Our Nig* and *The Garies* differ from most abolitionist and African American literature of the time in focusing on Northern racism rather than Southern racism or slavery. Consider how *Our Nig* exposes Northern prejudice while addressing a Northern white audience. Alternatively, compare this theme in either text to Frederick Douglass's descriptions of his experiences in the North in the second half of his narrative *My Bondage and My Freedom*, or to antislavery novels such as *Uncle Tom's Cabin* that locate racism primarily in the South.

4. Although many African American writers and abolitionists traveled abroad during the nineteenth century, Martin Delany was one of the first to imagine a transnational black identity. Both Katy Chiles and Jeffory Clymer analyze Delany's transnational vision. Compare his novel *Blake* work with later African American authors and activists like Richard Wright, Paul Robeson, and Marcus Garvey, who shared Delany's international perspective.

5. Think about how any of these novels use a variety of genres or blend genre categories. In particular, to what extent do they resemble slave narratives, domestic fiction, autobiography, Gothic fiction, or antislavery speeches and pamphlets? In each essay, what seems to be the author's intention in borrowing from these genres? Julia Stern's essay "Excavating Genre in *Our Nig*" offers a useful analysis of Wilson's mixture of various genres, and some of her insights might be applied to the other three novels discussed in this study guide.

RESOURCES

Primary Works

William Wells Brown, *Clotel; or, The President's Daughter: A Narrative of Slave Life in the United States. With a Sketch of the Author's Life* (London: Partridge & Oakey, 1853).

Martin Delany, *Blake; or the Huts of America, Anglo-African,* January–July 1859; *Weekly Anglo-African,* 23 November 1861–April 1862.

Frank J. Webb, *The Garies and Their Friends* (London: Routledge, 1857).

Harriet E. Wilson, *Our Nig; or, Sketches from the Life of a Free Black, in a Two-Story White House, North. Showing that Slavery's Shadows Fall Even There. By "Our Nig"* (Boston: George C. Rand & Avery, 1859).

Criticism

Katy Chiles, "Within and without Raced Nations: Intratextuality, Martin Delany, and *Blake; or the Huts of America*," *American Literature: A Journal of Literary History, Criticism, and Bibliography*, 80 (2008): 323–352.
Explores the relationship between Delany's serialized novel and other texts printed in those periodicals, and connects that relationship to the novel's stance toward black nationalism and transnationalism.

Jeffory A. Clymer, "Martin Delany's *Blake* and the Transnational Politics of Property," *American Literary History*, 15 (2003): 709–731.
Examines how Delany connects America's political and economic structure to ideas about property and international commerce in *Blake*.

Anna Mae Duane, "Remaking Black Motherhood in Frank J. Webb's *The Garies and Their Friends*," *African American Review*, 38 (2004): 201–212.
Examines Webb's positive depictions of black maternal empowerment and black domesticity.

R. J. Ellis, "Body Politics and the Body Politic in William Wells Brown's *Clotel* and Harriet Wilson's *Our Nig*," in *Soft Canons: American Women Writers and Masculine Tradition*, edited by Karen L. Kilcup (Iowa City: University of Iowa Press, 1999), pp. 99–122.
Analyzes and contrasts the writing styles of Brown's and Wilson's novels in depicting slavery and racial injustice.

M. Giulia Fabi, "The 'Unguarded Expressions of the Feelings of the Negroes': Gender, Slave Resistance, and William Wells Brown's Revisions of *Clotel*," *African American Review*, 27 (1993): 639–654.
Examines Brown's depictions of black resistance to slavery and racism such as passing, trickery, theft, and rebellion.

Henry Golemba, "Frank Webb's *The Garies and Their Friends* Contextualized within African American Slave Narratives," in *Lives Out of Letters: Essays on American Literary Biography and Documentation*, edited by Robert D. Habich (Madison, N.J.: Fairleigh Dickinson University Press, 2004), pp. 114–142.
Analyzes Webb's novel in connection to the novels of Brown, Delany, and Wilson and slave narratives by focusing on the author's persona, the author's sponsor, the audience, the literary marketplace, racial identity, and the cultural context.

Angelyn Mitchell, "Her Side of His Story: A Feminist Analysis of Two Nineteenth-Century Antebellum Novels—William Wells Brown's *Clotel* and Harriet E. Wilson's *Our Nig*," *American Literary Realism*, 24 (1992): 7–21.
Contrasts the two novels in their depictions of black women.

Eve Allegra Raimon, *The 'Tragic Mulatta' Revisited: Race and Nationalism in Nineteenth-Century Antislavery Fiction* (New Brunswick, N.J.: Rutgers University Press, 2004).
Includes a chapter on Brown's *Clotel* and another on Wilson's *Our Nig* that analyze each text's revision of the "tragic mulatta" convention.

Julia Stern, "Excavating Genre in *Our Nig*," *American Literature: A Journal of Literary History, Criticism, and Bibliography*, 67 (1995): 439–466.
Analyzes Wilson's mixture of Gothic elements with features of sentimental domestic fiction, slave narratives, and captivity narratives.

PEOPLE OF INTEREST

Frederick Douglass (1818–1895)
Probably the most prominent black man of the nineteenth century. Born a slave, Douglass first published his autobiography in 1845 and wrote prolifically the rest of his life, both in books and in the black-advocate periodicals he edited from 1847–1874, including *The North Star, Frederick Douglass' Paper*, and the *New National Era*. He was appointed consul to Haiti in 1889.

Frances Ellen Watkins Harper (1825–1911)
Author of poetry, short stories and four didactic novels, including *Minnie's Sacrifice, Sowing and Reaping, Trial and Triumph*, serialized in the *Christian Recorder* beginning in 1869, and *Iola Leroy; or, Shadows Uplifted* (1892).

Harriet Beecher Stowe (1811–1896)
The best known of the distinguished New England Beecher family, she wrote the sentimental antislavery novel *Uncle Tom's Cabin*, the best-selling novel of the nineteenth century.

The Birth of American Feminism

Aside from the antislavery movement, perhaps the most significant social activism in nineteenth-century America occurred within the women's movement. Many of America's earliest women's-rights activists, such as Lydia Maria Child, Lucretia Mott, and Elizabeth Cady Stanton, first became radicalized by the antislavery movement, one of the first social movements that accepted women as activists. By getting outside the domestic sphere and working for abolition, many American women realized the power of organization to transform society. Many also were drawn to abolitionism because they compared their own oppression to slavery. These parallels were especially clear to black women such as Sojourner Truth, an ex-slave turned abolitionist, feminist, and evangelist; her speech "Ar'n't I a Woman?" at the 1851 women's-rights meeting in Akron, Ohio, revealed how sexism combined with racism and slavery.

Historians of the American women's movement trace its beginning to the women's-rights convention in Seneca Falls, New York, in July 1848. This convention, led by Stanton and Mott, issued a Declaration of Sentiments that was modeled on the Declaration of Independence. The convention's philosophy and goals were influenced by Enlightenment thought, specifically John Locke's concept of "natural rights." The Declaration of Sentiments listed the many injustices suffered by women and their lack of political, economic, and educational rights and opportunities. Although the convention was organized and led by women, men attended, including abolitionist Frederick Douglass, and signed the declaration. Not surprisingly, it was widely criticized as a threat to the status quo of gender relations and roles.

The ideological context surrounding the American women's movement included two overlapping concepts that permeated American culture: the notion of "separate spheres" and what historian Barbara Welter has termed the "Cult of True Womanhood." Many Americans believed that there were two separate spheres appropriate for women and men—the woman's sphere was domestic, while the man's sphere was public. Women were expected to stay home, bear and raise children, and keep the house in order, while men were expected to be breadwinners in the workplace. Although many women were forced by economic necessity to go outside their sphere to find work to supplement their husbands' income, these realities did not alter the notion that women belonged at home. The Cult of True Womanhood was a set of ideologies that also defined "true" women as domestic, but also as pious, sexually pure, and submissive to men—to their fathers before marriage and to their husbands after. They were expected to be moral guides to their children, and while they could have a positive moral influence on their husbands, they could not refuse to obey them.

Compared to twenty-first-century feminism, the beliefs of some early women's-rights activists seem conservative and uncontroversial. While Margaret Fuller argued in *Woman in the Nineteenth Century* (1845) that "there is no wholly masculine man, no purely feminine woman," others, like Catharine Beecher, accepted the notion of separate spheres and merely wanted the two spheres to be considered on an equal level. Others, like Susan B. Anthony, were committed to the temperance movement, which they felt would help women who were abused by their alcoholic husbands. Unlike later feminists, most members of this first generation of feminists did not advocate abortion rights, fight for access to birth control, or accept lesbianism. Most of them were devoutly religious, though they rejected biblical sexism and argued that God created man and woman as equals. This first wave of American feminism was more concerned about domestic abuse, unequal pay for men and women, women's lack of property rights, educational opportunities, divorce rights, and voting rights. Many members of this movement were disappointed by the Fifteenth Amendment to the Constitution, which lifted racial barriers for voting but continued to exclude women from the polls. This fractured the coalition between the women's movement and the abolitionist movement, and some white feminists turned away from the fight for racial civil rights. Women were not given the right to vote until fifty years later, when the Nineteenth Amendment passed in 1920; this event signaled the end to the first wave of the American women's movement.

The women's movement encouraged many American women to enter the literary realm, and much of the best polemical and imaginative literature was from those who wrote about their experiences in a patriarchal society as well as other important issues. Although her novel *Uncle Tom's Cabin* is an abolitionist novel, Harriet Beecher Stowe emphasized the importance of the feminized domestic sphere as a site of resistance to slavery. The novel's phenomenal success, along with the popularity of Susan Warner's 1850 novel, *The Wide, Wide World*, and the works of Fanny Fern, encouraged other aspiring female writers. Although her novel *Hope Leslie* (1827) was written before the women's movement began, Catharine Maria Sedgwick's young female characters served as role models to her female readers. A later novelist, E. D. E. N. Southworth, also went against conventional gender notions with her young heroine Capitola Black in the 1859 novel *The Hidden Hand*. The extraordinary imagination and intellect manifested in the writings of Margaret Fuller and Emily Dickinson put to rest any notion of women's intellectual inferiority. The letters of Sarah and Angelina Grimké, daughters of a South Carolina slaveholder who became abolitionists, examined how the intersections of patriarchy and slavery denigrated both black women and white women. Sojourner Truth, despite her illiteracy, showed her cleverness and strong will in advocating women's rights as well as abolition, and the intersecting oppressions endured by enslaved women were eloquently expressed in Harriet Wilson's *Our Nig* (1859), Harriet Jacobs's *Incidents in the Life of a Slave Girl* (1861), and the works of Frances Ellen Watkins Harper. One of the most powerful depictions of industrial exploitation during this period is Rebecca Harding Davis's "Life in the Iron Mills" (1861).

TOPICS FOR DISCUSSION AND RESEARCH

1. Stanton, Anthony, Truth, the Grimké sisters, and other leaders of the early American women's movement hoped to improve conditions for women not only of their own time but also of future generations. To what extent do you think they succeeded? Consider the ways in which twentieth- and twenty-

first-century American society has been influenced by the women's movement and nineteenth-century women's literature.

2. Compare nineteenth-century literature written by women to literature written by their male contemporaries. Are the texts produced by each distinctive in terms of style or subject matter, or are they mostly similar? One pair of texts that might be interesting to compare are two slave narratives, Harriet Jacobs's *Incidents in the Life of a Slave Girl* and Frederick Douglass's *A Narrative of the Life of Frederick Douglass, an American Slave* (1845). Those who wish to learn more about sentimental literature (much of which was written by women) might consult Jane Tompkins's *Sensational Designs* and Shirley Samuels's *The Culture of Sentiment*.

3. To what extent are the issues raised by nineteenth-century American women writers specific to their time period? One might begin by examining primary texts such as Margaret Fuller's *Woman in the Nineteenth Century*, Truth's "Ain't I a Woman?" speech, or Sarah Grimké's *Letters on the Equality of the Sexes and the Condition of Women* (1838). Some helpful biographical and historical studies of the issues raised by women's rights advocates include Ellen Carol DuBois's *Feminism and Suffrage* and Judith Wellman's *The Road to Seneca Falls*.

4. As stated above, the American women's movement was in many ways born in the antislavery movement. Consider the similarities and differences between the two movements in terms of their beliefs, their rhetoric, their strategies, and the problems they addressed. DuBois's *Feminism and Suffrage* and Lawrence J. Friedman's *Gregarious Saints* are two useful starting points for research on these two movements. Jean Fagan Yellin and John C. Van Horne's *The Abolitionist Sisterhood* is a good source for those interested in the role of women in the American abolitionist movement.

5. To what extent did the early women's movement in America address the issues of race and slavery? What roles did African American women such as Sojourner Truth and Harriet Jacobs play in the movement, and what impact did they have? Students may wish to consult biographies of these two black feminists; see Nell Irvin Painter's *Sojourner Truth* and Yellin's *Harriet Jacobs: A Life*.

RESOURCES

Primary Works

Larry Ceplair, ed., *The Public Years of Sarah and Angelina Grimké: Selected Writings, 1835–1839* (New York: Columbia University Press, 1989).

A collection of documents by the sisters relating to women's rights and abolitionism.

Ellen Carol DuBois and Richard Cándida Smith, eds., *Elizabeth Cady Stanton, Feminist as Thinker: A Reader in Documents and Essays* (New York: New York University Press, 2007).

Contains eight recent essays about Stanton and several of her speeches, articles, and essays.

Biography

Pamela R. Durso, *The Power of Woman: The Life and Writings of Sarah Moore Grimké* (Macon, Ga.: Mercer University Press, 2003).
A biography of the elder Grimké sister that examines her feminist and antislavery writings.

Grace Farrell, "Beneath the Suffrage Narrative," *Canadian Review of American Studies/Revue Canadienne d'Études Américaines*, 36 (2006): 45–65.
Explains the role of feminist activist Lillie Devereux Blake in the American women's movement and her exclusion from feminist historiography in Susan B. Anthony's *History of Woman Suffrage*.

Elisabeth Griffith, *In Her Own Right: The Life of Elizabeth Cady Stanton* (New York: Oxford University Press, 1985).
The definitive Stanton biography.

Gerda Lerner, *The Grimké Sisters From South Carolina: Pioneers for Women's Rights and Abolition* (Chapel Hill: University of North Carolina Press, 2004).
A comprehensive biography of the Grimkés.

Nell Irvin Painter, "Difference, Slavery, and Memory: Sojourner Truth in Feminist Abolitionism," in *The Abolitionist Sisterhood: Women's Political Culture in Antebellum America*, edited by Jean Fagan Yellin and John C. Van Horne (Ithaca, N.Y.: Cornell University Press, 1994), pp. 139–158.
Examines Truth's relationship to the women's rights and abolitionist movements and the construction of her persona.

Painter, *Sojourner Truth: A Life, A Symbol* (New York: Norton, 1996).
The authoritative Truth biography.

Criticism

Naomi Greyser, "Affective Geographies: Sojourner Truth's *Narrative*, Feminism, and the Ethical Bind of Sentimentalism," *American Literature: A Journal of Literary History, Criticism, and Bibliography*, 79 (June 2007): 275–305.
Discusses Truth's ethical uses of sentimentalism and analyzes how it rhetorically confined her.

Mary Loeffelholz, "Posing the Woman Citizen: The Contradictions of Stanton's Feminism," *Genders*, 7 (March 1990): 87–98.
Examines Stanton's arguments for married women's property rights without denying their bodily nature in an 1860 speech.

Alison Piepmeier, "'As Strong as Any Man': Sojourner Truth's Tall Tale Embodiment," in *Women as Sites of Culture: Women's Roles in Cultural Formation from the Renaissance to the Twentieth Century*, edited by Susan Shifrin (Aldershot, U.K.: Ashgate, 2002), pp. 25–36.
Argues that Truth borrowed from the tall-tale genre to define herself as a female hero.

History

Ellen Carol DuBois, *Feminism and Suffrage: The Emergence of an Independent Women's Movement in America, 1848–1869* (Ithaca, N.Y.: Cornell University Press, 1999).
A history of the American women's movement from the Seneca Falls Convention to the passage of the Fifteenth Amendment.

Judith Wellman, *The Road to Seneca Falls: Elizabeth Cady Stanton and the First Woman's Rights Convention* (Urbana: University of Illinois Press, 2004).
A historical account of the birth of the American women's movement with an emphasis on Stanton.

Jean Fagan Yellin, *Women and Sisters: The Antislavery Feminists in American Culture* (New Haven, Conn.: Yale University Press, 1989).
Studies the intersections of gender, class, and racial ideologies in the activism of antislavery feminists.

PEOPLE OF INTEREST

Susan B. Anthony (1820–1906)
American abolitionist and leader in the women's movement who was best known for her advocacy of women's suffrage.

Catharine Beecher (1800–1878)
Sister of Harriet Beecher Stowe, an American educator who wrote about women's education and advocated kindergarten as part of each child's early education.

Lydia Maria Child (1802–1880)
American novelist, abolitionist, women's-rights activist, Indian-rights activist, novelist, and journalist, best known for her antislavery treatise *An Appeal in Favor of that Class of Americans Called Africans* (1833) and her historical romance *Hobomok* (1824).

Angelina Grimké (1805–1879)
American abolitionist, suffragist, lecturer, and writer who is best known for her antislavery pamphlet *An Appeal to the Christian Women of the South* (1836).

Sarah Grimké (1792–1873)
American abolitionist, writer, and suffragist who wrote *Letters on the Equality of the Sexes and the Condition of Woman.*

Frances Ellen Watkins Harper (1825–1911)
African American abolitionist, poet, and fiction writer whose best-known work is her novel *Iola Leroy* (1892).

John Locke (1632–1704)
English philosopher and one of the leading intellectuals of the Enlightenment; developed social contract theory, which formed the philosophical foundation for the American Declaration of Independence.

Lucretia Coffin Mott (1793–1880)
American abolitionist, social reformer, and advocate of women's rights instrumental in founding the American women's movement.

Emma Dorothy Eliza Nevitte Southworth (1819–1899)
Popular and prolific American novelist whose best-known work is *The Hidden Hand* (1859).

Elizabeth Cady Stanton (1815–1902)
American social activist, abolitionist, and leader of the American women's movement, authored the Declaration of Sentiments on behalf of women's rights.

Sojourner Truth (1797–1883)
Originally named Isabella Baumfree, an African American abolitionist, women's-rights activist, and evangelist, best known for her speech, "Ar'n't I a Woman?" which she delivered at a women's-rights convention in Akron, Ohio, in 1851.

Exploration, Expansion, and the Frontier

Exploration and expansion defined the Romantic era as both facts and metaphors. Between 1820 and 1860 the United States increased its size from 1.8 million to 3 million square miles and admitted eleven territories to statehood; some of them were part of the old Northwest Territory, others the result of territorial expansion following the Mexican-American War. Federal census data show the U.S. population more than tripling, from 9.6 million in 1820 to 31.4 million in 1860. When Lewis and Clark set out on their transcontinental expedition in 1803, much of the territory west of the Mississippi River was unmapped and largely unknown to white Americans. But by the time of the Civil War, westward expansion was a fact of American life, fueled by "gold rushes" in California (1849), Colorado, and Nevada (1858); federal land policies such as the 1862 Homestead Act, which offered 160 acres of farmland in return for five years of settlement and cultivation; and railroads that had begun to penetrate west past the Mississippi and south to New Orleans.

MANIFEST DESTINY AND TERRITORIAL EXPANSION

Territorial expansion was encouraged by Manifest Destiny, a political doctrine that became the subject of spirited debate. The exact term was probably first used in 1845, during the controversy over the proposed annexation of Texas, when the editor of the *United States Magazine and Democratic Review* (July/August 1845) declared it "the fulfillment of our manifest destiny to overspread the continent." The term had philosophical and political ramifications, associated as it was with freedom and the advance of democracy in territories held by Mexico and (in the case of Oregon) by Great Britain. However, it was a decidedly economic phenomenon as well. Rich farmlands and the prospect of immense mineral deposits lured individual "prospectors" to seek their fortunes. The war with Mexico (1846–1848) resulted in an increase of United States territory of nearly 1.2 million square miles, including the present states of Arizona, Nevada, California, Utah, and Texas, and parts of New Mexico, Colorado, and Wyoming. The acquisition of the southern part of the Oregon Territory (1846) and the Gadsden Purchase (1853) of the remaining parts of the American Southwest filled in the outline of the continental United States. Fed by a spirit of nationalism and a drive for imperialist conquest, Manifest Destiny certified a belief in American exceptionalism that held to the superiority of white culture and the beneficial effects of eradicating alternative views of the world. The period was marked by displacement of Native Americans and an increase in the American slave population, as well as vigorous opposition by those who felt that territorial expansion would upset the delicate balance between slave and free states. Henry David Thoreau's "Resistance to Civil Government" (1849; republished as "Civil Disobedience") is perhaps the most famous literary expression of that opposition.

EXPLORATION

The Lewis and Clark Expedition (1803–1804) explored the new Louisiana Purchase and inaugurated a period of frontier exploration that remained unabated until the Civil War and resulted in the increasing occupation and settlement of the new territories. Colonel John C. Frémont (1813–1890) made several important scientific journeys to the Rockies and on to the Sierra Nevada Mountains in the 1830s and 1840s; he later turned his wanderlust toward exploration of new railroad routes and parlayed his reputation as "The Pathfinder" into a political career. Frontiersmen like Daniel Boone and David Crockett took on legendary status as real-life examples of James Fenimore Cooper's Leather-Stocking hero. The settlement of the Oregon question in 1846, regarding disputed territory claimed by both the United States and Great Britain, led to the establishment of military garrisons and forts along the Oregon Trail, which served as outposts for both colonization and exploration.

THE FRONTIER

In 1893 the historian Frederick Jackson Turner famously analyzed the effects of the disappearing American frontier, calling unsettled territories necessary for encouraging self-reliance, individualism, democracy, free enterprise, and other national values. Already in the Romantic era, Americans were responding to the frontier in similar ways. On the one hand, it represented an egalitarian opportunity for wealth-gathering and land ownership. On the other hand, with the "taming" of the frontier came the forced removal of Native Americans, beginning in the 1830s; the reservation system, beginning in the late 1840s; and the systematic eradication of tribal resources and cultures in the years following the Civil War. Thoreau's ambivalent association of "wildness" and "wilderness" in *Walden* (1854) captures some of the contemporary anxiety of the age's view of the frontier, a place of freedom but also of lawlessness. So too does Mark Twain's *The Adventures of Huckleberry Finn* (1884), set in the 1840s, in which Huck vacillates between the civilizing effects of the land and the seductive "frontier" escapism of the river.

TOPICS FOR DISCUSSION AND RESEARCH

1. In what ways did American writers respond to real experiences of exploration and the frontier? For instance, Francis Parkman's *The California & Oregon Trail* (1849) chronicled his real-life adventures on the frontier but reflected cultural stereotypes of Indians and the savagery of the land. How might Herman Melville's early novels be read as cautionary statements about colonization? In what ways might *Moby-Dick* (1851) be an ecological statement about the exploitation of nature?

2. Writers were quick to see the metaphorical possibilities of expansion, in an era marked by increased attention to the possibilities of the self. Ralph Waldo Emerson's "American Scholar" address begins with calls for literary nationalism and the exploitation of indigenous material, language, and themes. Henry David Thoreau in *Walden* calls on readers to "explore whole new continents

and worlds within you." And Walt Whitman famously celebrates the expansion of the American spirit; in his preface to the 1855 edition of *Leaves of Grass* he wrote, "The largeness of nature or the nation were monstrous without a corresponding largeness and generosity of the spirit of the citizen." Consider how Romantic authors appropriate expansion as a trope for individualism.

3. In what ways did people of color respond in writing to Manifest Destiny? Do slave narratives, for instance, politicize the idea of geographic exploration and freedom in ways that are different from the definitions in writing by white males?

4. Consider the depictions in literature of the lives of frontier women. For instance, Caroline M. Kirkland in *A New Home—Who'll Follow? Or Glimpses of Western Life* (1839) blends careful details about domestic life in the Old Northwest with incisive social satire. How did other women writers use their experiences on the frontier to comment on life in more settled parts of the United States?

RESOURCES

"The American West" <http://www.vlib.us/americanwest/> [accessed 2 November 2009].
Hosted by the University of Kansas, this site contains extensive links to information organized by topic (from agriculture to wars), region, and date, with many useful timelines.

Edwin S. Fussell, *Frontier: American Literature and the American West* (Princeton: Princeton University Press, 1965).
Considers the depiction of the frontier—literally and metaphorically—in the works of Cooper, Hawthorne, Melville, Poe, Thoreau, and Whitman.

Mary Ellen Jones, *Daily Life on the Nineteenth Century American Frontier* (Santa Barbara, Cal.: Greenwood Press, 1998).
Describes the living conditions for miners, trappers, explorers, settlers, and the military, and their encounters with Native Americans.

Susan Cummins Miller, *A Sweet, Separate Intimacy: Women Writers of the American Frontier, 1800–1922* (Salt Lake City: University of Utah Press, 2000).
Essays on dozens of writers, including Caroline Kirkland, Margaret Fuller, Helen Hunt Jackson, Alice and Phoebe Cary, and Sarah Winnemukka Hopkins.

Vincent Ponko Jr., "The Military Explorers of the American West, 1838–1860," in *A Continent Comprehended*, volume 3 of *North American Exploration*, edited by John Logan Allen (Lincoln: University of Nebraska Press, 1997), pp. 332–411.
Detailed discussion of various expeditions, with maps.

Susan H. Armitage and Elizabeth Jameson, eds., *The Women's West* (Norman: University of Oklahoma Press, 1987).
Essays on women's life and experiences in the American West, primarily in the nineteenth century; covers topics such as work, family life, and gender roles.

PEOPLE OF INTEREST

Daniel Boone (1734–1820)
Explorer best known for his association with the Kentucky wilderness, achieved legendary status for his bravery, honesty, and wisdom, despite his lack of formal education.

David Crockett (1786–1836)
Frontiersman whose exploits were told in the "Crockett Almanacs," served with distinction as a soldier and congressman and died during the battle for the Alamo during the Texas Revolution.

John C. Frémont (1813–1890)
Made five expeditions to the American West, served as senator from California, and later ran for president.

Caroline M. Kirkland (1801–1864)
Novelist and magazine editor, moved with her family to Michigan, the setting of her most famous work, *A New Home—Who'll Follow?* (1839).

Francis Parkman (1823–1893)
Historian and writer who chronicled his early travels to the Pacific Northwest in *The California & Oregon Trail,* first published as a book in 1849.

Frederick Jackson Turner (1861–1932)
Educator and historian, is best known for his essay "The Significance of the Frontier in American History," which he presented before the American Historical Association in 1893.

The Fireside Poets

Note: The Fireside Poets are widely anthologized, and their works as a group may be found in most anthologies of nineteenth-century American poetry. The anthology listed below is a good general resource.

The Romantic view of the poet as a rebellious visionary whose work cuts across the grain of popular taste does not take into account the other strain in nineteenth-century poetry that confirmed cultural norms and rewarded writers who appealed to the sensibilities of a wide audience. Of these poets, few enjoyed the popularity and longevity of William Cullen Bryant, John Greenleaf Whittier, Henry Wadsworth Longfellow, Oliver Wendell Holmes Sr., and James Russell Lowell. These writers were known collectively as the Fireside Poets, so named because they often sang the praises of domestic themes of home and hearth, or the Schoolroom Poets, because generations of American schoolchildren were required to commit their poems to memory.

While the Fireside Poets differed from each other in significant ways, critics today see a pattern in their work that confirms a nineteenth-century aesthetic. According to Thomas Wortham, they "typified values and desires that in the minds of thoughtful men and women in the nineteenth century were synonymous with culture or civilization." In a culture of rapid change, art offered stability and escape, and the Fireside Poets provided "comfort in the familiar, the tried and true" in both their themes and their style. Their poems were marked by clarity and simplicity of expression, sentimentalism, serious moral purpose (even when delivered with wit and humor), and a generally conservative view of the past or of other cultures. Above all, their verse reflected the popular ideologies of domesticity, piety, common sense, courage, and the earnest pursuit of a life well lived. All of the Fireside Poets shared fairly conventional moral sensibilities that led them to oppose social injustice, but with some notable exceptions by Whittier and Lowell their poetry was largely concerned with the universal and the timeless, not with topics of immediate political relevance. The best poetic subjects, they believed, were those that were universal and close at hand, and the poet's task was to reintroduce readers to things they already knew and to phrase them memorably. As Lowell put it in *Among My Books, First Series* (1870), "Surely the highest office of a great poet is to show us how much variety, freshness, and opportunity abides in the obvious and familiar. He invents nothing, but seems rather to *re*-discover the world about him, and his penetrating vision gives to things of daily encounter something of the strangeness of new creation."

Lowell's pronouncement that the poet "invents nothing" unfairly minimizes the importance of originality for the Fireside Poets, for he also believed that "the changed conditions of modern life demand a change in the method of treatment." Led by Longfellow, a master of his craft, the Fireside Poets were skillful versifiers who excelled in a variety of modes of expression—didactic, inspirational, satiric, sentimental, fantastic, and realistic—as well as in diverse poetic genres, such as elegies, commemorative and occasional verse, meditations, ballads, idylls, pastoral romances, and lyric celebrations of nature. New Englanders all, and often considered together, in fact their lives and interests were significantly different. Bryant (1794–1878), who spent most of his life in New York, was a lawyer and newspaper editor. Whittier (1807–1892), a Quaker farmer and political activist, was distinguished for his abolitionism. Longfellow (1807–1882), like Lowell a classical scholar, taught languages and translated Dante. Holmes (1809–1894), famous for his wit and optimism, combined a celebrated career as a poet and novelist with a long tenure as a professor of medicine. Lowell (1819–1891) was an accomplished essayist, social critic, editor, diplomat, and teacher. Modern academic inattention to the Fireside Poets smacks of biographical irony, for Longfellow, Lowell, and Holmes all held prestigious academic appointments at Harvard.

Despite the enormous popularity of the Fireside Poets in the nineteenth century, their presence in American literature anthologies is dwindling today. There are ample reasons for both phenomena. In 1898 Professor William Cranston Lawton, citing literature's appeal to "universal human motives," maintained that poets like Longfellow "uttered the sincerest and purest feelings of the uncounted millions, all around the globe, that use our English speech." Much more recently, in her study of the place of poetry in American life, Joan Shelley Rubin argues that the Fireside Poets were "both icons and friends" for their nineteenth-century readers. But as Wortham points out, the values and aesthetic of the Fireside Poets run counter to contemporary literary preferences for "absurdity, irrationality, elliptical compression, multivalences of symbolic meaning, [and] solipsistic agony." Though the Fireside Poets are unlikely to enjoy a resurgence in popularity today, the poet Dana Gioia's tribute to Longfellow is a model of the careful reclamation work yet to be done on a group of poets whose "vitality . . . current critical instruments are not designed to register." Recent scholarship on their lives (by Gilbert Muller and Christoph Irmscher) and on their place in American culture (by Agnieszka Salska and Angela Sorby) suggests a renewed appreciation for their achievement. In their own century the Fireside Poets were a true national treasure, poets who spoke—as Walt Whitman hoped to—in the register of the people and to the highest aspirations of their readers.

TOPICS FOR DISCUSSION AND RESEARCH

1. Among the major themes of the Fireside Poets are the following:

- The life well lived, with emphasis on striving and acting, as exemplified in the final stanza of Longfellow's "Psalm of Life" (1838):

    Let us, then, be up and doing,
    With a heart for any fate;
    Still achieving, still pursuing,
    Learn to labor and to wait.

- Faith, endurance, and courage in the face of life's obstacles. As Bryant writes in "Thanatopsis," for instance, the fear of death is mediated by the knowledge that "All that breathe / Will share thy destiny." During a time of religious divisiveness, the Fireside Poets were mostly nondenominational, more concerned with piety than theology.

- An awareness of human foibles and pretensions. See for example Lowell's satiric *Fable for Critics* (1848) or Holmes's lighthearted "The Deacon's Masterpiece, or the Wonderful One-Hoss Shay" (1858), a reminder of the impermanence of human achievements.
- The importance of the historical past, which for the Fireside Poets revealed the enduring truths of human existence. Good examples are Longfellow's *Evangeline* (1847) and "Song of Hiawatha" (1855), which confirm national narratives of progress and loss, and Whittier's lyric "Snow-Bound: A Winter Idyl" (1866), a testimony to the value of the remembered past. Lowell's "Vision of Sir Launfel" (1849) combines the vogue for things medieval with the Fireside Poets' attention to moral lessons, as Sir Launfel ends his grail quest with the realization that inward charity and compassion are more significant than earthly accomplishments:

> The Holy Supper is kept, indeed,
> In whatso we share with another's need,—
> Not that which we give, but what we share,—
> For the gift without the giver is bare;

Students might consider tracing one of these themes in poems by at least two of the authors, arguing whether or not the Fireside Poets were essentially interchangeable in their sentiments. Consider, too, whether the theme is treated idealistically or more realistically. For arguments on both sides, see the studies by Wortham (who characterizes the Fireside Poets' verse as having "good feeling and hopeful expectations") and Justus (who sees their worldview as guardedly optimistic).

2. Another fruitful topic for research is the biographical intersection between the Fireside Poets and their less conventional Romantic contemporaries. Whitman found a mentor in Bryant; Emerson admired Holmes's wit and gifts for conversation; Hawthorne idolized Longfellow. How influential were the relationships among the Fireside Poets and the Romantic writers more often read today, and in what ways was their work similar? One way to approach this topic is to focus on the biography—whether two figures knew each other well, what characterized their relationship, and how each regarded the other. Another approach would be to focus on themes. Consider, for instance, a comparison of the attitudes toward death in Bryant's "Thanatopsis" and in Emerson's "Terminus" (1867) or between the politics in Thoreau's "Resistance to Civil Government" (1848) and Lowell's *The Biglow Papers* (1848), both of which express outrage at the Mexican-American War of 1846.

3. In a related vein, consider the work of the Fireside Poets alongside equally popular women poets of the time, such as Lydia Huntley Sigourney, the "Sweet Singer" of Hartford, Connecticut, or Alice and Phoebe Cary, two sisters from Cincinnati. Sigourney's "Pocahontas" (1841), for instance, might be profitably compared to Longfellow's "Song of Hiawatha." To what extent do construc-

tions of gender influence the choice and treatment of poetic subject matter, and is there evidence that either group wrote intentionally for a male or female readership?

4. The Fireside Poets achieved not only popular acclaim but also financial success, at a time when the profession of authorship offered new opportunities to make a living with one's pen. Rubin's study of poetry in American culture points out that by the 1840s poets could earn as much as $50 for a short poem published in a newspaper, and that editors were eager to include poems in annual gift books. Consider the ways in which the commercial considerations of book culture and publishing might have encouraged the writing of certain types of poetry and how a writer as different from the Fireside Poets as Poe might also have appealed to popular reading tastes in an effort to make money. Charvat's *Literary Publishing in America* treats the influence of commerce on the Fireside Poets and others.

RESOURCES

Primary Works

William Cullen Bryant, John Greenleaf Whittier, Henry Wadsworth Longfellow, Oliver Wendell Holmes Sr., and James Russell Lowell, *The New Anthology of American Poetry*, edited by Steven Gould Axelrod, Camille Roman, and Thomas Travisano (New Brunswick, N.J.: Rutgers University Press, 2003).

James Russell Lowell, *Among My Books*, 37th edition (1870; Boston: Houghton, Mifflin, 1893).

Biography

Christoph Irmscher, *Longfellow Redux* (Champaign: University of Illinois Press, 2006).

A reevaluation of Longfellow's career and his relationship with his readership.

Gilbert H. Muller, *William Cullen Bryant: Author of America* (Albany: State University of New York Press, 2008).

Examines Bryant's achievement as a poet, civic leader, and promoter of literary nationalism.

Criticism

William Charvat, *Literary Publishing in America, 1790–1850* (Philadelphia: University of Pennsylvania Press, 1959).

Considers the social and economic contexts for the rise of authorship as a profession in the United States.

Dana Gioia, "Longfellow in the Aftermath of Modernism," in *The Columbia History of American Poetry*, edited by Jay Parini and Brett C. Millier (New York: Columbia University Press, 1993), pp. 64–96.

An appreciative tribute, carefully detailing Longfellow's career and poetic accomplishments.

James H. Justus, "The Fireside Poets: Hearthside Values and the Language of Care" in *Nineteenth-Century American Poetry*, edited by A. Robert Lee (Totowa, N.J. & London: Barnes & Noble & Vision, 1985), pp.146–165.
Makes the case that in a world of grief and pain, the mission of the Fireside Poets was "to help assuage the received condition" of humanity. Excellent readings of the major poems.

William Cranston Lawton, *The New England Poets: A Study of Emerson, Hawthorne, Longfellow, Whittier, Lowell, Holmes* (1898; Plainview, N.Y.: Books for Libraries Press, 1972).
Presents the case for universality as the hallmark of the Fireside Poets.

Joan Shelley Rubin, *Songs of Ourselves: The Uses of Poetry in America* (Cambridge, Mass. & London: Belknap Press of Harvard University Press, 2007).
Examines the roles of poets and poetry for American readers, focusing on the 1880s through the 1950s. Chapter 2, "Amateur and Professional," is devoted to the Fireside Poets.

Agnieszka Salska, "From National to Supranational Conception of Literature: The Case of Henry Wadsworth Longfellow," *American Transcendental Quarterly*, 20 (December 2006): 611–628.
Traces the evolution of Longfellow's poetic program from nationalism to universalism.

Angela Sorby, *Schoolroom Poets: Childhood, Performance, and the Place of American Poetry, 1865–1917* (Durham: University of New Hampshire Press, 2005).
Examines the uses of the Schoolroom Poets, particularly Longfellow and Whittier, in American education, and the increasing child-centeredness of poetry in the nineteenth century.

Thomas Wortham, "William Cullen Bryant and the Fireside Poets," in *The Columbia Literary History of the United States*, edited by Emory Elliott (New York: Columbia University Press, 1987), pp. 278–288.
Argues that the Fireside Poets embodied "a unity of purpose and public success" because they affirmed the values of their culture and time.

PEOPLE OF INTEREST

William Cullen Bryant (1794–1878)
Author of "Thanotopsis" and "To a Water Fowl," he was among the most famous poets in America for some sixty-five years before his death. Publication of his *Poems* (1821) is regarded as a signal event in the maturation of the American poetic tradition.

Oliver Wendell Holmes Sr. (1809–1894)
Scientist, essayist, and novelist, as well as poet, Holmes is best known by present-day audiences for his poem "Old Ironsides." He studied law and medicine at Harvard University and was a member of the remarkable community of intellectuals in Cambridge at the end of the nineteenth century.

Henry Wadsworth Longfellow (1807–1882)

The only American writer honored in the Poets' Corner of Westminster Abbey, Longfellow was the most popular poet in America during his lifetime. His "Paul Revere's Ride," *Evangeline, A Tale of Acadie* (1847), "The Song of Hiawatha," and "The Courtship of Miles Standish" were extraordinarily popular poetic accounts of key events in New England history.

James Russell Lowell (1819–1891)

Remembered for his satirical poetry in *The Biglow Papers* (1848, 1862) and *A Fable for Critics* (1848), Lowell was influential as a poet and also as the editor of *The Atlantic Monthly*, which he played a role in founding and which he edited, championing the work of the Fireside Poets, among others.

John Greenleaf Whittier (1807–1892)

Remembered as the author of *Snow Bound. A Winter Idyll* (1866), Whittier was a sentimental poet who often wrote verses to promote his moral convictions, abolitionism in particular. He was an early contributor to *The Atlantic Monthly*, where one of his most anthologized poems, "Telling the Bees," was published.

Gothicism

The term Gothicism in its literary meaning derives not from the Goths, an ancient Germanic tribe, but from the sense of Gothic as medieval. This literary movement may be seen as a reaction against the rationalism of the Enlightenment and similar to the Romantic emphasis on emotion and sensation over reason and its depiction of exotic settings. Gothic literature shares some characteristics with the romance, a literary genre popular in the late medieval period that featured magic, battles between heroes and monsters, and an emphasis on chivalry. Like the romance, Gothic literature emphasizes the supernatural and often features a medieval setting such as decaying medieval castles, abbeys, and dungeons. In addition, Gothic literature may be identified by the following themes and features:

- Focus on mystery
- Depiction of physical and mental abnormality, such as insanity and physical deformity
- Emphasis on terror
- Emphasis on ambiguity (for example, events may be imprecisely described to the reader)
- Emphasis on the subconscious mind and dreams
- Importance of hereditary family curses
- Lack of didacticism
- Lack of realism
- Emphasis on the sublime in descriptions of setting (that is, things that inspire fear and awe such as thunderstorms, mountains, huge castles)

Many Gothic works also pair a character with a doppelgänger, that is, a "double," such as the protagonist and his monstrous alter ego in Robert Louis Stevenson's *The Strange Case of Dr. Jekyll and Mr. Hyde* (1886). The British developed the form. Horace Walpole's *The Castle of Otranto* (1764) is often cited as the first Gothic novel; other early examples include Ann Radcliffe's *The Mysteries of Udolpho* (1794) and Matthew Gregory Lewis's *The Monk* (1796). Mary Shelley's novel *Frankenstein; or, The Modern Prometheus* (1818) is perhaps the most famous example of the genre. Two of the earliest American works of Gothic fiction are Charles Brockden Brown's *Edgar Huntly* (1799) and "Somnambulism: A Fragment" (1805), in which sleepwalking characters act out their subconscious impulses. Washington Irving also included Gothic features in his tales, most famously in "Rip Van Winkle" (1819), in which ghostly figures appear, and "The Legend of Sleepy Hollow" (1819), in which the protagonist believes he is pursued by a headless ghost. During the mid nineteenth century, the best-known authors of the genre were Edgar Allan Poe and Nathaniel Hawthorne, some of whose works are discussed below. All of these works feature either supernatural occurrences or insanity, two hallmarks of the genre.

Hawthorne's novels *The Scarlet Letter* (1850) and *The House of the Seven Gables* (1851) both include several features of Gothic fiction. The latter novel is centered on the old Pyncheon mansion, and when Holgrave, a visitor to the mansion, first sees Clifford, an old inhabitant, he believes the man is a ghost. Like many Gothic novels, *The House of the Seven Gables* is concerned with a hereditary curse—in this case, a curse on the Pyncheon family and mansion. In *The Scarlet Letter*, an increasingly diabolical villain, Roger Chillingworth, becomes a doppelgänger to the pious yet hypocritical Reverend Dimmesdale. Chillingworth, like many Gothic villains, is physically deformed. The theme of witchcraft is embodied in Mistress Hibbins, a witch who often tempts Hester Prynne to join her in the forest.

Many of Poe's short stories also exemplify Gothic fiction. For example, "The Fall of the House of Usher" (1838) emphasizes Roderick Usher's insanity and his strange appearance. The Usher family also suffers from a hereditary curse that stems from several generations of incestuous marriage. The theme of premature burial, or the dead returning to life, emerges when Roderick's sister Madeleine—whom we might see as Roderick's doppelgänger—seems to die but bursts from her coffin and tomb near the end of the story. The setting of the story, the decaying Usher mansion, is typically Gothic in that it almost becomes a character, and it is inextricably tied to the Usher dynasty and its hereditary curse.

Though the Gothic works of Poe and Hawthorne are the most familiar examples of the genre in mid-nineteenth-century American literature, there are many others. George Lippard's *The Quaker City; or the Monks of Monk-Hall* (1844) was perhaps the most popular Gothic novel by an American during this period. Lippard's novel is noteworthy for adapting Gothic conventions to contemporary urban life as opposed to the distant past or exotic locations. Another best-selling novel of the period, Harriet Beecher Stowe's *Uncle Tom's Cabin* (1852), is primarily an antislavery novel, but it incorporates a subplot featuring a slave woman who is able to escape with a fellow slave by leading her cruel master to believe that his house is haunted. Herman Melville's novel *Moby-Dick* (1851) also includes Gothic elements such as deformity (for example, the white whale and Captain Ahab's amputated leg) and insanity (Ahab and Pip).

TOPICS FOR DISCUSSION AND RESEARCH

1. How does American Gothic literature compare to its European counterparts? How do American authors adopt and depart from the conventions of European Gothic literature? A good general resource on Gothic fiction is Jerrold Hogle's *The Cambridge Companion to Gothic Fiction* (2002), which includes chapters on German, British, Irish, and Scottish fiction. Those interested in focusing on the Gothic works of Poe should consult Benjamin Fisher's essay "Poe and the Gothic Tradition" in *The Cambridge Companion to Edgar Allan Poe* (2002).

2. Gothic literature is full of insanity, dreams, and strange behaviors motivated by subconscious desires and fears. Choose a Gothic fictional text by Poe, Hawthorne, or one of their American contemporaries and examine its relationship to theories of human psychology using David Punter's essay "Narrative and Psychology in Gothic Fiction" in *Gothic Fictions: Prohibition/Transgression* (1989).

3. How are female characters portrayed in nineteenth-century American Gothic literature? Are they passive victims, supernatural beings, brave heroines, or something else? Edgar Allan Poe's works are particularly interesting with regard to this topic. A good source regarding this topic is Joan Dayan's article "Poe's Women: A Feminist Poe?" (1993).

4. Many Gothic texts subliminally depict sexuality that is often seen as dangerous or abnormal. This theme is most prominent in works like Poe's "The Fall of the House of Usher" and "Ligeia." The first part of George Haggerty's *Queer Gothic* (2006) is a helpful general introduction to the theme of sexuality in Gothic literature, and Peter Coviello's essay "Poe in Love: Pedophilia, Morbidity, and the Logic of Slavery" (2003) focuses specifically on the sexual elements of Poe's works.

5. How has nineteenth-century American Gothic fiction influenced the works of twentieth-century American authors such as Flannery O'Connor and William Faulkner? How do the works of these later writers compare to their nineteenth-century predecessors? A good secondary source on O'Connor's and Faulkner's use of Gothic conventions is Margie Burns's essay "A Good Rose Is Hard to Find: 'Southern Gothic' as Social Dislocation in Faulkner and O'Connor" (1988).

RESOURCES

Kenneth W. Graham, ed., *Gothic Fictions: Prohibition/Transgression* (New York: AMS Press, 1989).
Includes fourteen essays about English Gothic fiction, a major influence on American Gothic literature.

George E. Haggerty, *Queer Gothic* (Urbana: University of Illinois Press, 2006).
A study of the links between Gothic literature and sexuality.

Jerrold E. Hogle, *The Cambridge Companion to Gothic Fiction* (Cambridge, England: Cambridge University Press, 2002).
A collection of essays about Gothic literature in various national contexts, including an essay on American Gothic literature.

Robert K. Martin and Eric Savoy, eds., *American Gothic: New Interventions in a National Narrative* (Iowa City: University of Iowa Press, 2009).
A collection of critical essays about American Gothic literature.

David Stevens, *The Gothic Tradition* (Cambridge, England: Cambridge University Press, 2000).
A useful overview of Gothic literature.

PEOPLE OF INTEREST

Charles Brockden Brown (1771–1810)
American novelist, historian, and editor, adopted Gothic conventions to an American setting in some of his fiction.

Washington Irving (1783–1859)
American fiction writer, biographer, and historian, is best known for his satire *A History of New-York* (1809) as well as *The Sketch Book* (1819), which included "Rip Van Winkle" and "The Legend of Sleepy Hollow."

Matthew Gregory Lewis (1775–1818)
English novelist and dramatist, wrote *The Monk* and other Gothic tales.

George Lippard (1822–1854)
American novelist, journalist, and social activist, became famous for *The Quaker City; or the Monks of Monk-Hall* (1844), a novel about urban crime with Gothic elements.

Ann Radcliffe (1764–1823)
English author of Gothic novels such as *The Mysteries of Udolpho* that featured virtuous female characters.

Mary Shelley (1797–1851)
English author, best known for her Gothic novel *Frankenstein; or, The Modern Prometheus* (1818).

Robert Louis Balfour Stevenson (1850–1894)
Scottish author, wrote *Treasure Island, The Strange Case of Dr. Jekyll and Mr. Hyde, David Balfour, Kidnapped,* and other popular novels.

Horace Walpole, fourth Earl of Orford (1717–1797)
English author and politician whose novel *The Castle of Otranto* became the model for later Gothic novels.

Literature of the American Women's Movement

The fact that the emergence of American women's literature coincided with the birth of the American women's movement is no mere coincidence. At a time when becoming an author was seen as a male prerogative, the women's movement gave American women the courage to take up the pen and in some cases become professional writers. Although not all works written by these women would be considered feminist by today's definitions, they nevertheless offered female perspectives that were mostly absent from earlier American literature. Conversely, the women's movement grew largely because many of its members had gained confidence through writing and used it to promote the cause. For a general summary of the early women's movement in America, see the essay "The Birth of American Feminism" in this volume. This essay is intended to supplement that overview by focusing on several of the most significant and representative activists and texts of the early American women's movement. (Margaret Fuller's "The Great Lawsuit," one of the most groundbreaking feminist texts from this period, is discussed in detail in a separate study guide.)

One of the most prominent leaders of the movement was Elizabeth Cady Stanton (1815–1902), author of the "Declaration of Sentiments," a foundational protofeminist text written for the 1848 Seneca Falls Women's Rights Convention. Stanton was an abolitionist as well as a feminist, and she wanted to eliminate racial and gender barriers that limited voting rights and civil rights. She and Susan B. Anthony were disappointed that the Fourteenth and Fifteenth Amendments (1868 and 1870, respectively) extended these rights to black men but not to white or black women, and argued that gender discrimination should also be unconstitutional. When their arguments failed to broaden these amendments, they opposed them, an act that created division within the women's movement and distanced them from their former ally Frederick Douglass and other abolitionists who supported the amendments. The two women founded the National Women's Suffrage Association (NWSA) in 1869, which soon split over the question of whether to support the Fourteenth and Fifteenth Amendments. Despite her focus on suffrage, Stanton differed from some leaders of the movement by extending her activism beyond this issue by advocating reform of divorce laws, birth control practices, and women's economic rights. Another issue that separated her from others in the movement was her stance on Christianity, which she criticized for relegating women to subservient roles; she expressed these views in her book *The Woman's Bible* (1895). Between 1868 and 1870 she and Anthony worked with Parker Pillsbury in founding *The Revolutionary*, the NWSA's official periodical that was devoted to women's issues.

Stanton was introduced to Anthony (1820–1906) in 1851, though both had attended the Seneca Falls Convention three years earlier. Anthony did not produce as much as Stanton in terms of printed texts, but she was an indefatigable speaker on behalf of women for over half of her life. Like Stanton and many other women's rights activists of the time, Anthony was active also in the temperance and abolitionist movements. However, after breaking with abolitionists over the Fourteenth and Fifteenth Amendments, she focused exclusively on women's rights, especially suffrage. She also allied herself with conservative suffragists and reunited the NWSA with the more conservative American Women's Suffrage Association in 1890, a move that displeased the more radical Stanton. Despite their differences, both women worked together with Matilda Joslyn Gage in writing three volumes of *History of Woman Suffrage* during the 1880s.

Joining Stanton and Anthony in rejecting the Fourteenth and Fifteenth Amendments for their failure to enfranchise women was Sojourner Truth (circa 1797–1883), the most famous African American women's rights advocate of her time. Although many white feminists were also abolitionists who sympathized with African Americans, Truth brought the perspective of a black former slave to the movement. Truth, whose original name was Isabella Baumfree, was born in a Dutch-speaking area of New York State. She ran away from her second master in 1826, a year before slavery ended in New York. In 1843 Isabella felt a spiritual calling, renamed herself, and began a career as a wandering evangelist in New York and New England. While in Massachusetts she became involved in the abolitionist movement and met Olive Gilbert, who wrote Truth's biography *Narrative of Sojourner Truth: A Northern Slave* (1850). Although Truth was illiterate, her wit and strong personality made her a powerful force in the women's and antislavery movements. She attended the women's rights convention in Akron, Ohio, in May 1851, where she delivered her most famous speech, commonly titled "Ar'n't I a Woman?" Truth's speech, which was summarized in the *Anti-Slavery Bugle* and later transcribed by the convention chairperson Frances D. Gage in 1863, used self-deprecating, folksy humor in refuting the arguments of clergymen who used Scripture to justify the subordination of women. She also pointed out how the notions regarding "true womanhood" did not extend to enslaved women like herself who were forced to perform hard work outside the home and were not allowed to keep and nurture their children. In addition, the tall, muscular Truth countered the traditional notion of women as naturally weak, timid, and submissive, and as Alison Piepmeier notes, she presented herself as a sort of "tall tale" hero. Truth reentered the national spotlight in Harriet Beecher Stowe's 1863 essay *The Lybian Sybil*, which depicts Truth as simple and unlettered yet powerful, devout, and humorous. During the Civil War she helped to recruit African American soldiers for the Union army, and after the war she continued to lecture on behalf of various reform movements until a year before her death in 1883.

Although most women's rights activists were from the North, two of its most influential leaders, Sarah Grimké (1792–1873) and her sister Angelina (1805–1879), grew up on their father's Charleston, South Carolina, plantation before moving to Philadelphia during the 1820s and converting to Quakerism, a religion known for its opposition to slavery. Like many women's-rights activists of their time, they also supported the antislavery movement, largely because they saw their own subjugation under patriarchy as parallel to the oppression of slaves. Their involvement in both movements was a major reason for leaving Charleston, where they were shunned for their radical views. For both sisters, speaking out against slavery in public required them to reject the patriarchal belief that women should restrict themselves to domestic matters. Although their comparative freedom in the North inspired them to express their beliefs, their lectures throughout New England drew criticism from Catharine Beecher (sister of Harriet Beecher Stowe, author of *Uncle Tom's Cabin*), who argued that women should stay out of the public sphere and focus on their domestic duties. Angelina responded with *Letters to Catharine Beecher* (1837), one of which compares the women's movement to the Founding Fathers' fight for independence from British rule (much like Stanton did a decade later in her "Declaration of Sentiments"). In another letter she brings feminist and abolitionist concerns together by deploring the sexual abuse of slave women by white men, and declares, "the investigation of the rights of the slave has led me to a better understanding of my own." That same year Sarah wrote *Letters on the Equality of the Sexes, and the Condition of Woman* (published serially in *The Spectator* and as a book a year later), which criticized the popular concept of "separate spheres" for each sex and used the notion that women are moral guides to their husbands in order to argue that women should have more freedom to exert their moral influence in the public sphere. Angelina ended her lecturing career soon after marrying the abolitionist Theodore Dwight Weld in 1838; that same year, Sarah also retired from the lecture circuit. Nevertheless, both women continued to support women's rights and abolitionism throughout the rest of their lives, and their fearless activism and insightful arguments on behalf of women and African Americans profoundly shaped both movements for decades to come.

TOPICS FOR DISCUSSION AND RESEARCH

1. Because of the close ties between the women's movement and abolitionism, the central ideas of both movements inevitably overlap. Students may be interested in doing research on the legal restrictions placed on women and comparing them to the laws governing slaves and free African Americans in order to see both parallels and differences between these two forms of oppression. One helpful source on subjugation of women in nineteenth-century America is Ellen Carol DuBois and Lynn Dumenil's *Through Women's Eyes: An American History with Documents* (2008). Kathryn Kish Sklar's *Women's Rights Emerges within the Anti-slavery Movement, 1830–1870* (2000) is useful in drawing connections between the two movements.

2. In many ways, the women's movement in nineteenth-century America focused mostly on improving the lives of free white women. However, African American feminists such as Sojourner Truth brought the issues of race and slavery into feminist discussions. Consider how Truth, as a formerly enslaved black woman, approached the issues of women's oppression and women's rights from a different perspective than that of middle-class white women. Students might also explore the impact that Truth had upon the women's movement in broadening its focus to include black women, including those who were enslaved. Nell Irvin Painter's *Sojourner Truth: A Life, A Symbol* (1996) and her

essay "Difference, Slavery, and Memory" (1994) contain useful information about Truth's involvement in women's rights and abolitionism.

3. Leaders of the women's movement in nineteenth-century America were often criticized not only for challenging patriarchal oppression but also for expressing their views publicly. The American public's reaction to the Grimké sisters is a case in point. What obstacles did they face in speaking out in favor of women's rights, and how did they respond to these challenges? Pamela Durso's biography of Sarah Grimké, *The Power of Woman* (2003), and Gerda Lerner's biography of both sisters, *The Grimké Sisters of South Carolina* (2009), are both excellent resources, as is Larry Ceplair's collection of their writings in *The Public Years of Sarah and Angelina Grimké* (1989). In addition, Jean Fagan Yellin's *Women and Sisters* (1989) includes a chapter that examines Angelina Grimké's comparison of slavery to the subjugation of women.

4. Elizabeth Cady Stanton's "Declaration of Sentiments" borrowed the phrase "all men and women are created equal" from the Declaration of Independence and recast the complaints of oppressed colonists against King George III in gendered terms, with subjugated women demanding rights from their patriarchal rulers. Compare the two documents and analyze their similarities and differences. Also consider the ways in which the "Declaration of Sentiments" might be considered a critique of the Declaration of Independence for failing to promote equality between women and men. The "Declaration of Sentiments" may be found online at <http://www.usconstitution.net/sentiments.html#sent>; the Declaration of Independence is available at <http://www.ushistory.org/declaration/document/index.htm>.

5. Although Stanton's friendship with Susan B. Anthony was central to the success of the American women's movement, the two women sometimes disagreed about which issues they should address, and these disagreements were paralleled by conflicts within the movement. One possible research topic is to explore these philosophical and strategic differences and consider the impact that these differences had on the movement. Two useful biographical sources for researching this topic are Elisabeth Griffith's *In Her Own Right* and *Elizabeth Cady Stanton: Feminist As Thinker* (1985) and Kathleen Barry's *Susan B. Anthony: A Biography of a Singular Feminist* (2000).

RESOURCES

Primary Works

Larry Ceplair, ed., *The Public Years of Sarah and Angelina Grimké: Selected Writings, 1835–1839* (New York: Columbia University Press, 1989).

A collection of documents by the sisters relating to women's rights and abolitionism.

Ellen Carol DuBois and Richard Cándida Smith, eds., *Elizabeth Cady Stanton, Feminist as Thinker: A Reader in Documents and Essays* (New York: New York University Press, 2007).

Contains eight recent essays about Stanton and several of her speeches, articles, and essays.

Angelina E. Grimké, *Letters to Catherine E. Beecher, In Reply to An Essay on Slavery and Abolitionism, Addressed to A. E. Grimke. Revised by the Author* (Boston: Isaac Knapp, 1838); and Sarah Moore Grimké, *Letters on the Equality of the Sexes and the Condition of Woman; Addressed to Mary S. Parker, President of the Boston Female Anti-Slavery Society* (Boston: Isaac Knapp, 1838).

History of Woman Suffrage, volumes 1–3, edited by Elizabeth Cady Stanton, Susan B. Anthony, and Matilda Joslyn Gage (New York: Fowler & Wells, 1881–1886).

Narrative of Sojourner Truth, A Northern Slave, Emancipated from Bodily Servitude by the State of New York, in 1828, told to and edited by Olive Gilbert (Boston: For the author, 1850).

Biography

Pamela R. Durso, *The Power of Woman: The Life and Writings of Sarah Moore Grimké* (Macon, Ga.: Mercer University Press, 2003).
A biography of the elder Grimké sister that examines her feminist and antislavery writings.

Grace Farrell, "Beneath the Suffrage Narrative," *Canadian Review of American Studies/Revue Canadienne d'Études Américaines*, 36, 1 (2006): 45–65.
Explains the role of feminist activist Lillie Devereux Blake in the American women's movement and her exclusion from feminist historiography in Anthony's *History of Woman Suffrage*.

Elisabeth Griffith, *In Her Own Right: The Life of Elizabeth Cady Stanton* (New York: Oxford University Press, 1985).
The definitive Stanton biography.

Gerda Lerner, *The Grimké Sisters From South Carolina: Pioneers for Women's Rights and Abolition* (Chapel Hill: University of North Carolina Press, 2004).
A comprehensive biography of the Grimkés.

Nell Irvin Painter, "Difference, Slavery, and Memory: Sojourner Truth in Feminist Abolitionism," in *Abolitionist Sisterhood: Women's Political Culture in Antebellum America*, edited by Jean Fagan Yellin and John C. Van Horne (Ithaca, N.Y.: Cornell University Press, 1994), pp. 139–158.
Examines Truth's relationship to the women's rights and abolitionist movements and the construction of her persona.

Painter, *Sojourner Truth: A Life, A Symbol* (New York: Norton, 1996).
The authoritative Truth biography.

Criticism

Ellen Carol DuBois, *Feminism and Suffrage: The Emergence of an Independent Women's Movement in America, 1848–1869* (Ithaca, N.Y.: Cornell University Press, 1999).
A history of the American women's movement from the Seneca Falls Convention to the passage of the Fifteenth Amendment.

Naomi Greyser, "Affective Geographies: Sojourner Truth's *Narrative,* Feminism, and the Ethical Bind of Sentimentalism," *American Literature: A Journal of Literary History, Criticism, and Bibliography,* 79 (2007): 275–305.
Discusses Truth's ethical uses of sentimentalism and analyzes how it rhetorically confined her.

Mary Loeffelholz, "Posing the Woman Citizen: The Contradictions of Stanton's Feminism," *Genders,* 7 (Spring 1990): 87–98.
Examines Stanton's arguments for married women's property rights without denying their bodily nature in an 1860 speech.

Alison Piepmeier, "'As Strong as Any Man': Sojourner Truth's Tall Tale Embodiment," in *Women as Sites of Culture: Women's Roles in Cultural Formation from the Renaissance to the Twentieth Century,* edited by Susan Shifrin (Aldershot, U.K.: Ashgate, 2002), pp. 25–36.
Argues that Truth borrowed from the tall-tale genre to define herself as a female hero.

Judith Wellman, *The Road to Seneca Falls: Elizabeth Cady Stanton and the First Woman's Rights Convention* (Urbana: University of Illinois Press, 2004).
A historical account of the birth of the American women's movement with an emphasis on Stanton.

Jean Fagan Yellin, *Women and Sisters: The Antislavery Feminists in American Culture* (New Haven, Conn.: Yale University Press, 1989).
Studies the intersections of gender, class, and racial ideologies in the activism of antislavery feminists.

PEOPLE OF INTEREST

Matilda Joslyn Gage (1826–1898)
Women's-rights activist and prolific essayist. She was a founding member in 1869 of the National Woman Suffrage Association and served as president for twenty years. She wrote *Woman, Church and State: A Historical Account of the Status of Woman though the Christian Ages: With Reminiscences of the Matriarchate* (1893).

Sarah Moore Grimké (1792–1873) and **Angelina Grimkè** (1805–1879)
The Grimkè sisters were energetic advocates for social causes, particularly abolition and women's equality. Sarah's *Letters on the Equality of the Sexes* (1838) is regarded as the pioneering argument for women's rights.

Elizabeth Cady Stanton (1815–1902)
One of the organizers of The First Woman's Rights Convention at Seneca Falls, New York, on 19–20 July 1848. She collaborated with Susan B. Anthony in editing the weekly womens'-rights newspaper *The Revolution* from 1868 to 1870. She was president of the American Woman Suffrage Association from 1887 to 1889, and she wrote *The Woman's Bible* in two volumes (1895, 1898).

Literary Professionalism and Organizations: Tours, Clubs, the Lyceum Movement

In the four decades before the Civil War, literary authorship in the United States moved from an avocation to a profession. With the notable exceptions of Washington Irving and James Fenimore Cooper, most earlier authors wrote as an adjunct to their "real" professions or politely disguised their writings with pseudonyms. But during the Romantic era, the means developed for American writers to begin making a living from their pen alone. There were a variety of contributing, interlinked factors in a developing commercial market for literature. The U.S. population was increasingly literate; in 1850, an estimated ninety percent of white American adults could read. Magazines grew in popularity among a busy class of readers, and editors were willing to pay for short stories, sketches, and poems. More efficient transportation and postal systems formed a national distribution network for print literature. A growing and geographically dispersed American population was more and more bound together by what Ronald J. Zboray calls, in *A Fictive People: Antebellum Economic Development and the American Reading Public* (1993), a new community of words. Public attitudes toward literary authorship, formerly viewed as a frivolous pastime or the province of the elite, were changing, as were the attitudes toward literature itself, particularly fiction-writing. Admittedly, the old proscriptions against novel-reading died hard: in 1852, Daniel Smith in the influential *Book of Manners* decried, "Many people lose a great deal of time by reading; for they read frivolous or idle books, such as absurd romances, where characters that never existed are insipidly displayed" (quoted in Zboray). But the public appetite for long fiction would not be denied. In 1870, fiction accounted for seventy percent of the purchases of the New York Mercantile Library, the fourth largest in the United States.

The careers of professional writers were supported by several cultural institutions during the Romantic era. The growth of railroads and improved riverboat travel made author tours increasingly popular. Charles Dickens's American tours in 1842 and again in 1867 not only sold books; they augured the new celebrity for writers and modeled a new multimedia approach for commercially successful writers—the text, the oral presentation, and the personal appearance. Ralph Waldo Emerson, for instance, supported himself primarily as a lecturer from the 1830s to the 1860s, turning his lectures into published essays.

Reading tours benefited from a larger public initiative called the lyceum movement. Named for the school where Aristotle taught the youth of ancient Athens, the lyceum movement was a democratic form of education that provided average American adults the opportunity to attend and participate in debates on topics of current interest. According to some estimates, about three thousand local lyceums existed in the United States by the middle 1830s. By mid century the lyceum movement had become more professional and provided touring authors with a ready-made audience and venue for reading their work. Emerson, Frederick Douglass, and to some extent Henry David Thoreau and Nathaniel Hawthorne all traveled the lyceum circuit.

Literary clubs supported the professionalization of authorship by legitimizing public interest in reading and literature and sustaining the conversation among writers. Literary clubs had flourished in the United States since its beginnings; among the more notable was the Friendly Club of New York City, which flourished in the 1790s and numbered among its members the novelist Charles Brockden Brown and the dramatist William Dunlap. Possibly the most famous group was the Transcendental Club, established in 1836 by Emerson and others to provide a venue for discussing "new views" in philosophy, religion, and literature. As was often the case, the club published a literary magazine, the *Dial* (1840–1844), edited first by Margaret Fuller and later by Emerson. The functions of most literary clubs were social, intellectual, and civic—to provide camaraderie, to encourage the production of indigenous writing, and to elevate the reputation of the host town. The Semi-Colon Club of Cincinnati is a good example. Founded in 1829 to provide "evenings of social relaxation and rational amusement," it flourished until about 1846 and included many of the city's literary figures, such as the Reverend Lyman Beecher and his daughter Harriet (later Harriet Beecher Stowe). One of its members described a typical meeting in 1839, when the club could boast more than thirty members: "The plan of it is that its members shall voluntarily contribute original pieces which are read in the early part of the evening, with intervals for conversation & music" (quoted in Habich).

Among the most influential and durable literary associations was the Saturday Club of Boston (at first called the "Atlantic Club," after the magazine for which most of its members wrote). Founded around 1856 by a group of New England writers and civic leaders, it endured into the twentieth century. Members of the club met monthly for dinner at Boston's Parker House hotel, there to enjoy each other's company and share their writing. Among the most famous authors in the Saturday Club were Emerson, Oliver Wendell Holmes, James Russell Lowell, Henry Wadsworth Longfellow, and John Greenleaf Whittier.

TOPICS FOR DISCUSSION AND RESEARCH

1. Women authors, particularly fiction writers in the 1850s, were financially very successful. Can any of that success be explained by the growth of new reading audiences? By the subjects of their work? By women's issues that were reflected or dramatized in their best-selling novels? Refer to reviews at the time, as well as commentary in letters or diaries by women.

2. To what extent were American authors aware of readers' interests, and to what extent did they write to appeal to particular audiences? Focus on a specific author or two, and examine their writing process for evidence that they had certain audience taste in mind—for instance, Hawthorne as he wrote *The House of the Seven Gables* or Susan Warner as she wrote *The Wide, Wide World*.

3. The photograph changed celebrity to a visual phenomenon. How did American writers (Whitman is a good example) capitalize on visual celebrity to further their careers and promote themselves as professional authors? Using online and print sources, find photographs of Romantic authors, and using

biographies and editions of their letters, try to discover whether they planned or controlled those photographs.

4. In what ways did literary clubs serve as "workshops" for American writers? Consult their letters or diaries or (if available) published editions of their manuscripts to see how they presented their work for discussion and how they might have changed it as a result.

5. Leo Braudy, in his study *The Frenzy of Renown* (1986), argues that Romantic writers such as Emerson, Whitman, and Dickinson tried to "combat commercialism, technology, and the flatness of constant change" while still being successful in the literary marketplace. Investigate the career of a Romantic author, perhaps using personal letters or journals, to see how he or she negotiated the practical demands of publication while seeming to remain outside the commercial sphere.

RESOURCES

William Charvat, *The Profession of Authorship in America, 1800–1870. The Papers of William Charvat*, edited by Matthew J. Bruccoli (Columbus: Ohio State University Press, 1968).
Essays on the conditions for authorship, studies of individual authors (Poe, Longfellow, Cooper, and Melville, among others), and other examinations of "literary economics."

Michael Newbury, *Figuring Authorship in Antebellum America* (Stanford, Cal.: Stanford University Press, 1997).
Examines the ways in which Romantic authors sought to define themselves in a newly emerging industrial economy.

Angela G. Ray, *The Lyceum and Public Culture in the Nineteenth-Century United States* (East Lansing: Michigan State University Press, 2005).
Argues for the increasing commercialization of the lyceum movement.

Ronald J. Zboray, *A Fictive People: Antebellum Economic Development and the American Reading Public* (New York: Oxford University Press, 1993).
Traces patterns in publication, taste, reading habits, and book distribution.

PEOPLE OF INTEREST

Lyman Beecher (1775–1863)
Father of the novelist Harriet Beecher Stowe, was a Calvinist minister who wrote an anti-Catholic tract, *A Plea for the West* (1835).

Charles Brockden Brown (1771–1810)
Often called America's first professional novelist, was famous for *Wieland* (1798) and *Edgar Huntly* (1799), which combined Gothic elements with American landscapes and characters.

Charles Dickens (1812–1870)
Enormously successful English writer of *David Copperfield* (1849–1850) and *Great Expectations* (1860–1861), made two reading tours of the United States.

William Dunlap (1766–1839)
Playwright and historian of drama, achieved his greatest success with his Revolutionary War drama *André* (1798).

Washington Irving (1783–1859)
Arguably America's most famous author before James Fenimore Cooper, published *The Sketch Book* in 1819 under the pseudonym "Geoffrey Crayon" and wrote such famous American tales as "The Legend of Sleepy Hollow" and "Rip Van Winkle."

Native American Oral Literature

The first-time student of Native American oral literature confronts at once two daunting, though not insurmountable, facts. First, there is the incredible variety of Indian oral culture; by some estimates, at the beginning of European exploration more than five hundred indigenous languages were spoken in what is today the United States and Canada, and over two hundred remain, each with distinctive cultural features. Second, the expectations for literary forms and techniques do not necessarily transfer from one culture to another, so that Native American literature can be misinterpreted or misunderstood if cast in the terms of other literatures. But these problems are also opportunities, for to examine the rich literary traditions of First People is to open the doorway to worldviews, languages, and aesthetics that challenge and enrich an understanding of more commonly canonized Western literature.

Orality was not, of course, a feature only of the Romantic era; most oral literature replicated stories and myths from the timeless past, and so to see it as originating in a particular period would be a mistake. But Native American spoken expression was put in the spotlight by historical changes in Indian treatment and policies in antebellum America that threatened the use of indigenous languages and the cultures they represented. In the nineteenth century, conceptions of the "noble savage" collided with the political and ethnocentric realities of Manifest Destiny. Indian relocation had begun under Thomas Jefferson, who wished Native Americans to occupy a buffer zone between the United States and territories held by Spain and England. After the War of 1812, increased white migration beyond the Alleghenies pressured the United States to push Native Americans to territories beyond the Mississippi River. Enforcement of the Indian Removal Act of 1830 under President Andrew Jackson resulted in the forced relocation of perhaps 100,000 Native Americans. Weather, mistreatment, inadequate nutrition, and sheer exhaustion made conditions brutal on these forced marches: some 3,500 Creeks died in Alabama, and from 1838 to 1839 the infamous "Trail of Tears" took the lives of an estimated 4,000 Cherokees, nearly a fifth of the total Cherokee population. Following the discovery of gold in California in 1848, the United States began stationing troops along the Oregon Trail to protect immigrants traveling westward, a military occupation that further exacerbated relations with Plains tribes.

Ethnographic attention by European Americans to Native Americans and their languages increased during the period, spurred by the work of ethnologists John Heckewelder and Henry Rowe Schoolcraft. But even serious researchers showed little interest in the aesthetics of oral literature, valuing it not as art but as a literal record of Native American ideas and customs. Among the casualties of these policies and attitudes were indigenous languages and oral traditions. Efforts to acculturate Native Americans following the Civil War led to measures like those of the 1868 Commission on Indian Affairs, which recommended the eradication of Native American languages.

With few exceptions, in antebellum America there was little printed literature by Native Americans. Elias Boudinot's pamphlet, *An Address to the Whites*

(1826), argued for white support as the Cherokees acculturated. William Apess wrote *A Son of the Forest* (1829), the first full-length Native American autobiography published in the United States. His essay "An Indian's Looking-Glass for the White Man," part of his collection *The Experiences of Five Christian Indians of the Pequo'd Tribe* (1833), offered a powerful religious condemnation of white prejudice. In their depictions of the brutal treatment of Native Americans, the narratives of Occom and Apess resembled the slave narratives of the time, albeit with a decidedly Christian perspective. Both Boudinot and Apess were powerful orators whose speeches appeared in print. But American Indian literature was overwhelmingly oral until after the Civil War, not just because Native Americans had little access to the business of publishing but because orality had always been the preferred means to share, preserve, and transmit Indian cultures.

While acknowledging the dangers of imposing Western definitions of genre, scholars such as Andrew Wiget identify some common forms of Native American oral literature as creation/origin narratives, trickster tales, oratory, and poetry or songs.

CREATION/ORIGIN NARRATIVES

Varied and widespread across Indian cultures, creation narratives commonly involve a supreme force or deity, a mediating figure who brings about the creation or renewal of the earth, and a narrative movement across time and space. Not merely teleological explanations of the universe, creation myths provide an emotionally resonant sense of unity, a rationale for life and death, and a paradoxical coexistence of both the temporal and the eternal. Among the many examples are the "Old Man" stories of the Blackfeet, in which Na'pi travels the world transforming its geography and creating humans out of clay, and the Zuni story "When Newness was Made."

TRICKSTER NARRATIVES

As Jarold Ramsey notes, the trickster figure appears in many guises, depending upon tribal traditions: Coyote (Plateau, Great Basin, and Rocky Mountain Indians), Raven (North coast groups), Blue Jay, Raccoon, Dragonfly, Spider, Hare, and others. The trickster may be creative or destructive, cautionary or exemplary, antisocial or divine. The intent of trickster narratives varies as well, from pointing out human pretensions to satirizing social institutions or those who ignore them. Barbara Babcock calls the trickster figure a "'criminal' culture-hero" who "embodies all possibilities—the most positive and the most negative—and is paradox personified."

ORATORY

In the nineteenth century some believed that Native Americans had a gift for inspired eloquence. Wiget distinguishes ritual oratory from secular. An example of the first would be ceremonial addresses such as the Iroquois Thanksgiving address that precedes ritual gatherings in the tribal longhouse. (An excellent translation and discussion by Michael K. Foster appears in Brian Swann's 1994 anthology.) The second would be exemplified by the eulogies and political speeches of orators like Boudinot and Apess.

POETRY AND SONG

Distinguished from other oral performance less by their subject than by their form and conventions, Native American poetry and song rely on meter, repetition, figures, and other lyrical devices. Sung verse was sometimes performed by shamans, other times by a singer/poet commemorating an event or offering a kind of prayer or "formula." William Bright's translation and discussion of a Karuk "love medicine" poem in Swann's anthology is an example of the fluid combination of verse and song.

TOPICS FOR DISCUSSION AND RESEARCH

1. A frequent controversy in the discussion of Native American oral literature centers on the political implications of translation. This is particularly problematic when the translation cuts across both language and culture. The autobiography of Black Hawk (Sauk), for instance, published in 1833, was transcribed by a white newspaper editor, who heard it dictated by Black Hawk to an interpreter. At its worst, the act of translation may be seen as a type of colonization, according to Margara Averbach. A more pragmatic position is represented by Jarold Ramsey, who argues that ignoring translated texts poses a greater problem, for it accelerates the disappearance of Native American voices. Students can examine the issue by choosing a single text and researching the circumstances of its translation: who translated it, when, and for what purposes.

2. Translation from the oral to the writtten can also distort by its literalness, ignoring the performative features of spoken art that are difficult to reproduce in print. Many nineteenth-century translations, following the lead of the influential American anthropologist Franz Boas, emphasized literal renderings of the spoken word with an emphasis on accuracy and content, not artistry. In an important revisionist approach, Dennis Tedlock shows the importance of linguistic signals (such as pitch, grammar, archaisms, and interjections) and "oral" or "paralinguistic" features (such as voice quality, loudness, and pausing) to our appreciation of oral texts. Barre Toelken (in the Swann anthology) extends these performative features to include audience responses such as laughter. Examine several examples that include the directions and paralinguistic signals to see how this information is recorded, and consider the effects of inserting a non-narrative voice into the printed text.

3. A similar issue is the use of Westernized genres to categorize Native American oral literature. Critics such as Wiget point out the insuitability of using Western genres and the aesthetics of written texts to categorize oral ones. Babcock maintains, however, that cross-cultural analysis reveals some pro-

nounced similarities between, for example, the trickster figure and Western literary heroes that make a comparative, generic approach legitimate. Using a single text, compare and contrast the interpretation of it when it is defined in Western terms (that is, as an elegy) or in Native American terms (that is, as a "formula"). Alternatively, locate a video reproduction of a poetic performance such as those in *Words and Place: Native Literature from the American Southwest* and compare its effectiveness to a written text.

4. To what extent can we finally ask conventional Western questions of value—about artistic originality, for instance, or authorial intent—of literatures that are essentially collaborative and often ritualized? Even formulaic texts depend upon the individual artistry of the speaker or singer, as Michael K. Foster notes in his work on Iroquoian oratory. However, failure to appreciate the distinctive conventions of Native American spoken literature—what Tedlock calls "a pervasive deafness to oral qualities"—can result in dismissing the texts as repetitive or simplistic. For instance, in Navajo stories, the frequent refrain "it is said" (*jiní*) may strike the Western ear as redundant, but it serves a crucial purpose, to indicate that the narrator is retelling someone else's story and to lend cultural authority to the tale. The structures set out by the anthropologist Dell Hymes provide a strategy and a vocabulary for analyzing oral prose without imposing Western aesthetics on it. One way to investigate this phenomenon would be to locate reviews of published translations and trace the comments, negative and positive, about the presence of such ritualistic phrasings.

5. Despite the difficulties of translation and the loss of performative aspects of the works, critics have stressed the need to include Native American oral literature alongside other Western canonical texts. Arnold Krupat makes the important argument that modern theorists from Michel Foucault to Raymond Williams have challenged key concepts such as authorship, definitions of literature, and canonicity in ways that admit the distinct contributions of Native American oral literature and justify their inclusion in the American classroom.

RESOURCES

Primary Works

Brian Swann, ed., *Coming to Light: Contemporary Translations of the Native Literature of North America* (New York: Random House, 1994).

A comprehensive collection of translated Native American texts, organized by region, with contextual commentary by the translators and an informative editorial introduction.

Lawana Trout, ed., *Native American Literature: An Anthology* (Lincolnwood, Ill.: NTC Publishing Group, 1999).

A collection of Native American songs, tales, and poetry from a range of tribal cultures, including some from the oral tradition of the nineteenth century.

Words and Place: Native Literature from the American Southwest <http://wordsand-place.arizona.edu/index.html> [accessed 3 November 2009].

Produced at the University of Arizona, this site includes filmed performances of Native American oral tales and songs, with English subtitles and commentary.

Criticism

Margara Averbach, "Translation and Resistance in Native North American Literature," *The American Indian Quarterly*, 24 (Spring 2000): 165–181.
Argues that the act of translation is a kind of cultural imperialism that perverts the original by placing it in terms that may not be appropriate.

Barbara Babcock, "'A Tolerated Margin of Mess': The Trickster and His Tales Reconsidered," *Journal of the Folklore Institute*, 9 (1975): 147–186.
Shows the variety of trickster tales across cultures and analyzes the paradoxical nature of the trickster. Reprinted in Wiget, pp. 153–185.

Dell Hymes, *"In Vain I Tried to Tell You": Essays in Native American Ethnopoetics* (Philadelphia: University of Pennsylvania Press, 1981).
Examines the grammatical and semantic structures commonly found in Native American oral literature.

Arnold Krupat, "An Approach to Native American Texts," *Critical Inquiry*, 9 (1982): 323–338.
Defends attention to printed texts and argues for the need to systematize inquiry into Native American literature by examining modes of production and the concepts of authorship, literature, and canonicity in light of current critical theory. Reprinted in Wiget, *Critical Essays*, pp. 116–131.

Jarold Ramsey, *Reading the Fire: The Traditional Indian Literatures of America*, revised and expanded edition (Seattle & London: University of Washington Press, 1999).
Includes essays about representative Native works from a range of Indian communities across the country, concentrating on the Far West. Discusses, among others, origin narratives and trickster tales.

Dennis Tedlock, "On the Translation of Style in Oral Narrative," *The Journal of American Folklore*, 84 (January–March 1971): 114–133.
Argues for "treatment of oral narrative as dramatic poetry" and defends the stylistic complexity of Native American oral literature, using examples from the Zuni tradition.

Andrew Wiget, *Native American Literature* (New York: Twayne, 1985).
A mature scholarly overview of the literature from its beginnings to the present, as well as the theoretical and scholarly contexts.

Wiget, ed., *Critical Essays on Native American Literature* (Boston: G. K. Hall, 1985).
An important collection that includes essays on methodological approaches and an excellent survey of nineteenth-century published literature by Native Americans.

PEOPLE OF INTEREST

William Apess (1798–1839)
Mother was a Pequot, was a staunch defender of Indian rights.

Black Hawk (1767–1838)
Sauk chief, was an opponent of United States expansion into his tribe's territory; his views appear in his autobiography, which was dictated to a government interpreter and published in 1833.

Elias Boudinot (circa 1804–1839)
Cherokee, edited the *Cherokee Phoenix*, the first Native American newspaper in the United States.

John Heckewelder (1743–1823)
Moravian missionary whose *Account of the History, Manners, and Customs of the Indian Nations* (1819) influenced the Leather-Stocking tales of James Fenimore Cooper.

Samson Occom (1723–1792)
Mohican, wrote a famous autobiography that was written sometime after 1768 but not printed in its entirety until 1982.

Henry Rowe Schoolcraft (1793–1864)
An ethnographer whose *Algic Researches* (1839) included translated texts.

Romanticism

The terms "Romanticism" and "Romantic" should not be confused with the popular meaning, as pertaining to love. "Romanticism" derives from the genre of the medieval romance, a heroic narrative emphasizing the importance of chivalry and valor in battle. Many Romantic authors, artists, and composers were fascinated by the Middle Ages and its legends of fair maidens, valiant knights, and evil villains. This fixation was part of Romanticism's reaction against the materialism and ordinariness of modern life, particularly the Industrial Revolution and the Enlightenment. Otherwise, Romanticism is defined by the following characteristics:

- Promotion of individualism and celebration of eccentric individuals who refuse to conform to social norms or accede to traditional authority figures
- Celebration of nature's beauty and its ability to enhance human spirituality
- Interest in imagination (as opposed to reason, logic, and empirical observation)
- Interest in emotions, especially emotional extremes
- Celebration of the rural life and the "common folk" living in rural areas
- Celebration of Native Americans and other non-European groups as "noble savages"
- Support for revolution, especially the French Revolution

In addition to these features, Romanticism is characterized by its emphasis on the sublime and picturesque. These terms were used by the aesthetic theoretician Edmund Burke, whose essay "A Philosophical Enquiry into the Origin of Our Ideas of the Sublime and Beautiful" (1757) set the terms for later Romantic authors and artists. Burke defined the sublime as a quality that invokes awe and even terror in the human mind. The sublime refers to objects that are immense in scale, and often these objects are not entirely visible. Examples from the natural world include oceans, mountains, glaciers, and storms—all of which are huge, overwhelming, menacing, and fascinating. On the other hand, the beautiful—often termed the picturesque—includes small, smooth, delicate objects that are easy and pleasant to observe such as flowers, calm winding streams, and small, harmless creatures. Romantic works set in medieval locations that emphasize the sublime often overlap with Gothicism and its fascination with the supernatural.

The Romantic movement may be traced to Germany in the mid eighteenth century, where its tenets were expressed especially in the works of Johann Wolfgang von Goethe, whose novel *The Sorrows of Young Werther* (1774) celebrated the unrestrained emotional expressions of its protagonist. Literary Romanticism soon spread to England and was embraced by writers such as William Blake, William Wordsworth, and Samuel Taylor Coleridge. The Scottish author Sir Walter Scott was among the foremost Romantic novelists. Romantic texts that incorporate

Gothic elements include Mary Shelley's *Frankenstein* (1818) and John William Polidori's "The Vampyre" (1819). One of the first American writers to adopt Romanticism was the poet Philip Freneau, author of "The Power of Fancy" (1770) and "The Wild Honey-Suckle" (1786). However, Romanticism did not take serious hold in American literature until the early nineteenth century.

It is not surprising that Romanticism had a profound impact on American literature throughout much of the nineteenth century. The landscape in many parts of the United States and its surrounding frontiers was often beautiful and awe inspiring, and those regions lying to the west of the frontier stirred the imaginations of many Americans. The presence of Native Americans prompted Romantics to view them as noble savages, a motif borrowed from the French Romantic author Jean-Jacques Rousseau. Although American authors did not look to the Middle Ages as much as their European counterparts did, they often set their works in America's colonial past. Furthermore, the fact that the nation began in a revolution appealed to many Romantic nationalists. Finally, the American support for individual freedom and expression overlapped extensively with Romanticism, which shared some of the features of Transcendentalism, such as individualism and glorification of Nature. The two movements are not identical, though.

Several major American authors from this period were deeply influenced by Romanticism. Some fictional examples of American Romanticism include the tales of Washington Irving (the most famous of which are "Rip Van Winkle" and "The Legend of Sleepy Hollow") and the historical romances of Catharine Maria Sedgwick (for example, *Hope Leslie*, 1827), James Fenimore Cooper (*The Pioneers*, 1823; *The Last of the Mohicans*, 1826; *The Prairie*, 1827; *The Pathfinder*, 1840; and *The Deerslayer*, 1841), and Nathaniel Hawthorne (for example, *The Scarlet Letter*, 1850). Romanticism's glorification of Nature permeated many of these works. For instance, Irving's tales abound with lush descriptions of the beauty of the Hudson River valley in New York, while Sedgwick's *Hope Leslie* paints vivid pictures of the gorgeous scenery of colonial New England. The noble-savage motif is also evident in *Hope Leslie* as well as Cooper's novels. Herman Melville's descriptions of the noble savages of Tahiti in *Typee* (1846) and his use of the concept of the sublime in describing the ocean and the white whale in *Moby-Dick* (1851) also reveal his debt to Romanticism. Both Hawthorne and Melville share Romanticism's emphasis on individualism in *The Scarlet Letter* and *Moby-Dick*, respectively, as do the essays of Transcendentalists Ralph Waldo Emerson and Henry David Thoreau and the poetry of Walt Whitman and Emily Dickinson. The poetry and fiction of Edgar Allan Poe is also characteristic of Romanticism in its emphasis on emotion and imagination, and the medieval settings of some of his Gothic tales are also characteristic of the movement. Most American poets of this time, including Emerson, Whitman, and the so-called "Fireside Poets" of New England—Henry Wadsworth Longfellow, John Greenleaf Whittier, William Cullen Bryant, James Russell Lowell, and Oliver Wendell Holmes—also relied on Romantic conventions.

TOPICS FOR DISCUSSION AND RESEARCH

1. Choose a text by Cooper, Sedgwick, or Irving and examine how it depicts America's colonial past. Which elements of America's past do these authors seem to long for? Conversely, which aspects do they depict negatively? See William Kelly's book *Plotting America's Past: Fenimore Cooper and the Leatherstocking Tales* (1983), Amanda Emerson's essay "History, Memory, and the Echoes of Equivalence in Catharine Maria Sedgwick's *Hope Leslie*" (2007), and Howard Horowitz's article "'Rip Van Winkle' and Legendary National Memory" (2004).

2. Many Romantic American authors, such as Cooper, Longfellow, Sedgwick, and William Gilmore Simms, often depicted American Indians as noble savages. Which positive and negative characteristics do these writers ascribe to this group? In what ways do these authors use these depictions to comment on their own society and culture? *An Early and Strong Sympathy* (edited by John Caldwell Guilds and Charles Hudson, 2003) includes writings by Simms about American Indians. See Richard Shaner's article "Simms and the Noble Savage" (1976) and Susanne Opfermann's essay "Lydia Maria Child, James Fenimore Cooper, and Catharine Maria Sedgwick: A Dialogue on Race, Culture, and Gender" (1999). Gaile McGregor's *The Noble Savage in the New World Garden* (1988) also includes a chapter on Cooper's depictions of American Indians.

3. In what ways do American Romantic authors adapt Romanticism to American culture and geography? Which elements of English Romanticism are they borrowing, and in which ways do they depart from English Romanticism? One might compare Poe's Gothic fiction to Shelley's *Frankenstein,* or compare Wordsworth's poetry to poems by Emerson or the Fireside Poets in their glorification of nature. One starting point for researching this topic is Lance Newman's electronic book *Sullen Fires Across the Atlantic: Essays in Transatlantic Romanticism* (2006; http://www.rc.umd.edu/praxis/sullenfires/intro/intro.html).

4. How has American Romantic literature influenced later American literature? Consider how Romantic themes such as individualism, imagination, emotional expression, rebellion, and natural beauty are used by twentieth century authors. For example, explore the similarities between Walt Whitman and Allen Ginsberg, or examine Henry David Thoreau's impact on Gary Snyder or Robinson Jeffers. See John Osborne's essay "The Beats" in *A Companion to Twentieth-Century Poetry* (2001) or Patrick Murphy's article "Robinson Jeffers, Gary Snyder, and the Problem of Civilization" in *Robinson Jeffers and a Galaxy of Writers* (1995).

5. What are the parallels between American Romantic literature and American Romantic art? For instance, compare the celebration of natural beauty in works by Cooper, Irving, Sedgwick, or Thoreau to the landscape paintings of Thomas Cole. To learn more about the paintings of Cole and the Hudson River School, consult Barbara Babcock Milhouse's *American Wilderness: The Story of the Hudson River School of Painting* (2007).

RESOURCES

William L. Andrews, ed., *Literary Romanticism in America* (Baton Rouge: Louisiana State University Press, 1981).
Includes seven essays focusing on the Romantic elements in the works of Emerson and Hawthorne, early African American fiction, and the concept of the "self-made man" in American autobiography.

Edward Halsey Foster, *The Civilized Wilderness: Backgrounds to American Romantic Literature, 1817–1860* (New York: Free Press, 1975).
A helpful introduction to American Romantic literature.

Michael T. Gilmore, *American Romanticism and the Marketplace* (Chicago: University of Chicago Press, 1985).
Examines the works of Emerson, Thoreau, Hawthorne, and Melville and connects their attitudes toward the commodification of literature to the shift from an agrarian to a market economy in antebellum America.

Jennifer A. Hurley, *American Romanticism* (San Diego, Cal.: Greenhaven Press, 2000).
A collection of articles that places romanticism within social, political, literary, and philosophical contexts.

Gaile McGregor, *The Noble Savage in the New World Garden: Notes Toward a Syntactics of Place* (Bowling Green, Ohio: Bowling Green State University Popular Press, 1988).
Includes a long section on the noble savage in American culture and literature.

Lance Newman, Chris Koenig-Woodyard, and Joel Pace, eds., *Sullen Fires across the Atlantic: Essays in Transatlantic Romanticism* (College Park: University of Maryland Press, 2006) <http://www.rc.umd.edu/praxis/sullenfires> [accessed 20 October 2009].
A Web-based electronic book of essays examining transatlantic connections in Romantic literature.

PEOPLE OF INTEREST

William Blake (1757–1827)
English poet, painter, and printmaker, was one of the first writers and visual artists to embrace Romanticism. His best-known literary work is his collection of poems *Songs of Innocence and of Experience* (1789).

Edmund Burke (1729–1797)
Anglo-Irish statesman, author, political theorist, and philosopher, lived much of his life in England and was a prominent critic of the French Revolution.

Samuel Taylor Coleridge (1772–1834)
English poet, literary critic, and philosopher, collaborated with William Wordsworth in writing *Lyrical Ballads* and is best known for his poems "The Rime of the Ancient Mariner" and "Kubla Khan."

Philip Morin Freneau (1752–1832)
American poet, political writer, and newspaper editor who supported the American Revolution.

Johann Wolfgang von Goethe (1749–1832)
German poet, novelist, dramatist, essayist, and philosopher, was a pioneer of Romantic literature.

Washington Irving (1783–1859)
American fiction writer, biographer, and historian, is best known for his satire *A History of New-York* (1809) as well as *The Sketch Book* (1819), which included "Rip Van Winkle" and "The Legend of Sleepy Hollow."

John William Polidori (1795–1821)
Italian-English physician and author, is known for his 1819 short story "The Vampyre," the first vampire story in English.

Jean-Jacques Rousseau (1712–1778)
French philosopher and author whose ideas inspired the French Revolution, is known for his novels *Julie, ou la nouvelle Héloïse* (1761) and *Emile: or, On Education* (1762).

Sir Walter Scott (1771–1832)
Scottish author who wrote narrative poems such as *Marmion* (1808) and *The Lady of the Lake* (1810) as well as prose historical romances such as *Waverly* (1814) and *Ivanhoe* (1819).

Mary Shelley (1797–1851)
English author, best known for her Gothic novel *Frankenstein: or, The Modern Prometheus* (1818).

William Wordsworth (1770–1850)
English poet, is best known for his Romantic lyric poetry. His most famous volume of poetry, *Lyrical Ballads* (1798), was written with Samuel Taylor Coleridge.

Slavery and Abolitionism

Antislavery literature can be traced as far back as Samuel Sewall's 1700 tract "The Selling of Joseph." Some Founding Fathers, such as Thomas Jefferson and Benjamin Franklin, also wrote against slavery in *Notes on the State of Virginia* (1785) and "On the Slave Trade" (1790), respectively, though Jefferson's antislavery commitments did not extend to manumitting his own slaves. However, the American abolitionist movement was not significantly organized until around 1830. In 1831, William Lloyd Garrison began publishing his antislavery newspaper *The Liberator*, and he became the most powerful abolitionist in America.

Although Garrison and many other leaders of the movement were white, the efforts of African American abolitionists were crucial to the eventual success of the movement, and many of them contributed through literature. During the mid nineteenth century, the slave narrative became one of the fastest growing literary genres in America. While Frederick Douglass's 1845 *Narrative* and his 1855 *My Bondage and My Freedom* are the most famous examples, other popular slave narratives were written or told by Moses Roper, Sojourner Truth, Henry Bibb, William Wells Brown, Harriet Jacobs, and dozens of others. Part autobiography and part antislavery propaganda, slave narratives were the movement's most popular form of literature. Many abolitionists, both black and white, also wrote anti-slavery fiction and poetry. Some examples include Lydia Maria Child's stories "Mary French and Susan Easton" (1834) and "The Black Saxons" (1841), Richard Hildreth's novel *The Slave: or Memoir of Archy Moore* (1836), John Greenleaf Whittier's poems "The Hunters of Men" (1835) and "The Farewell" (1838), and Frances Ellen Watkins's poem "The Slave Mother" (1857). Another antislavery text, Brown's 1853 *Clotel; or The President's Daughter* (discussed in the study guide "Antebellum African American Novels" in section II of this volume), was the first novel written by an African American. The most famous antislavery novel was Harriet Beecher Stowe's *Uncle Tom's Cabin*, originally published in serial form in the Free Soil newspaper *The National Era* in 1851-1852 and later in book form in March 1852. The novel was dramatized countless times and also inspired many imitations as well as many proslavery novels written as "corrections" to Stowe's work, such as William Gilmore Simms's *The Sword and the Distaff* (1852; republished as *Woodcraft* in 1854) and Caroline Lee Hentz's *The Planter's Northern Bride* (1854).

TOPICS FOR DISCUSSION AND RESEARCH

1. What role did civil disobedience play in the abolitionist movement? Henry David Thoreau's essay "Resistance to Civil Government" (1849) is a logical starting point for understanding the concept of civil disobedience. It might also be interesting to compare the abolitionist movement to the twentieth-century civil-rights movement, particularly the philosophy of Martin Luther King Jr., with regard to civil disobedience. Consulting Henry Mayer's *All on Fire: William Lloyd Garrison and the Abolition of Slavery* and James M. Washington's collection of King's essays and speeches in *A Testament of Hope*

will help students see how both Garrison and King believed in the power of civil disobedience.

2. Which rhetorical strategies did slave narratives use to argue against slavery? In researching this question, one might examine not only the well-known narratives of Douglass and Jacobs but also the dozens of lesser-known narratives that may be found in the "North American Slave Narratives" section of the University of North Carolina Library's database *Documenting the American South* <http://docsouth.unc.edu/neh/>. Helpful secondary sources about slave narratives include William L. Andrews's *To Tell a Free Story* and Charles T. Davis and Henry Louis Gates's *The Slave's Narrative.*

3. How did proslavery authors respond to *Uncle Tom's Cabin* and other abolitionist literature? In addition to the novels by Simms and Hentz mentioned above, George Fitzhugh's book-length essay *Sociology for the South* (1854) is typical of much proslavery literature. Thomas F. Gossett's essay "Anti-Uncle Tom Literature," which can be found in the Norton Critical Edition of *Uncle Tom's Cabin*, is a helpful overview of this genre, as is the website "Anti Uncle Tom Novels" <http://utc.iath.virginia.edu/proslav/antitoms.html>.

4. How do early antislavery texts like Sewall's "The Selling of Joseph," Franklin's "On the Slave Trade," and the "Manners" chapter in Jefferson's *Notes on the State of Virginia* compare to nineteenth-century abolitionist propaganda? One approach would be to consider both the religious and secular elements to arguments in both eighteenth- and nineteenth-century antislavery writing. Another approach would be to consider these works in their historical contexts to see how slavery evolved from the eighteenth century to the nineteenth century. Charles Johnson and Patricia Smith's *Africans in America* is an excellent historical source about American slavery.

5. Although slavery in the United States was abolished about a century and a half ago, it still exists in other parts of the world today, often in the form of child labor or prostitution. How do the efforts to end present-day slavery compare to those of nineteenth-century America? Students can find out about one such organization, the Anti-Slavery International, from their website "Abolish Slavery—Soon" <http://www.abolishslaverysoon.webs.com>; another abolitionist organization, the American Anti-Slavery Group, also has a website <http://www.iabolish.org>.

RESOURCES

William L. Andrews, *To Tell a Free Story: The First Century of Afro-American Autobiography, 1760-1860* (Urbana: University of Illinois Press, 1986).
Analyzes the freedom and constrictions facing authors of slave narratives and other African American autobiographies.

Charles T. Davis and Henry Louis Gates Jr., eds., *The Slave's Narrative* (New York: Oxford University Press, 1985).
Includes ten contemporary reviews of slave narratives and several essays analyzing slave narratives as historical documents and literary texts.

Thomas F. Gossett, "Anti-Uncle Tom Literature," *Uncle Tom's Cabin: Authoritative Text, Backgrounds and Contexts, Criticism*, edited by Elizabeth Ammons (New York: Norton, 1994), pp. 442–453.
Examines the novels written in the wake of *Uncle Tom's Cabin* that countered Stowe's depictions of slavery by depicting it positively.

Charles Johnson, Patricia Smith, and the WGBH Series Research Team, *Africans in America: America's Journey through Slavery* (New York, San Diego, & London: Harcourt Brace, 1998).
A companion text to the PBS series *Africans in America* that traces the history of African Americans from the beginning of the Atlantic slave trade through the abolition of slavery in the United States. Includes illustrations and features historically based short stories by Charles Johnson depicting slaves.

Henry Mayer, *All on Fire: William Lloyd Garrison and the Abolition of Slavery* (New York: Norton, 1998).
A thorough biography of Garrison that focuses on his role in the antislavery movement and analyzes his writings in *The Liberator*.

James M. Washington, ed., *A Testament of Hope: The Essential Writings and Speeches of Martin Luther King, Jr.* (New York: Harper Collins, 1990).
Contains over fifty speeches, essays, and other writings by King.

PEOPLE OF INTEREST

Henry Bibb (1815–1854)
African American abolitionist, author, and journalist born into slavery, wrote *Narrative of the Life and Adventures of Henry Bibb, an American Slave* (1849) and founded the antislavery newspaper *Voice of the Fugitive* in Canada in 1851.

Lydia Maria Child (1802–1880)
American novelist, abolitionist, women's-rights activist, Indian-rights activist, novelist, and journalist, is best known for her antislavery treatise *An Appeal in Favor of that Class of Americans Called Africans* (1833) and her historical romance *Hobomok* (1824).

Benjamin Franklin (1706–1790)
American diplomat, statesman, printer, inventor, scientist, and writer, is well known for his *Autobiography* (1791), his role in the movement for American independence from Britain, and his experiments with electricity.

William Lloyd Garrison (1805–1879)
American social reformer, orator, and journalist, founded the abolitionist periodical *The Liberator* in 1831 and the American Anti-Slavery Society in 1833.

Caroline Lee Hentz (1800–1856)
American novelist, wrote the proslavery novel *The Planter's Northern Bride* (1854).

Richard Hildreth (1807–1865)
American author, journalist, and historian, wrote the antislavery novel *The Slave: or Memoir of Archy Moore* (1836).

Thomas Jefferson (1743–1826)
American statesmen, diplomat, and author who wrote the Declaration of Independence (1776) and served as president of the United States (1801–1809).

Moses Roper (circa 1815–1891)
African American abolitionist and lecturer born into slavery, wrote *Narrative of the Adventures and Escape of Moses Roper from American Slavery* (1838).

Samuel Sewall (1652–1730)
Massachusetts judge, essayist, and diarist who participated in the Salem witch trials and wrote the antislavery tract "The Selling of Joseph" (1700).

Frances Ellen Watkins Harper (1825–1911)
African American abolitionist, poet, and fiction writer whose best-known work is her novel *Iola Leroy* (1892).

Southwestern Humor

Southwestern humor is geographically misnamed, as its most prominent writers (not all of them Southwesterners) resided in states and territories as far east as Georgia and as far north as Tennessee. It is sometimes called "frontier" humor, because its plots and characters typically reflect rural values and offer critiques of mid-century ideas of civilization. The movement flourished at the height of American Romanticism, from the 1830s through the 1860s, and coincided with both the rise of sectarian conflict in the United States and the development of a magazine culture. In fact, one of the most prominent "sporting magazines" (so named because they often included stories about hunting and fishing), William T. Porter's *Spirit of the Times* (1831–1861), was published in New York; it became the chief outlet for Southwestern humor, publishing many of the movement's most important writers before they went on to collect their tales in book form.

Southwestern humor is indebted to an antebellum interest in American regionalism, as well as the popularity of the David Crockett Almanacs (1835–1856), narratives written in the first person as if by Crockett (though not by him; he died in 1836) which mythologized the hero of the Alamo and promoted exaggerated tales of his bravery, prowess, and heroism. Characters in Southwestern tales are usually extreme, from the ribald vengeance of Sut Lovingood (made famous in a series of tales by George Washington Harris) or the scheming selfishness of Simon Suggs (a creation of Johnson Jones Hooper). Plots usually revolve around the exaggerated conflict, violence, and improbabilities associated with the tall-tale tradition. The protagonists are frontier types, usually poor and uneducated, who are shown to be superior to the ostensibly more powerful members of their society by tricking them and thus revealing the illusory nature of social power and rank. The disparity between appearance and reality is also reflected in the form of most Southwestern humor, the framed tale, a story within a story reported by an outside narrator in which the differences between the two narrators are revealed. In his *Native American Humor* (1937), Walter Blair identifies three underlying incongruities that often define Southwestern humor narratives:

- Between grammatical language of the frame and dialect of the internal tale
- Between situation of the tale and situation of the telling
- Between the realism of the frame and the fantasy of the tale itself.

One of the most famous tales of the genre, "The Big Bear of Arkansas" (1841) by Thomas Bangs Thorpe, illustrates some of these features. Its frontier narrator entertains a cabin full of travelers on their way down the Mississippi River with an increasingly outlandish hunting tale about a mythical bear who manages to elude him year after year. The frontiersman's story is itself narrated by an unnamed traveler, whose language clearly marks him as educated but unfamiliar with frontier ways. Like the other travelers, he is naively tricked into listening to the outlandish tale until the anticlimactic ending—the bear gives up and dies simply because its time had come. While the narrator interprets the story as the simple superstition of frontier "children of the wood," in fact it is the supposedly sophisticated travelers who are gullible enough to listen to the tale and then reward its teller with drinks. The joke is finally on them; the humor resides not in the tale but the telling of it; the powerful are shown to be foolish and the unsophisticated to be shrewd and powerful. In many ways Southwestern humor reflects Romantic anxieties over the power of the individual and critiques the viability of pluralism as an American value.

Johnson Jones Hooper (1815–1862) and George Washington Harris (1814–1869) are arguably the best exemplars of the tradition of Southwestern humor. Hooper, a lawyer and newspaper editor, is today best known for his 1846 collection, *Some Adventures of Captain Simon Suggs, Late of the Tallapoosa Volunteers; Together with "Taking the Census," and Other Alabama Sketches.* Harris's work ranges from playful sketches of rural Tennessee life to scathing political satire to the extravagant humor of his most enduring creation, the titular hero of Harris's 1867 collection *Sut Lovingood. Yarns Spun by a "Nat'ral Born Durn'd Fool["].* With their comic exaggerations, tall tales, rural dialects, and subversive challenges to authority by backwoods tricksters, the tales by Hooper and Harris have earned a minor, but firm, place in the history of American literature.

The tales of Hooper, like Harris a Southerner and secessionist, originated in topical criticism of recent political events, mostly from the Andrew Jackson presidency. But like Harris's Sut Lovingood, Hooper's Simon Suggs transcends the narrowly political to make a statement about the human condition. Born in Wilmington, North Carolina, in 1815, Hooper lived most of his life in Alabama; a lawyer and newspaper editor, he published his first humorous sketch in 1843. The tale was reprinted in William T. Porter's *Spirit of the Times.* In 1844 Hooper published the first of his Simon Suggs stories, and their popularity led to the collection *Some Adventures of Captain Simon Suggs.* For the remainder of his career Hooper divided his time between writing, the law, and newspaper journalism. His later tales are collected in *A Ride with Old Kit Kuncker* (1849), enlarged as *The Widow Rugby's Husband* (1851).

Simon Suggs is the ultimate political scammer who exposes fraud and hypocrisy while at the same time benefiting himself financially or socially. Among the most famous of the adventures are "Simon Becomes Captain" and "The Captain Attends a Camp-Meeting." In the first, Suggs capitalizes on false rumors of an Indian insurgency to establish martial law and set himself up as head of the Tallapoosa Volunteers, a group of predatory scoundrels. (The frame narrator wryly comments that their nickname, "The Forty Thieves," was inaccurate because they never numbered more than thirty-nine.) Trading on the community's gullibility and fear, Suggs is opposed by a cowardly skeptic named Yellow Legs (Suggs calls him a "durned, little, dirt-eatin' deer-face") and the belligerent Widow Haycock, who is mistakenly shot in a mock battle whose only other casualties are "a poney and a yoke of steers, haltered to their owner's carts in the road." In "The Captain Attends a Camp-Meeting," Suggs dupes a local gathering of religious revivalists into donating money for the reform of pirates. Fools and hypocrites all, from the lecherous preacher to the pious slave owner, the crowd is an easy and deserving mark for Suggs, as is the Reverend Bela Bugg, a fraud himself. Amoral and conniving, the ultimate confidence man, Suggs takes as his motto, "It is good to be shifty in a new country."

George Washington Harris was born near Pittsburgh, Pennsylvania, on 20 March 1814, but spent most of his life in Knoxville, Tennessee, where he was apprenticed in his brother's jewelry-making business. He married in 1835, and during his lifetime he was variously employed as a steamboat captain, gentleman farmer, metalworker, surveyor, and businessman. After an apprenticeship as a contributor to local newspapers, in 1843 Harris published his first full-length story in the most important venue for the Southwestern humorists, Porter's *The Spirit of the Times*. Writing as "Mr. Free" and "Sugartail" (a local name for a jackass), Harris wrote sporadically for Porter's magazine until 1854, when he wrote his final piece for Porter and the first to feature the backwoods rascal who would make Harris famous: "Sut Lovingood's Daddy, Acting Horse." With the plowing horse dead and planting time come, Dad decides to play the horse's role to prompt the other family members to get to work, and he takes the acting too far. As Sut's mother tells Dad, "Yu plays hoss better nur yu dus husban." Barging through a stand of sassafras, Dad upsets a hornets' nest, strips off the horsehide disguise, and heads naked for the safety of the creek, kicking and squealing "jis es natral es yu ever seed any uther skeer'd hoss du" as the hornets swarm around him.

The tale, which opened the 1867 *Yarns*, introduces some of the signature features of the Lovingood collection: the powerful made powerless, the bestial nature of mankind, Sut's tendency to perpetrate "skeers" as a way of asserting his place in society, and the citified outside narrator who frames Sut's stories. In later yarns this narrator is called "George," probably a thinly veiled persona for the author himself, and he is occasionally a character as well as a scene setter. In this story, his role is merely to prepare the reader for Sut's entrance and provide a vivid description of Sut: "a queer looking, long legged, short bodied, small headed, white haired, hog eyed, funny sort of a genius."

Two of Harris's most often discussed Lovingood stories are "Parson John Bullen's Lizards" and "Hen Baily's Reformation." In the first, Sut plots revenge on the minister who has humiliated him when he catches Sut in the huckleberry bushes with a young woman. Sut attends one of the parson's camp meetings, pretending to be moved to conversion so he can sidle close to the stage; at the moment of the parson's greatest triumph—the regeneration of the sinner—Sut stuffs lizards up Bullen's pantlegs, tormenting him with a real-world equivalent of the devil's serpents in Bullen's sermon. Bullen's gyrations, the antics of the lizards, and the crowd's prurient joy when the parson strips off his clothing and runs off in terror call forth some of Harris's most breathless and lively prose. "Hen Baily's Reformation" recounts another representative "skeer." A secret drunkard, Hen mistakenly drinks turpentine and swallows a live lizard while quenching himself with a gourdful of water. In a bizarre "cure,"

Sut and his cohorts stuff a mole up Baily's pantleg—hoping, they claim, that Hen will mistake it for an escaping lizard. But the mole enters Hen through his anus, chasing the lizard out his mouth, and the terrified Baily afterward joins a temperance society, where he claims ("the cussed hippercrit!") to have been avoiding liquor all along.

TOPICS FOR DISCUSSION AND RESEARCH

1. A major theme in Southwestern humor is the democratic reversal of power, seemingly a testimony to faith in the "common man." The plots, however, are often racist and misogynistic. In what ways do the tales critique the evils of racism and misogyny, and in what ways do they reflect them? See Richard Boyd Hauck, *A Cheerful Nihilism* (1971), for some of the political and social subversions of American humor.

2. Walter Blair and Hamlin Hill in *America's Humor: From Poor Richard to Doonesbury* (1978) discuss "the most enduring American comic type: the homespun, unlettered, but shrewd man of common sense." Does this description seem to fit the protagonists of the Southwestern humor tales? Consider how much of their humor turns on the reversal between those who are "unlettered, but shrewd" and those who are educated but gullible, and examine this put-down of education in the context of the rise of public school education in the United States.

3. As Jesse Bier points out in *The Rise and Fall of American Humor* (1968), common targets of Southwestern humor are pretension, complacency, and conformity. But the protagonists are themselves sometimes petty, cruel, and selfish. Are they examples of Romantic individualism and antisocialism, or are they merely eccentric?

4. While the Southwestern humor tradition seems to have died out after the American Civil War, its legacy clearly extends to works like *The Adventures of Huckleberry Finn* (1884). In form and theme, how did the tradition of Southwestern humor influence later writers like Mark Twain, William Faulkner, and Flannery O'Connor?

5. Critical reception of the Southwestern humorists has always been divided between those like Edmund Wilson, who dismissed Harris's tales as "crude and brutal" in his *Patriotic Gore* (1962), and those like Brom Weber, who praised them in his 1954 edition of *Sut Lovingood* for representing "traditional and wholesome values" like justice and protection of the weak. With reference to the stories, to the criticism, or to both, what are the arguments on both sides?

6. The boundary between historical fact and fiction is particularly permeable in Harris's and Hooper's work. Like much of the Southwestern humor tradition, it relies on exaggeration rather than imagination. Sut Lovingood's tall tales are in the tradition of the David Crockett Almanacs, which retold and stretched the exploits of the real-life Crockett and the riverboat man Mike Fink. Some of Suggs's military adventures are satiric reimaginings of episodes in the early career of Andrew Jackson, and the entire collection has been seen

as a burlesque of nineteenth-century campaign biographies. How are historical events represented in the tales, and to what effect?

7. Students might investigate the ways in which Harris and Hooper influence later American writers. Mark Twain, whose brief review of the Lovingood *Yarns* commended the book's humor but predicted—rightly—that Eastern readers "will find it coarse and possibly taboo it," put the trickster figure to good use in *The Adventures of Huckleberry Finn* (1884), particularly in the figures of the fraudulent King and Duke. Simon Suggs lives on in the scheming members of William Faulkner's Snopes family and in the comic avengers who populate the stories of Flannery O'Connor.

RESOURCES

Primary Works

George Washington Harris, *Sut Lovingood. Yarns Spun by a "Nat'ral Born Durn'd Fool.["] Warped and Wove for Public Wear* (New York: Dick & Fitzgerald, 1867).

Johnson Jones Hooper, *Some Adventures of Captain Simon Suggs, Late of the Tallapoosa Volunteers; Together with "Taking the Census," and Other Alabama Sketches* (Philadelphia: Carey & Hart, 1846).

Biography

W. Stanley Hoole, *Alias Simon Suggs: The Life and Times of Johnson Jones Hooper* (University: University of Alabama Press, 1952).
The standard biography.

Angel Price, "Southwestern Humor and Mark Twain," *Mark Twain in His Times* (2007) <http://etext.virginia.edu/railton/projects/price/southwes.htm> [accessed 4 November 2009].
Useful brief biographies of the Southwestern humorists, along with selected texts.

Milton Rickels, *George Washington Harris* (New York: Twayne, 1966).
An accurate biography combined with an analysis of the works.

Paul Somers, *Johnson J. Hooper* (Boston: Twayne, 1984).
Combines biography and criticism.

Criticism

Jesse Bier, *The Rise and Fall of American Humor* (New York: Holt, Rinehart & Winston, 1968).
Traces the history of American humor as antithetical to American values.

Walter Blair and Hamlin Hill, *America's Humor: From Poor Richard to Doonesbury* (New York: Oxford University Press, 1978).

Part Two, "The Golden Age of American Humor," examines exaggeration, anti-intellectualism, and native speech in antebellum humor.

James E. Caron and Thomas M. Inge, eds., *Sut Lovingood's Nat'ral Born Yarnspinner: Essays on George Washington Harris* (Tuscaloosa & London: University of Alabama Press, 1996).
Essays on a variety of perspectives; includes a useful bibliography of work on Harris.

M. Thomas Inge, *The Frontier Humorists: Critical Views* (Hamden, Conn.: Shoe String Press, 1975).
Reprints twenty important essays on the Southwestern humorists, prefaced by a valuable introductory survey of the group. Excellent bibliography of criticism through the early 1970s.

M. Thomas Inge and Edward J. Piacentino, eds., *The Humor of the Old South* (Lexington: University of Kentucky Press, 2001).
Essays exploring the influence of Harris and Hooper on later American writers and comic traditions.

Lawrence E. Mintz, ed., *Humor in America: A Research Guide to Genres and Topics* (Westport, Conn.: Greenwood Press, 1988).
Essays on a variety of approaches, including film, ethnic humor, and women's humor; see especially the sections on literary humor and humor in periodicals for some contexts for Southwestern humorists.

Noel Polk, "The Blind Bull, Human Nature: Sut Lovingood and the Damned Human Race," in *Gyascutus: Studies in Antebellum Southern Humorous and Sporting Writing,* edited by James L. W. West (Atlantic Highlands, N.J.: Humanities Press, 1978), pp. 13–49.

Johanna Nicol Shields, "A Sadder Simon Suggs: Freedom and Slavery in the Humor of Johnson Hooper," in *Humor of the Old South* (Lexington: University Press of Kentucky, 2001), pp. 130–153.
Argues for Hooper's political vision of "a new moral order in which good men must earn the right to organize a progressive society."

Southwestern Humor, 1830–1860 <http://www.wsu.edu/~campbelld/amlit/swhumor.htm> [accessed 2 November 2009].
A website maintained by Donna M. Campbell of Washington State University, containing reliable notes about the movement and links to texts and author information.

Southwestern Humor: Criticism and Defense of an American Character <http://xroads.virginia.edu/~HYPER/DETOC/sw/front.html> [accessed 2 November 2009].
A website assembled by John Molinaro that reproduces representative texts, discusses the cultural aspects of Southwestern humor, and provides links to brief critical biographies of the major Southwestern humorists.

Edmund Wilson, "Poisoned!" in his *Patriotic Gore: Studies in the Literature of the American Civil War* (New York: Oxford University Press, 1962), pp. 507–519.
A generally unsympathetic view of the Southwestern humorists.

PEOPLE OF INTEREST

Augustus Baldwin Longstreet (1790–1870)
Author of *Georgia Scenes* (1835), was a lawyer and Methodist minister who later served as a college president in Georgia, Mississippi, and South Carolina.

William Trotter Porter (1809–1858)
Editor of *The Spirit of the Times* from 1831 until his death, provided a venue for publishing many of the Southwestern humorists.

William Tappan Thompson (1812–1882)
Newspaper editor in Georgia, wrote *Major Jones's Courtship* (1843), *Major Jones's Chronicles of Pineville* (1843), and *Major Jones's Sketches of Travel* (1848).

Thomas Bangs Thorpe (1815–1878)
Author of "The Big Bear of Arkansas," was a painter and journalist.

Technology and Industrialization

While more accelerated growth in technology and industrialization occurred in the years following the Civil War, Americans during the Romantic era saw great changes in everyday life as the result of technical developments in communication, transportation, and industry. While these advances spurred the growth of a literary culture that helped to promote American writing, many authors were skeptical of the new developments and examined in their work the human costs of technology and industrial culture.

COMMUNICATIONS TECHNOLOGIES

Telegraphy

The first successful telegraph communication in the United States occurred in 1844, when Samuel F. B. Morse, who developed the dot-dash code that bears his name, sent his famous message, "What hath God wrought," between Baltimore and Washington, D.C. During the antebellum period, technical problems continued to plague the medium: attempts to lay transatlantic cables were hampered by breakage and deterioration of insulation, and inventors struggled to perfect the "duplex telegraph," which permitted messages to be sent both ways at once on the same wire. But the "Victorian Internet," as modern scholars sometimes call the telegraph, continued to spread. In 1861 the first transcontinental telegraph cable began service, increasing the speed and efficiency of war-time communications. By 1868, the first successful transatlantic cable revolutionized information transfer between the United States and Europe.

Photography

Though experiments with the "camera obscura" dated to the 1500s, and various people claimed to have developed photographic technologies in the early nineteenth century, photography in the Romantic Age reached the popular consciousness in 1839, when the French Academy of Science announced Louis-Jacques-Mandé Daguerre's invention of the daguerreotype, in which an image was exposed directly onto a polished silver surface. In the years following, the development of photographic negatives and reproducible prints and the gradual movement of photography from the studio to the outdoors brought about a popularization of the art, which now produced not just portraits of famous people but landscapes, family members, and news events. During the Civil War, Mathew Brady's battlefield photographs helped bring home the horrors of combat.

Photographic technology prompted a prolonged debate about the representation and communication of truth. Compared to portraits in oil, which were too expensive and formal to capture the continuum of a subject's life, photography was seen as a more accessible, honest, and natural medium for recording reality. (The common synonym for photography was "sun painting.") American writers joined the debate over photography's value. Walt Whitman preferred the photograph to the painting, telling his friend Horace Traubel, "artists fool with nature—reform it, revise it, to make it fit their preconceived notions of what it should be." By the middle 1860s, cheaply reproduced photographs called *cartes de visite* (due to their similarity in size to Victorian "calling cards") and cabinet-card photos brought the technology within reach common people. Photography was a democratic medium of communication, allowing Americans even of modest means to record and share the events of history, own pictures of themselves and others, and appreciate visually places and people they might never actually visit in person.

TRANSPORTATION TECHNOLOGIES

Concurrent with the revolution in information technologies were new developments in transportation. The 1810s saw a boom in paved turnpikes linking American cities and towns; chief among these commercial toll roads was the National Road, which eventually ran for some seven hundred miles from Maryland to Illinois. Efforts to construct a nationwide series of canals flourished in the 1820s, with one of the longest, the Erie Canal in New York State, completed in 1825. Steamboats plied the Mississippi and Ohio rivers in increasing numbers, opening up the West to commerce and travel. None of these transportation technologies could compete, however, with the railroad, which expanded with incredible speed after the development of the first steam locomotives in the 1830s. Miles of track in the United States grew from only thirty in 1830 to thirty thousand by the beginning of the Civil War.

INDUSTRIAL TECHNOLOGIES

As Daniel Walker Howe has pointed out in *What Hath God Wrought* (2007), the United States at the beginning of the Romantic era shared many of the characteristics of developing nations today, including poor transportation and communication systems, a primarily agricultural economy, the need for an effective education system, the growth of cities, and the challenges of industrialization. Restrictions on sea trade during the War of 1812 encouraged the growth of domestic industry instead, particularly in such areas as textile production. Steam began to supplant water as the source of industrial power. Thanks to improvements in automated looms, by the 1830s the first factory towns appeared in New England, most famously in Lowell, Massachusetts, offering opportunities for rural girls to achieve some measure of economic independence, in return for grueling days laboring in textile mills.

New industrial technologies mechanized production, which in turn eroded the "home work" economy: products formerly made one-at-a-time, from clothing to shoes to firearms, were increasingly mass-produced. Among the most significant inventions of the period those that increased the efficiency of American industry: for instance, the steam locomotive, the automatic reaper, and the steel plow in the 1830s, the typewriter and sewing machine in the 1840s and 1850s.

TOPICS FOR DISCUSSION AND RESEARCH

1. American writers responded to technological change with a mixture of wonder and concern. Oliver Wendell Holmes, in his 1859 essay "The Stereoscope and the Stereograph," welcomed the accuracy of photography: as he put it, "the very things which an artist would leave out, or render imperfectly, the photograph takes infinite care with, and so makes its illusions perfect." Emily Dickinson playfully celebrated the railroad in "I like to see it lap the Miles." What aspects of technology did American writers find encouraging?

2. How does industrialization function thematically in the literature of the Romantic period? For instance, Rebecca Harding Davis dramatized the misery of industrial workers in her short story, "Life in the Iron Mills." Consider how the rise of industrialization was seen as antithetical to the virtues of living in nature as depicted, in the works of James Fenimore Cooper. Leo Marx's famous study *The Machine in the Garden: Technology and the Pastoral Ideal in America* (1964) is a useful starting place.

3. In what ways did the rise of industrial technologies challenge the faith in moral agrarianism that was an important part of the American ethos? Henry David Thoreau worried about the "quiet desperation" of people unprepared for a world of technology, industry, and trade as he watched the commercialization of his home town of Concord. Based on reviews and other responses, did nineteenth-century readers agree with such worries, or did they find Romantic texts out-of-step with the times?

4. Developments in transportation and communication helped to bring American writing to a larger and more diverse market, particularly through newspapers and magazines but also through the mass production of books. Using a resource such as *The Industrial Book, 1840–1880*, edited by Scott E. Casper et al., volume three of *A History of the Book in America* (2007), investigate how some technological development in printing or publication affected the spread of literature during the Romantic period. You might, for instance, investigate how the mass production of paperbacks brought literature to Civil War soldiers or how railroad and canal systems enabled paper to be shipped cheaply to Western cities and readers.

RESOURCES

Scott E. Casper, et al., eds., *The Industrial Book, 1840–1880*, volume 3 of *A History of the Book in America* (Chapel Hill: University of North Carolina Press, 2007).
Authoritative essays on various topics in book history, including discussions of manufacturing, publishing, authorship, copyright, and reading patterns.

Walter Licht, *Industrializing America: The Nineteenth Century* (Baltimore & London: Johns Hopkins University Press, 1995).
Examines the effects of market forces on the social history of the United States. Chapters 2 and 3 cover American economic development during the Romantic era and Americans' responses to industrialization.

Leo Marx, *The Machine in the Garden: Technology and the Pastoral Ideal in America*, thirty-fifth anniversary edition (New York: Oxford University Press, 2000). Examines the contradictory attitudes expressed in nineteenth-century American writing toward pastoralism and mechanization, with special reference to Romantic authors.

Carroll W. Pursell, *The Machine in America: A Social History of Technology*, second edition (Baltimore: Johns Hopkins University Press, 2007). Examines the interplay between technology and social change, especially the growth of cities, changes in agriculture, and improvements in transportation.

PEOPLE OF INTEREST

Mathew B. Brady (1823–1896)
Daguerreotypist and commercial photographer, was famous for his dramatic battlefield photographs of the Civil War and the portraits in his *Gallery of Illustrious Americans* (1850).

Louis-Jacques-Mandé Daguerre (1757–1851)
French photographer and inventor, revealed the process for making daguerreotypes before a joint session of the Académie des Sciences and the Académie des Beaux-Arts in 1839.

Samuel F. B. Morse (1791–1872)
Artist and inventor, developed the telegraph in the 1840s.

Transcendentalism

Transcendentalism is a philosophical and religious way of thinking that manifested itself in particular, if not necessarily uniform, ways. Though some of its ideas about individualism and nature can be traced to the late eighteenth century and to European thinkers such as Samuel Taylor Coleridge and Immanuel Kant, Transcendentalism flourished as an indigenous American movement from the 1830s through the 1860s. It overlapped chronologically with Romanticism, with which it shared some key concepts, and was identified with a group of New England writers, chief among them Ralph Waldo Emerson, Henry David Thoreau, Margaret Fuller, the theologian and social reformer Theodore Parker; the educator Elizabeth Palmer Peabody; and the visionary philosopher Amos Bronson Alcott.

Pressed to explain themselves, those associated with Transcendentalism offered various definitions at the time. Emerson, in his lecture "The Transcendentalist" (1842), called it "Idealism as it exists in 1842." William Henry Channing, in his section of the *Memoirs of Margaret Fuller Ossoli* (1852), called it "a vague yet exalting conception of the godlike nature of the human spirit." One of the first historians of the movement, Octavius B. Frothingham, called it in *Transcendentalism in New England* (1876) "an assertion of the immanence of divinity in instinct." What emerges from these contemporary definitions, and from the writings of the Transcendentalists themselves, are some recurring ideas:

- The indwelling of the divine in the human soul
- The superiority of the individual over society or its institutions
- Intuition, imagination, and vision as the ways of understanding the world,
- Nature as both a field of study and an inspiration to self-development
- A confidence that the universe is organic, welcoming, and inherently good.

These ideas are interconnected. Because the divine dwelled within every soul, Transcendentalists generally accepted the paramount importance of each human being. (Alcott called the individual "a god in ruins.") Therefore, in Emerson's term, the watchword of life was "self-reliance," not reliance on society, its institutions, its traditions, or its ideas. Because logic and sensory knowledge limited what the individual could know to the realm of experience, the Transcendentalists believed that intuition—a higher, mystical, poetic awareness—revealed a truer sense of the world as organic and divine. With that bracing revelation about the world came the challenge to live up to our place in it. As Thoreau put it in *Walden* (1854), "Our whole life is startlingly moral"—that is, our every action either advances or retards our spiritual development.

Though the Transcendentalists gravitated toward certain important topics, it is impossible to define Transcendentalism with complete accuracy. First, it was a term of disparagement that most members of the group disliked, and it implied a coherent dogma that all of them rejected. Second, defining Transcendentalism is an inherently contradictory act, for to *define* means to fix the limits of something and to *transcend* means to go past them. One of the most famous brief definitions was reportedly offered by one of Emerson's friends in 1836; the term *Transcendentalism* meant, she supposed, "a little beyond." The Transcendentalists themselves preferred terms like "the new school" or "the newness."

Transcendentalism was a product of its times. As a "creedless" religious phenomenon, Transcendentalism reacted to some of the dogmatism and sectarianism that characterized American Protestantism in the mid nineteenth century. The Unitarian theologian William Ellery Channing promoted the idea that individual people had a "likeness to God," but it remained for the Transcendentalists to assert the true divinity of human beings, and many of them would have agreed with Emerson in his "Divinity School Address" (1838) in finding contemporary religion too scholastic, dogmatic, and emotionally cold. As a philosophy, Transcendentalism accepted the Enlightenment idea that nature reveals the divine will, while recognizing a higher "Reason" than mere scientific observation.

Most characteristically, the Transcendentalists valued individualism, expressed in a variety of ways. Fuller referred to "self-dependence," Thoreau to "living deliberately," Emerson to "the infinitude of the private man." Yet, Transcendentalism had some definite social manifestations. The Transcendental Club flourished from 1836 to about 1848, a loose confederation of the "like-minded" who met in the Boston area for conversation and inspiration. One of the Club's main projects was the *Dial* (1840–1844), a magazine of literature and ideas edited by Emerson and Fuller. In 1840, George and Sophia Ripley founded the Brook Farm community in West Roxbury, Massachusetts, a working farm and communal society intended to fuse intellectual and manual labors. Largely skeptical of existing social institutions, Transcendentalists were active in the reform movements of the day that promised to free individuals from the constraints of unfair laws and practices. Thoreau claimed in "Resistance to Civil Government" (1848) that our proper duty was to our selves, not to remedying evil; yet, he became one of the most committed opponents of slavery. Fuller and Sophia Ripley championed women's rights; Parker and Emerson advocated abolitionism; Alcott and Peabody pioneered educational reform.

After the Civil War, Transcendentalism's influence began to wane. Individual Transcendentalists like Emerson were upheld as cultural icons; less popular ones like Fuller and Thoreau were rediscovered and had their reputations adjusted to meet the genteel standards of the Gilded Age. But in the face of industrialization, big business, and new science, particularly evolutionism and its outgrowth "Social Darwinism," Transcendentalism seemed to some a quaint irrelevance. Yet, the Transcendentalists' ideas about self-reliance, the beauty of nature, and the importance of principled living continue to animate and inspire readers.

TOPICS FOR DISCUSSION AND RESEARCH

1. Walt Whitman's poetry shows definite Emersonian influence, while Herman Melville's short story "Bartleby, the Scrivener" (1853) may be read as a critique of Transcendental individualism. What other authors reacted to the Transcendentalists, in their time and later? Begin with Roger Asselineau's *Transcendentalist Constant in American Literature* (1980).

2. While scholars and teachers often focus on the American phenomenon of Transcendentalism and its expression by Emerson and others, in fact the movement was influenced by thinkers from Great Britain and continental Europe. Consider what the Transcendentalists were reading as they wrote. What was the effect of Samuel Taylor Coleridge, Thomas Carlyle, and Johann Wolfgang von Goethe on Transcendentalism?

3. Transcendentalism flourished at the same time as the antislavery, the women's-rights, and the educational reform movements. What assumptions did these movements share? Compare and contrast, for instance, the views of an educator such as Alcott, who entered into mature dialog with his students, with the more common views of the time that education meant discipline and memorization. See the comprehensive discussions in Anne C. Rose, *Transcendentalism as a Social Movement, 1830–1850* (1981).

4. Frothingham wrote in 1876 of Transcendentalism's far-reaching influence: "It affected thinkers, swayed politicians, guided moralists, inspired philanthropists, created reformers." To what extent are the Transcendental writers still influential? Using a single text such as Thoreau's *Walden* or "Civil Disobedience," Emerson's "Self-Reliance," or Fuller's *Woman in the Nineteenth Century*, trace its continuing effect in the twentieth and twenty-first centuries. Who in the political, environmental, or reform arenas today has cited the text, and for what reasons? You might begin by searching indexes to contemporary newspapers and periodicals for references to the works. Alternatively, you might search online to see in what contexts certain key phrases from the Transcendentalists (Thoreau's "The mass of men lead lives of quiet desperation," for instance) show up on the Internet. Michael Meyer's study *Several More Lives to Live: Thoreau's Political Reputation in America* (1977) is a model of this type of investigation.

RESOURCES

Paul F. Boller Jr., *American Transcendentalism, 1830–1860: An Intellectual Inquiry* (New York: Putnam's, 1974).
Traces the development of American Transcendentalism and its religious, philosophical, and social origins.

Philip F. Gura, *American Transcendentalism: A History* (New York: Hill & Wang, 2007).
An essential introduction to the movement as a conscious redirection of the American democratic experiment, placing authority in the human heart. Detailed and grounded in individual thinkers and their lives.

Gura and Joel Myerson, eds., *Critical Essays on American Transcendentalism* (Boston: G. K. Hall, 1982).
A comprehensive collection of commentary and analysis, from the earliest reactions to modern scholarship.

Barbara Packer, *The Transcendentalists* (Athens: University of Georgia Press, 2007).

A thoughtful and gracefully written introduction, focusing on social and religious reform. Originally published in *The Cambridge History of American Literature*, volume 2, edited by Sacvan Bercovitch (New York: Cambridge University Press, 1995).

PEOPLE OF INTEREST

Amos Bronson Alcott (1799–1888)
Philosopher and educator whose radical Temple School in Boston challenged prevailing views about the educability of young children. His daughter Louisa May Alcott (1832–1888) was the author of the popular adolescent novels *Little Women* (1868) and *Little Men* (1871).

William Ellery Channing (1780–1842)
Leading Unitarian minister, was revered by the Transcendentalists for his progressive theology and opposition to slavery.

William Henry Channing (1810–1884)
Nephew of the famous Dr. William Ellery Channing and a protégé of Emerson, was a Unitarian minister and active social reformer who spent much of his career after the 1850s preaching in Liverpool, England.

Samuel Taylor Coleridge (1772–1834)
Influential British poet and critic known for poems such as "The Rime of the Ancient Mariner" and "Kubla Khan," helped to bring German literature and philosophy to the attention of the Transcendentalists.

Octavius B. Frothingham (1822–1895)
Biographer and second-generation Transcendentalist, was the founder and first president of the Free Religious Association, which attempted to reconcile religion with evolutionary science.

Immanuel Kant (1724–1804)
German philosopher, influenced the Transcendentalists with his arguments for the individual construction of truth in works such as his *Critique of Pure Reason* (1781, revised 1787).

Theodore Parker (1810–1860)
Radical Unitarian theologian, minister, and abolitionist whose sermon *A Discourse on the Transient and Permanent in Christianity* (1841) challenged the historicity of biblical miracles.

Elizabeth Palmer Peabody (1804–1894)
Assisted Alcott in his Temple School, was instrumental in bringing educational reforms such as the kindergarten to American public education.

George Ripley (1802–1880)
Transcendentalist, minister, editor, and literary reviewer, founded Brook Farm in 1840 with his wife Sophia Dana Ripley (1803–1861), an educational reformer and advocate of women's rights.

Wars and Peace

From the 1820 Missouri Compromise to the end of the Civil War in 1865, the United States was torn by sectional conflict over slavery and its expansion into new territories. These tensions shaped both the Mexican War and the fighting between proslavery and antislavery settlers in the Kansas Territory; they also led the nation to the Civil War, perhaps the most devastating event in American history. Although war was not one of the more common themes in mid-nineteenth-century American literature, several American authors wrote about the subject or used it as a backdrop for their works.

The Mexican War of 1846–1848 was supported both by proponents of Manifest Destiny and by Southern Democrats who wished to expand slavery into Texas and northern Mexico. Such expansion would allow more representatives from slaveholding states in Congress to balance the growth of representatives from free states in the northwest. However, many antislavery writers criticized the war because they opposed the expansion of slavery. For example, in his essay "Resistance to Civil Government" (1849), Henry David Thoreau described his refusal to pay a federal tax because it supported the war against Mexico, and Ralph Waldo Emerson also expressed his opposition to the war and to slavery in his poem "Ode Inscribed to W. H. Channing" (1847). During the war, David Wilmot, a Democratic Congressman from Pennsylvania, proposed legislation to outlaw slavery in any lands acquired from Mexico, but his bill failed to pass the Senate. Walt Whitman, while serving as editor of the Brooklyn *Daily Eagle*, endorsed the Wilmot Proviso, though he also expressed support for the war.

The sectional and partisan conflicts over the expansion of slavery continued into the following decade. During the mid 1850s proslavery settlers in the Kansas-Nebraska Territories battled against "Free Staters" led by John Brown (see the study guide for "Thoreau's Political Essays") to determine the question of whether slavery would be permitted in the territory. The fighting followed the passage of the 1854 Kansas-Nebraska Act, which ruled that the slavery issue would be determined by the settlers, a policy termed "popular sovereignty." This series of conflicts was called "Bleeding Kansas" and foreshadowed the Civil War. Brown's unsuccessful raid on the federal arsenal at Harpers Ferry, Virginia, in 1859 and his capture and execution further escalated tensions over slavery throughout the nation. In his essay "A Plea for Captain John Brown" (1860), Thoreau defended Brown's actions and his commitment to abolitionism.

Not surprisingly, the two major wars of this period, as well as earlier conflicts, found their way into several American literary texts of the time. For instance, stanza 34 of Whitman's "Song of Myself" describes a battle at the Alamo in which Texan settlers fought for independence from Mexico. He also wrote about the Civil War, which he witnessed as a nurse in a military hospital, in his collection of poems *Drum-Taps* (1865). More authors wrote about wars that had occurred in the past. Washington Irving, for instance, referred to the American Revolutionary War in "The Legend of Sleepy Hollow" (1819), in which the "Headless Horseman" is thought to be the ghost of a Hessian soldier killed during the war. Whitman also referred to the Revolutionary War in stanza 35 of poem "Song of Myself" (1855), which describes the naval battle that occurred in 1779 between the American ship *Bonhomme Richard* and the British ship *Serapis*. William Gilmore Simms wrote more extensively about this war in several novels, including *The Partisan: A Tale of the Revolution* (1835), *Katharine Walton* (1851), and *Woodcraft, or Hawks about the Dovecote* (1854). The abolitionist author Lydia Maria Child set her story "The Black Saxons" (1841) in South Carolina during the War of 1812, which is also the backdrop for Mordecai Manuel Noah's play *She Would Be a Soldier* (1819). Catharine Maria Sedgwick went back further in time in her novel *Hope Leslie* (1827), which is set during the Pequot War, which took place in New England in 1637. James Fenimore Cooper also wrote about frontier conflict between whites and American Indians in his novel *The Last of the Mohicans* (1826), which takes place during the French and Indian War (1756–1763). Aside from fiction and poetry focusing on war, other American writers such as Simms wrote biographies of Revolutionary War heroes such as Nathanael Greene and Francis Marion.

TOPICS FOR DISCUSSION AND RESEARCH

1. In what ways did mid-nineteenth-century American authors respond to the Mexican War? Was there consensus among these authors in their attitudes toward the war, or did they voice differing opinions? Students can read about Emerson's reactions in John Q. Anderson's essay "Emerson on Texas and the Mexican War," and Len Gougeon's essay "The Anti-Slavery Background of Emerson's 'Ode Inscribed to W. H. Channing.'" William Cullen Bryant's reactions are discussed in Bernard Weinstein's article "Bryant, Annexation, and the Mexican War."

2. Examine the representations of the American Revolutionary War in mid-nineteenth-century American literature. To what extent are these depictions an expression of the authors' nationalism? William Kelly's essay "Republican Fictions: Cooper and the Revolution" in *Reading Cooper, Teaching Cooper*, edited by Jeffrey Walker, is a good source for Cooper's attitudes toward the American Revolution. For a discussion of Simms's depictions of this war, see Roger Bresnahan's essay "William Gilmore Simms's Revolutionary War: A Romantic View of Southern History."

3. Both Sedgwick and Cooper describe conflicts between white settlers and American Indians in their fiction. Are there any significant differences or similarities between the two authors in their attitudes toward American Indians, white settlers, and the conflicts between them? Two essay collections that may help in researching this topic are *Catharine Maria Sedgwick: Critical Perspectives*, edited by Lucinda L. Damon-Bach and Victoria Clements, and *James Fenimore Cooper: New Critical Essays*, edited by Robert Clark.

4. Most stories about war focus primarily on men, but some American literary works written during the mid nineteenth century, including Simms's *Katharine Walton* and Sedgwick's *Hope Leslie*, feature female protagonists. How do these texts represent women and their relationships to war? Two essays dealing with this topic are Patricia Okker's "Gender and Secession in Simms's *Katha-*

rine Walton," and Judith Fetterley's "'My Sister! My Sister!': The Rhetoric of Catharine Sedgwick's *Hope Leslie."*

5. Choose an American literary work from the mid nineteenth century that depicts the American Revolutionary War, the War of 1812, or the Mexican War, and compare its depictions of war with the historical facts. What seems to be the author's purpose in describing the war? In what ways does the author depart from historical fact, and to what apparent purpose? Some good historical studies of these wars include Samuel Griffith's *War for American Independence,* Walter Borneman's *1812: The War That Forged a Nation,* and John Eisenhower's *So Far From God: The U.S. War with Mexico, 1846–1848.*

RESOURCES

John Q. Anderson, "Emerson on Texas and the Mexican War," *Western Humanities Review,* 13 (1959): 191–199.
Provides information about Emerson's attitude toward the Mexican War.

Walter R. Borneman, *1812: The War That Forged a Nation* (New York: Harper-Collins, 2004).
A historical study of the War of 1812 that argues for its importance in American history.

Roger J. Bresnahan, "William Gilmore Simms's Revolutionary War: A Romantic View of Southern History," *Studies in Romanticism,* 15 (1976): 573–587.
Discusses Simms's depictions of the Revolutionary War

Robert Clark, ed., *James Fenimore Cooper: New Critical Essays* (London: Vision Press, 1985).
Includes information about Cooper's depictions of armed conflicts between American Indians and European settlers.

John S. D. Eisenhower, *So Far From God: The U.S. War with Mexico, 1846–1848* (Norman: University of Oklahoma Press, 2000).
A historical study of the political, diplomatic, and military dimensions of the Mexican War.

Judith Fetterley, "'My Sister! My Sister!': The Rhetoric of Catharine Sedgwick's *Hope Leslie,"* in *Catharine Maria Sedgwick: Critical Perspectives,* edited by Lucinda L. Damon-Bach and Victoria Clements (Boston: Northeastern University Press, 2003), pp. 78–99.
Analyzes Sedgwick's depictions of women in the Pequot War in her novel *Hope Leslie.*

Len Gougeon, "The Anti-Slavery Background of Emerson's 'Ode Inscribed to W. H. Channing,'" in *Studies in the American Renaissance,* edited by Joel Myerson (Charlottesville: University Press of Virginia, 1985), pp. 63–77.
Includes information about Emerson's opposition to the Mexican War and expansion.

Samuel B. Griffith, *The War for American Independence: From 1760 to the Surrender at Yorktown in 1781* (Urbana: University of Illinois Press, 2002).
A thorough and well-documented history of the Revolutionary War.

William Kelly, "Republican Fictions: Cooper and the Revolution," in *Reading Cooper, Teaching Cooper*, edited by Jeffrey Walker (New York: AMS, 2007), pp. 95–123.
Includes information about Cooper's attitudes toward the American Revolution.

Patricia Okker, "Gender and Secession in Simms's *Katharine Walton*," *Southern Literary Journal*, 29.2 (Spring 1997): 17–31.
Analyzes Simms's depiction of women in his novel about the Revolutionary War.

Bernard Weinstein, "Bryant, Annexation, and the Mexican War," *ESQ*, 63 (1971): 19–24.
Analyzes Bryant's reactions to the Mexican War.

PEOPLE OF INTEREST

John Brown (1800–1859)
American abolitionist, led an antislavery militia in the Pottawatomie Massacre in the Kansas-Nebraska Territory in 1856 and led a raid on the U.S. military arsenal at Harpers Ferry, Virginia, in 1859.

Lydia Maria Child (1802–1880)
American novelist, abolitionist, women's-rights activist, Indian-rights activist, novelist, and journalist, is best known for her antislavery treatise *An Appeal in Favor of that Class of Americans Called Africans* (1833) and her historical romance *Hobomok* (1824).

Nathanael Greene (1742–1786)
Major general of the Continental Army during the American Revolutionary War.

Washington Irving (1783–1859)
American fiction writer, biographer, and historian, is best known for his satire *A History of New-York* (1809) as well as *The Sketch Book* (1819), which included "Rip Van Winkle" and "The Legend of Sleepy Hollow."

Francis Marion (1732–1795)
Military officer who served in Continental Army during the American Revolutionary War, was instrumental in resisting British military forces in South Carolina.

Mordecai Manuel Noah (1785–1851)
Jewish American playwright, diplomat, and newspaper editor best known for his play *She Would Be a Soldier* (1819).

David Wilmot (1814–1868)
Congressman and senator representing Pennsylvania, proposed a bill in 1846 that would prevent the extension of slavery into new territories acquired by the United States.

Part III
Study Guides
on Works and Writers

James Fenimore Cooper, The Leather-Stocking Tales (1823–1841)

James Fenimore Cooper (1789–1851) was among the most acclaimed and pro-lific American prose writers of the Romantic era. But for readers today, as James D. Wallace points out, Cooper—like his most famous character, Natty Bumppo, "The Leather-Stocking"—exists mainly on the margins, "never quite central to anyone's notion of what American literature is all about." His reputation rests largely on his five "Leather-Stocking tales," with their adventurous plots, innu-merable adaptations pitched to young readers, and enduring film versions.

He was born James Cooper in New Jersey in 1789 to Elizabeth and William Cooper. (He took his mother's maiden name as his middle name later in life.) His father, who prospered in business and land speculation, moved the family to the upstate New York village of Cooperstown, on Lake Otsego, where he was landlord, judge, and later member of Congress. After a short stint at Yale, in 1806 James Cooper went to sea as a merchant sailor to prepare himself for a naval career. In 1810 he left the service to help his brothers manage his father's legacy; the next year, he married Susan De Lancey and formally resigned from the navy. During their long and happy marriage the Coopers had seven children, five of whom survived to adulthood.

A political conservative who believed in the prerogatives of the landowning class, Cooper was financially unsuccessful, and his inherited fortunes disappeared. Around 1820 he had settled on a literary career. *The Spy,* his second novel, was an encouraging success in 1821, and *The Pioneers,* the first of the Leather-Stocking tales, appeared in 1823. For the next decade Cooper wrote historical romances set on the frontier and at sea. In 1826 he and his family moved abroad, where he began to write more stridently political novels set in Europe. His American audience found them not to their taste, and Cooper began a lifelong quarrel with his readership. In 1834, back in the United States, he published *A Letter to His Countrymen,* promising to stop writing for an unappreciative audience. Despite continuing tension between the patrician Cooper and the tastes of his popular audience, he never made good on his pledge to put aside his pen. At his death in Cooperstown in 1851, Cooper left a corpus numbering 32 novels and 18 volumes of history, travel, and social commentary.

The Leather-Stocking series comprises *The Pioneers* (1823), followed by *The Last of the Mohicans* (1826), *The Prairie* (1827), *The Pathfinder* (1840), and *The Deerslayer* (1841). (The books as published do not follow Natty Bumppo's devel-opment chronologically. He is youngest in the last novel, *The Deerslayer;* a mature warrior in *The Last of the Mohicans* and *The Pathfinder;* a grizzled veteran in *The Pioneers;* and an enfeebled old man in *The Prairie,* at the end of which he dies.) Cooper himself referred to the series in the 1841 preface to *The Deerslayer* as "something like a drama in five acts; complete as to material and design." Readers of only the most famous of the tales, *The Last of the Mohicans,* may be surprised to learn that the heroic Natty Bumppo (variously named Hawk-Eye, Leather-Stocking, Deerslayer, or Pathfinder) begins in *The Pioneers* as a peripheral, almost comic figure, as does the Delaware chief Chingachgook, who as "John Indian" is aged and compromised by drunkenness. The friendship of these two loyal companions endures throughout the Leather-Stocking series, as they brave the threats of vengeful Iroquois and the equally threatening encroachment of European American civilization. In Natty and Chingachgook, Cooper inscribed his respect for talent, loyalty, plain speaking, courage, and reverence for the natural world.

Readers of the entire series will recognize other repeated character types: motherless daughters (Elizabeth Temple in *The Pioneers*, Elizabeth Wade of *The Prairie*, and Mabel Dunham of *The Pathfinder*) or pairs of sisters with opposite temperaments (Alice and Cora Munro of *The Last of the Mohicans* and Judith and Hetty Hutter in *The Deerslayer*) who triumph over circumstance to reveal their heroic dimensions; evil Indians (variously named Magua, Mahtoree, and Arrowhead) who pose an overtly physical and covertly sexual threat to the white characters; and the "noble" young men of both races (Hard Heart and Uncas among the Indians, for instance, and Major Duncan Heywood and Jasper Western among the European Americans) whose similarities complicate racial stereotypes in the novels. Also repeated throughout the series are strong but self-centered white men such as Hurry Harry Marsh and Tom Hutter of *The Deerslayer*, the belligerent settler Ishmael Bush of *The Prairie*, and the egotistical Charles Cap of *The Pathfinder*; and characters comically out of place on the frontier, such as the bookish Doctor Obad Battius of *The Prairie* or the bumbling singing-master David Gamut of *The Last of the Mohicans*. Leslie A. Fiedler contends that "the essential fable of the historical romance" is the triumph of good over evil, and the continuing plot thread of pursuit/captivity/escape/revenge in all five Leather-Stocking novels supports that view. But the series' diverse cast of characters and panoramic view of early American settlement from the 1740s through the early 1800s are reminders that Cooper's Leather-Stocking tales are also about the varying responses to the American frontier, the meaning of law and ethics in a developing society, and the disputed points of contact between civilization and the wilderness, male and female, European American and Indian, exploitation and preservation.

TOPICS FOR DISCUSSION AND RESEARCH

1. Examine Cooper's biographical connection with his subject matter as a way to comment on the authenticity of the novels. Characters like Judge Marmaduke Temple of *The Pioneers*, with his incongruous frontier mansion and his benevolent insistence that the natural environment be protected by law, are clearly based upon Cooper's father, and the entire series (except for *The Prairie*) is set in and around Cooper's ancestral home in upstate New York. For a discussion of Cooper's alienation from the ethos of success and power that his father embraced, see Robert H. Zoellner's essay. But Cooper's political stance on property and wealth is more complicated. Steven Watts traces Cooper's shifting politics thematically in the Leather-Stocking tales, where he "struggled to sort out the conflicting claims of virtue and commerce, community and individualism."

2. Critical opinion is divided on Cooper's social criticism. Generally, for Leather-Stocking, social laws are intrusive and inappropriate to life in nature. Geoffrey Rans argues that Natty Bumppo and Chingachgook may be seen as early victims of industrialization. But critics such as William P. Kelly see Cooper's criticism moderating in the later tales, with a more realistic appraisal of the possibilities of progress. Using his essays and political writings, examine what Cooper considers important social improvements and how those ideas manifest themselves in the novels.

3. The Leather-Stocking tales offer an extensive critique not only of American society but also of American social attitudes toward gender and ethnicity. Readers have long noted the stereotypical qualities of Cooper's women and ethnic characters, even in Cooper's own century. In "A Fable for Critics" (1848) the poet James Russell Lowell called Cooper's female characters "all sappy as maple and flat as the prairie," and Mark Twain made hilarious fun of the "Cooper Indians" who (to Twain's more realistic tastes) served only to confirm existing stereotypes. But modern critics have found more complexity in those characters. For a defense of Cooper's "females," see Nina Baym, who makes the case that women are significant because Cooper defines them as "the nexus of social interaction," and Jane Tompkins, who sees in Cooper's stereotypes a reflection of Romantic anxiety over gender roles. Cooper's often conventional depiction of gender relationships is complicated by Leather-Stocking's refusal to marry and by the prevalence of male-male friendships. In an important mythic reading of the tales, Leslie A. Fiedler sees in the relationship of Leather-Stocking and Chingachgook a renunciation of civilization and evidence of "Cooper's secret protest against the gentle tyranny of home and woman." Choose one of these positions and test it with a close reading of one of the novels.

4. Cooper's treatment of ethnicity is sometimes more enlightened and nuanced than the novels' concern with "blood" might suggest. Hurry Harry of *The Deerslayer* illustrates outright racism in his brutish condemnation of all Indians, and Leather-Stocking's insistent claim in *The Last of the Mohicans* that he is "a man without a cross" points out a pervasive fear of miscegenation, but Cooper just as often shows tolerance in the views of Natty Bumppo, who says in *The Pathfinder*, "each color has its gifts, and its laws, and its traditions; and one is not to condemn another because he does not exactly comprehend it." To examine race and ethnicity in the novels, choose two characters who seem to exemplify opposing positions; then argue which position is borne out in the novel itself. Do racist characters come to recognize their racism? Is ethnocentrism shown to be faulty? Alternatively, investigate Cooper's own attitudes, using biographies and letters, and see which characters seem to speak for the author on the issues of race and ethnicity. Probably the most influential discussion of the implications of race in the tales is by D. H. Lawrence, who finds in the mixed-race friendship of Leather-Stocking and Chingachgook "a new human relationship" that is "deeper than property, deeper than fatherhood, deeper than marriage, deeper than love." For other discussion of the Leather-Stocking tales

in the context of race issues of the time, see the analysis by Michael Schnell and the essays in *A Historical Guide to James Fenimore Cooper*.

RESOURCES

Primary Works

The Pioneers (New York: Charles Wiley, 1823).
The Last of the Mohicans: A Narrative of 1757 (Philadelphia: Carey & Lea, 1826).
The Prairie (London: Henry Colburn, 1827).
The Pathfinder; or, The Inland Sea (London: Richard Bentley, 1840).
The Deerslayer: or, The First War-Path (Philadelphia: Lea & Blanchard, 1841).

Biography

Wayne Franklin, *James Fenimore Cooper: The Early Years* (New Haven, Conn.: Yale University Press, 2007).
Covering Cooper's life through 1826 and taking economics as its driving force, this will be the standard biography when completed by volume 2.

Donald A. Ringe, *James Fenimore Cooper*, revised edition (Boston: Twayne, 1988).
Bio-critical study that treats Cooper's fiction in chronological order.

Robert H. Zoellner, "Fenimore Cooper: Alienated American," *American Quarterly*, 13 (Spring 1961): 55–66.
Considers Cooper's "gradual but unmistakable alienation from the American ethos."

Criticism

Martin Barker and Roger Sabin, *The Lasting of the Mohicans: History of an American Myth* (Jackson: University Press of Mississippi, 1995).
Traces "the Mohican myth" through popular culture.

Nina Baym, "The Women of Cooper's Leatherstocking Tales," *American Quarterly*, 23 (December 1971): 696–709.
Defends Cooper's female characters.

George Dekker and John P. McWilliams, eds., *Fenimore Cooper: The Critical Heritage* (London & Boston: Routledge & Kegan Paul, 1973).
Contemporary reviews of each of Cooper's major novels.

Leslie A. Fiedler, *Love and Death in the American Novel*, revised edition (New York: Stein & Day, 1966).
Sees in Cooper's male-male friendships the working out of mythic conflicts between "corruption and innocence, sophistication and naivete, aesthetics and morality."

William P. Kelly, *Plotting America's Past: Fenimore Cooper and the Leatherstocking Tales* (Carbondale & Edwardsville: Southern Illinois University Press, 1983).
Shows the development of Cooper's views of history.

D. H. Lawrence, "Fenimore Cooper's Leatherstocking Novels," in *Studies in Classic American Literature* (1923; rpt. New York: Viking, 1961), pp. 47–64.
Argues for the relationship between Leather-Stocking and Chingachgook as "the nucleus of a new society" in America.

Leland S. Person, ed., *A Historical Guide to James Fenimore Cooper* (Oxford, England: Oxford University Press, 2007).
Includes essays on Cooper's women characters and race in the novels, an appreciation of his literary achievements, an excellent brief biography, and a bibliographical survey.

Geoffrey Rans, *Cooper's Leather-Stocking Novels: A Secular Reading* (Chapel Hill & London: University of North Carolina Press, 1993).
Sees Leather-Stocking and Chingachgook as victims of industrialization.

Michael Schnell, "The For(e)gone Conclusion: The Leatherstocking Tales as Antebellum History," *American Transcendental Quarterly*, 10 (December 1996): 331–348.
Examines race in the tales.

Jane Tompkins, "No Apologies for the Iroquois: A New Way to Read the Leatherstocking Novels," in *Sensational Designs: The Cultural Work of American Fiction 1790–1860* (New York & Oxford, England: Oxford University Press, 1985), pp. 94–121.
Argues for Cooper's stereotypical characters as markers of his society's concern for cultural difference.

Mark Twain, "Fenimore Cooper's Literary Offences," *North American Review*, 161 (July 1895): 1–12.
A comic treatment of Cooper's style and characters.

W. M. Verhoeven, ed., *James Fenimore Cooper: New Historical and Literary Contexts* (Amsterdam, N.Y.: Rodopi, 1993).
Includes essays on *The Last of the Mohicans*, *The Pathfinder*, and the frontier myth.

James D. Wallace, "Leatherstocking and His Author," *American Literary History*, 5 (Winter 1993): 700–714.
Argues for the importance of Cooper's work for contemporary cultural theorists.

Steven Watts, "'Through a Glass Eye, Darkly': James Fenimore Cooper as Social Critic," *Journal of the Early Republic*, 13 (Spring 1993): 55–74.
Traces Cooper's developing social vision, particularly his views of commerce.

Rebecca Harding Davis, "Life in the Iron Mills,"

The Atlantic magazine (April 1861); collected in *Life in the Iron Mills and Other Stories*, edited by Tillie Olsen (New York: Feminist Press, 1972)

Rebecca Blaine Harding Davis (1831–1910) chronicled the transition to industrialism in the United States during the Romantic period in ways that anticipated by more than a decade the drift toward Realism in the later nineteenth century. Born in western Pennsylvania, she was an avid reader as a child, discovering early the fiction of Nathaniel Hawthorne, whom she later claimed as an important influence. She spent her childhood years in Alabama and, after age six, in Wheeling, Virginia (now West Virginia), a city on the political border of North and South as well as at the forefront of American industrialization, thanks to vast nearby supplies of coal. She graduated from the Washington (Pennsylvania) Female Seminary in 1848, returned to her family in Wheeling to help manage the household, and there began a writing apprenticeship with a local newspaper.

Her career changed dramatically when the leading editor James T. Fields accepted one of her short stories for publication in the prestigious *The Atlantic Monthly* for April 1861. With its unflinching depiction of the gritty world of the industrial poor, its ironic treatment of Romantic moral platitudes, and a distinctive narrative voice that vacillated between scathing sarcasm and bathetic emotionalism, "Life in the Iron Mills" was an immediate literary sensation. "Life in the Iron Mills" is set in the early years of the Industrial Revolution in the United States. The unnamed narrator recalls the story of Hugh Wolfe, a Welsh immigrant who labors as a "puddler" in an iron mill (his job was to stir the vats of molten iron as it cured), and his cousin Deborah, who works in a textile mill. They struggle without hope of bettering themselves until one day, when Deborah overhears a mill visitor remark sarcastically that money cures all ills, she steals his wallet and gives it to Hugh. After a moral crisis of the soul, Hugh is caught with the stolen money, convicted of grand larceny, and sentenced to nineteen years in prison, where he takes his own life. Rescue comes to Deborah only through the agency of a Quaker woman, who brings her from the city to a country retreat.

This compelling but sentimental plot is enriched by the pervasive symbolism of the characters and setting. Desperately poor and broken by their work—Deborah is literally hunchbacked—the two cousins are emotionally impoverished: Deborah pines for love, Hugh for the chance to develop his artistic talents. In his off hours he sculpts korl, an industrial byproduct, into pleading human figures that represent either his own frustrated hopes or the fulfillment of his dreams. The story's setting is similarly oppressive, from the hellish atmosphere of the iron mill itself, to the sooty haze that hangs over the town, where "masses of men" march mechanically from home to work, to Hugh's filthy hovel, where he collapses exhausted at the end of each day. Even the sluggish river that meanders through the town promises only an ironic commentary on the life of mill workers, for as the narrator points out, it represents "no type of such a life. What if it be stagnant and slimy here? It knows that beyond there waits for it odorous sunlight, quaint old gardens, dusky with soft, green foliage of apple-trees, and flushing crimson with roses,—air, and fields, and mountains. The future of the Welsh puddler passing just now is not so pleasant. To be stowed away, after his grimy work is done, in a hole in the muddy graveyard, and after that,—*not* air, nor green fields, nor curious roses."

So impressed was Fields with "Life in the Iron Mills" that he offered to double the $50 he paid Davis for it if she would contribute to the *Atlantic* again. The result was her first novel, *Margret Howth*, a realistic look at class warfare and industrialization and the struggle to find meaning in life outside of materialism. Fields serialized the book in the *Atlantic*, publishing it as a novel in 1862. But he dictated changes in the story, notably a "happy ending" with an improbable marriage, that point out the concessions beginning authors were forced to make, particularly those whose purposes were to examine realistically the truths of a new industrial economy. Davis's sudden success led Fields and his wife, Annie, to introduce her to the New England coterie of writers that included Ralph Waldo Emerson, the Alcotts, and most notably Hawthorne. Significantly, they came to find her attention to social injustice uncomfortable, and for her part she grew impatient with their sometimes one-sided optimism, especially about the Civil War.

During the 1860s Davis's personal and professional lives competed for her attention. She married the journalist Lemuel Clarke Davis of Philadelphia in 1863, suffered an illness that was treated with the infamous "rest cure," and gave birth in 1864 to her first child, Richard Harding Davis, who grew up to become a popular literary figure like his mother. Despite the competing demands of motherhood—Richard was followed by brother Charles in 1866 and sister Nora in 1872—Davis insisted upon also maintaining her literary career, and throughout the 1860s and 1870s she regularly published short stories in the *Atlantic* and elsewhere, treating the Civil War, slavery, Reconstruction politics, sectionalism, and industrialization with her characteristic candor and realism. Later in life, driven sometimes by financial needs and at other times by her concern for the social conditions of women and the poor, Davis added new genres such as children's literature and crusading journalism to her work in fiction; for several years she wrote for Horace Greeley's progressive *New York Tribune*. Her son Richard joined his mother as a literary celebrity, and by the 1890s the Davis family moved in important social circles, numbering among their friends presidents Grover Cleveland and Theodore Roosevelt.

Davis's husband, Clarke, died in 1904, the same year that her autobiography was published. In *Bits of Gossip* appears Davis's artistic credo, which combined her aesthetics with her social conscience:

> It has always seemed to me that each human being, before going out into the silence, should leave behind him, not the story of his own life, but of the time in which he lived,—as he saw it,—its creed, its purpose, its queer habits, and the work which it did or left undone in the world. Taken singly, these accounts might be weak and trivial, but together they would make history live and breathe.

When Davis died in 1910, her friend Elizabeth Stuart Phelps, herself a prominent novelist, attested to the lasting power of Davis's fiction. "Life in the

Iron Mills," Phelps maintained, resonated after nearly fifty years with "a certain grim picturesqueness," and its characters "breathed and suffered, loved and missed of love, won life or wasted it with an ardor that was human and a power that was art." Known today primarily for her pioneering story of industrial injustice and frustrated hope, Rebecca Harding Davis stands at the beginning of the Realist movement in America.

TOPICS FOR DISCUSSION AND RESEARCH

1. With its self-conscious and distinctive narrative voice, "Life in the Iron Mills" is not only a story about industrialization but also the story of the narrator's reaction to the narrative of Hugh and Deborah and an invitation for readers to examine their own stance toward the subject. "Stop a moment," the narrator addresses the reader.

> I am going to be honest. This is what I want you to do. I want you to hide your disgust, take no heed to your clean clothes, and come right down with me,—here, into the thickest of the fog and mud and foul effluvia. I want you to hear this story. There is a secret down here, in this nightmare fog, that has lain dumb for centuries: I want to make it a real thing to you.

Consider what is known about this narrator and speculate about his or her motives. It may be the education of the reader, who is referred to as an "amateur psychologist," into a world of experience and complexity; or, as some critics have speculated, the telling of the story may be therapeutic for the narrator, even redemptive. Some research into contemporary reviews might suggest how Davis's readers interpreted the story's purpose. See Walter Hesford's article for some possible approaches.

2. As a social statement, "Life in the Iron Mills" is clearly a commentary on the consequences of industrialism. Consider how it is also a critique of Romantic optimism and individualism. There are Thoreauvean echoes throughout, for example—from the initial descriptions of "masses of men" to the final, perhaps ironic paragraph, which sounds in its reference to "the promise of the Dawn" very much like the ending of *Walden*. Examine these parallels, or echoes, of earlier Romantic writers and, perhaps using Davis's biography for evidence, investigate whether "Life in the Iron Mills" represents the same skepticism toward Romantic optimism and individualism that Davis felt toward the Concord writers. Or consider where the story fits in the supposed transition from Romanticism to Realism by applying working definitions of each term to the text. Sharon Harris's critical biography helps to position "Life" in nineteenth-century literary history.

3. "Life in the Iron Mills" is a prescient statement of the ways later-nineteenth-century America would respond to the new problems of the industrial poor. This economic critique is embodied in the conversation of three men who visit the mill and debate the issue in Hugh's and Deb's hearing. Kirby, the mill owner, limits his responsibility to paying wages; Dr. May counsels individual "bootstrapping"; and Mr. Mitchell sees no solution other than com-

munal action. With this conversation Davis anticipates the three main social responses to poverty in the last decades of the nineteenth century: laissez-faire capitalism and contract relationships, self-improvement, and unionism. Which of these Davis endorses is a difficult question, since none is finally effective in changing conditions for Deborah and Hugh. Give context to the discussion by investigating one or all of those historical solutions and seeing which of them might be best articulated in the story.

4. Walter Hesford points out, "Davis writes, as it were, on the border of her world—the middle-class world shared by the majority of her readers—and the unknown, mysterious world of the workers." Investigate industrial conditions in the 1830s, at the dawn of the Industrial Revolution in the United States, as well as the attempts by mid-century reformers to improve the lives of workers. Does Davis accurately represent the historical realities or does she distort them for sentimental effect? There remains a great deal of ambiguity in the story, perhaps understandable for one that appeals to both the head and the heart. As Phelps put it, the story exists "at the point where the intellect and the moral nature meet." Davis's particular challenges were to understand new industrial realities that readers and other writers would have found foreign and to depict them both realistically and affectedly.

RESOURCES

Biography

Sharon Harris, *Rebecca Harding Davis and American Realism* (Philadelphia: University of Pennsylvania Press, 1991).
An accurate biography and examination of Davis's place in literary history.

Criticism

Walter Hesford, "Literary Contexts of 'Life in the Iron Mills,'" *American Literature: A Journal of Literary History, Criticism, and Bibliography*, 49 (March 1977): 70–85.
Places "Life in the Iron Mills" in three contexts: Davis's reading of Hawthorne, her reaction against the social novel, and mid-nineteenth-century religiosity.

Elizabeth Stuart Phelps, "Stories That Stay," *Century*, 81 (November 1910): 118–124.
Examines the way "Life in the Iron Mills" affected Phelps's attitudes toward the poor.

William H. Shurr, "'Life in the Iron Mills': A Nineteenth-Century Conversion Narrative," *American Transcendental Quarterly*, 5 (December 1991): 245–257.
Argues that Mitchell is the narrator and that "Life in the Iron Mills" is the story of his religious conversion.

⌒◇◇⌒

Frederick Douglass,
Narrative of the Life of Frederick Douglass, an American Slave, Written by Himself
(Boston: Anti-Slavery Office, 1845); and
My Bondage and My Freedom
(New York & Auburn, N.Y.: Miller, Orton & Mulligan, 1855).

Born into slavery in rural Maryland, Frederick Douglass became perhaps the most historically significant African American of nineteenth-century America, and his career as an antislavery lecturer, newspaper editor, author, activist, statesman, and diplomat is remarkable. He was born Frederick Augustus Washington Bailey in February 1818 in Talbot County, Maryland. His father was a white man, perhaps his master Aaron Anthony, and after he was separated from his slave mother, Harriet, during his infancy, he was raised by her mother until he was taken to Wye plantation at age six. After Anthony's death Frederick became the property of Lucretia Auld, wife of Thomas Auld, and later he was taken to Baltimore to live with Thomas's brother Hugh Auld. Hugh's wife, Sophia, taught Frederick the alphabet despite a law against teaching literacy to slaves. After Hugh put an end to Sophia's teaching, Frederick continued to learn how to read and write from local white boys. Literacy led the young slave to question slavery and eventually enabled him to read antislavery texts. He later shared this knowledge with other slaves. Frederick returned in 1833 to Thomas Auld, who found him difficult to manage and hired him out to Edward Covey in January 1834 to "break" him. Covey failed to subdue Frederick, who returned to Thomas Auld only to be hired out to William Freeland the next year. Frederick tried unsuccessfully to escape with four other slaves. Later he was taken back to Baltimore to live with Hugh Auld, who hired him out to a shipbuilder as an apprentice. While in Baltimore Frederick met Anna Murray, a free black woman, whom he later married.

He began his escape on 3 September 1838, disguised as a sailor, eventually reaching New York City. There he was aided by David Ruggles, a black abolitionist. Murray met him there, and they were married by another black abolitionist, James W. C. Pennington. At Ruggles's suggestion, the newlyweds moved to New Bedford, Massachusetts, where they were taken in by Nathan and Mary Johnson. Frederick had already assumed the surname Johnson after his escape, but at Nathan's suggestion he changed it to Douglass.

Douglass began attending antislavery meetings in 1841 and subscribed to William Lloyd Garrison's newspaper *The Liberator*. He made his first speech at an abolitionist meeting in Nantucket, and was encouraged to become a lecturer. In 1843 he participated in an abolitionist lecture tour throughout the Northeast and Midwest. During the following year he began writing his first narrative, which was published by the American Anti-Slavery Society in May 1845. It became a best seller, but many readers doubted that such a well-written narrative was written by a former slave. The publication of the *Narrative* also jeopardized Douglass's freedom, so he sailed for Ireland in August 1845 and spent eighteen months traveling as an abolitionist lecturer throughout the British Isles, where the antislavery movement was very popular. He noticed a lack of racial prejudice among the British and was treated as a celebrity. Several of his new British abolitionist friends raised money to buy his freedom, and they also contributed toward a printing press that Douglass planned to use in starting an abolitionist newspaper.

In 1847 he returned to America as a free man, but his former mentor Garrison did not support Douglass's newspaper project. Undaunted, Douglass started *The North Star* in Rochester, New York, which in 1851 merged with Gerrit Smith's *Liberty Party Paper* to form *Frederick Douglass' Paper*. In addition to promoting abolition, *The North Star* also supported women's rights, and Douglass attended the first Women's Rights Convention in Seneca Falls, New York, in 1848.

As the controversy over slavery escalated throughout the 1850s, Douglass became increasingly active and independent. He disagreed with Garrison's belief that abolitionists should avoid politics and that the Constitution supported slavery. He also recognized the destructive power of racism in the North and spoke out for desegregating public schools. During this decade, Douglass wrote a novella, *The Heroic Slave* (1853), and in his second autobiography, *My Bondage and My Freedom*, he expanded his earlier narrative by describing his experiences as a freedman. He also made a famous speech, "What to the Slave Is the Fourth of July?" in Rochester on 5 July 1852. During the Civil War, Douglass urged President Lincoln to admit black men to the Union Army, and after the war he encouraged President Johnson to pass a voting rights act for blacks.

During the final three decades of his life Douglass was appointed to several high-level positions: federal marshal and recorder of deeds for the District of Columbia, president of the Freedman's Bureau Bank, consul to Haiti, and chargé d'affaires for the Dominican Republic. He expanded his earlier autobiographies and published *Life and Times of Frederick Douglass* in 1881, which he further expanded and republished in 1892. He had five children with Anna, who died in 1882; in 1884 he married Helen Pitts, a white woman. He died in February 1895.

TOPICS FOR DISCUSSION AND RESEARCH

1. Douglass's *Narrative* is often taken as representative of slave narratives because it includes most of the features that characterized abolitionist literature. It describes the heartrending separation of slave families, depicts the physical and sexual brutality of slaveowners, chastises professing Christians for owning and abusing slaves, and emphasizes the power of literacy among slaves. It also resembles most other slave narratives by including authenticating documents from respected white men—in this case, a preface by Garrison and a letter from Wendell Phillips. Students might look at the database "North American Slave Narratives" <http://docsouth.unc.edu/neh/> or consult *William Lloyd Garrison and the Fight against Slavery* (1994) to trace the influence of earlier slave narratives or Garrison's writings on Douglass's *Narrative* and analyze how he departs from their conventions.

2. One reason that the *Narrative* was so effective lies in Douglass's awareness of his audience. This intended audience was predominantly Northern, white, Protestant, middle-class, and pro-temperance. In targeting this audience, Douglass avoided making blanket judgments against whites, and all the whites portrayed negatively are Southern. He took a risk in one aspect of his narrative, however, in that he did not explicitly endorse Christianity in the main part of the text and frequently denounced hypocritical Christians. Douglass's appendix to the narrative explains that he does not oppose Christianity itself but rather those who use Christianity to justify slavery, a subject that Shaindy Rudoff discusses in his essay "Tarring the Garden." Beginning with Rudoff's essay, students might wish to examine Douglass's religious views and explore how he works within the Christian framework of his audience in arguing against slavery.

3. Douglass ends his 1845 *Narrative* with the 1841 abolitionist meeting in Nantucket, but by the mid 1850s he had experienced legal freedom for almost a decade. As the essays in *Liberating Sojourn* reveal, Douglass's travels in Britain after the *Narrative* was published radicalized him and gave him confidence. *My Bondage and My Freedom*, published in New York City in August 1855, is balanced between his life as a slave and his life as a freedman. The second half narrates his tour of Great Britain as well as his encounters with American abolitionists, some of whom resented Douglass's fame and were threatened by his independent spirit. Unlike the *Narrative, My Bondage* does not include prefatory documents from his white mentors Garrison and Phillips; instead, it includes a foreword by the black abolitionist James McCune Smith. This change signals Douglass's break with the Garrisonians earlier in the decade and reveals a more confident, less deferential author than the *Narrative* does. *My Bondage* also differs from the earlier text in its criticism of Northern racism, both within the abolitionist movement and more generally, and as Eric Goldman points out, it is less opposed to violence as a means to end slavery than the *Narrative*. One potential essay topic would be a comparative analysis of the two texts to trace Douglass's evolution as a writer and abolitionist. Alternately, students could research the racial attitudes of Garrison and his followers by consulting John L. Thomas's biography *The Liberator* (2008) and examine how *My Bondage* addresses those issues.

4. As Vince Brewton has observed, *My Bondage* portrays Douglass as a self-made man, much like Benjamin Franklin's *Autobiography*, and it conforms to the tradition of individualism in American culture that was embodied in Ralph Waldo Emerson's essay "Self-Reliance" and the writings of Henry David Thoreau. In this sense, Douglass comes across as quintessentially American, and students might examine how *My Bondage* overlaps thematically with these American Renaissance texts and how it extends or revises these notions of selfhood.

5. Self-reliance was often described in gendered terms in Douglass's day; for this reason, it is not surprising that Douglass emphasizes his masculinity in both narratives. This issue is particularly prominent in his fight with Edward Covey and his invocation of Patrick Henry's famous declaration, "Give me liberty, or give me death!" The turning point of the narrative focuses on masculinity

as well: "You have seen how a man was made a slave; you shall see how slave was made a man." As Kimberly Drake argues, Douglass was influenced by prevailing ideologies of masculinity, and both narratives emphasize Douglass's struggle to attain manhood. Students interested in masculinity studies might explore the representations of black masculinity in Douglass's time and analyze how his narratives respond to these images. Consult the introduction of Darlene Clark Hine and Ernestine Jenkins in *A Question of Manhood: A Reader* in *U.S. Black Men's History and Masculinity* (1999).

RESOURCES

Biography

Philip S. Foner, ed., *The Life and Writings of Frederick Douglass* (New York: International Publishers, 1975).
Each of the first four volumes of this five-volume series focuses on one period of Douglass's life and includes biographical information as well as Douglass's speeches, editorials, and letters from that period. Volume five includes other writings by Douglass written between 1844 and 1860.

Waldo E. Martin Jr., *The Mind of Frederick Douglass* (Chapel Hill: University of North Carolina Press, 1984).
An intellectual biography of Douglass.

William S. McFeely, *Frederick Douglass* (New York: Norton, 1991).
The definitive biography of Douglass.

Criticism

Vince Brewton, "'Bold Defiance Took Its Place': 'Respect' and Self-Making in *Narrative of the Life of Frederick Douglass, an American Slave*," *Mississippi Quarterly*, 58 (June 2005): 703–717.
Analyzes how Douglass's identity in the *Narrative* is shaped by the interactions between the values of slaveholding whites and those of black slaves.

Jeannine DeLombard, "'Eye-Witness to the Cruelty': Southern Violence and Northern Testimony in Frederick Douglass's 1845 *Narrative*," *American Literature*, 73 (June 2001): 245–275.
Analyzes Douglass's attempts in his narrative to move from the embodied subjectivity of a former-slave eyewitness of slavery to the universal, disembodied subjectivity of an abolitionist.

Kimberly Drake, "Rewriting the American Self: Race, Gender, and Identity in the Autobiographies of Frederick Douglass and Harriet Jacobs," *MELUS*, 22 (1997): 91–108.
Examines how the nineteenth-century norms of masculine and feminine identity formation that influence the slave narratives of Douglass and Jacobs illustrate the psychoanalytic theories of Sigmund Freud and Jacques Lacan about the role of language in identity construction.

"Frederick Douglass, 1818–1895," in *Documenting the American South*, University
    Library, University of North Carolina at Chapel Hill, 2004 <http://docsouth.
    unc.edu/neh/douglass/bio.html> [accessed 17 April 2009].
A brief biography of Douglass with links to electronic versions of his three autobiographies and his novella *The Heroic Slave*.

Eric A. Goldman, "Spilling Ink and Spilling Blood: Abolitionism, Violence and
    Frederick Douglass's *My Bondage and My Freedom*," *A/B: Auto/Biography
    Studies*, 17 (2002): 276–295.
Argues that *My Bondage* differs from Douglass's 1845 *Narrative* in revealing his
belief that violence rather than moral suasion was necessary to end slavery.

Alan J. Rice and Martin Crawford, eds., *Liberating Sojourn: Frederick Douglass and
    Transatlantic Reform* (Athens: University of Georgia Press, 1999).
A collection of ten historical essays focusing on how Douglass's experiences in
Britain during 1845–1847 radicalized him and made a significant impact on
British society.

Shaindy Rudoff, "Tarring the Garden: The Bible and the Aesthetics of Slavery
    in Douglass's *Narrative*," *ESQ: A Journal of the American Renaissance*, 46, 4
    (2000): 213–237.
Analyzes Douglass's biblical allusions in the 1845 *Narrative* and his criticism of
proslavery uses of the Bible to justify slavery.

Eric J. Sundquist, ed., *Frederick Douglass: New Literary and Historical Essays*
    (Cambridge, England: Cambridge University Press, 1900).
A collection of thirteen essays that focus on Douglass's career as a journalist, editor, author, orator, and politician within his historical contexts.

⌒◈⌒

Ralph Waldo Emerson, Early Addresses and Lectures
(1837–1844)

Ralph Waldo Emerson (1803–1882) graduated from Harvard College in 1821
and after a brief tenure as a teacher began to study for the ministry. He was named
associate pastor in 1829 of Boston's Second Church, a Unitarian congregation,
but after his wife's death from tuberculosis in 1831, Emerson resigned his pastor-
ate and travelled to Europe. Upon his return, he began a career as a lecturer.

Following the publication of *Nature* in 1836, Emerson delivered a series of
addresses that capitalized on his growing reputation as a speaker. Unlike his lectures,
which were often organized in series and delivered repeatedly, Emerson's addresses
were usually more topical, often delivered only once, and focused on applying some
of his broader generalizations to particular social problems of the day.

The poet and biographer Oliver Wendell Holmes, who was on the program
when Emerson delivered the 1837 Phi Beta Kappa address (or the American
Scholar address, as it is commonly known), years later, in 1885, recalled it as "our

intellectual Declaration of Independence." Given at the invitation of the Phi Beta Kappa society at Harvard College, the address begins with a by-then standard call for a bold new national literature free from British influence. Emerson goes on to consider why the young scholars sitting in front of him are so unlikely to answer that call: they have been encouraged by their teachers not to think and create but to parrot the thoughts of others, to be bookworms and "bibliomaniacs" rather than aspiring to the more active and meaningful calling of the true scholar, which Emerson calls "Man Thinking." In a series of redefinitions, Emerson calls upon his student audience to use books wisely (in their "idle times," for inspiration), to be creators of knowledge rather than just consumers of it, and to embrace a life of intellectual activity.

A year later Emerson was once again invited back to the Harvard campus, this time to deliver the customary address in July 1838 in honor of the graduating class of Divinity School students. As with the Phi Beta Kappa event, this one was intended to be ceremonial, not controversial; but the choice of Emerson, we now know, was an intentional affront to the school's president, who had recently denied a student group the right to invite an abolitionist speaker to campus. Emerson's address, it turned out, was no less inflammatory. In the crowded inner sanctum of Harvard's Divinity Hall, before the seven assembled seniors, their faculty, and numerous guests, Emerson pronounced contemporary Christianity "corpse-cold" and dead, a victim of an overreverence for Jesus as a person (rather than his teachings) and an overreliance on forms and ceremony. Repeating in the Divinity School address some of the same indictments of education that he had voiced in "American Scholar," Emerson counseled the students to ignore what their professors had taught them; recognize the workings of the divine in all things, not just in the biblical miracles (which he called "monsters"—freakish and unnatural things); and instead be true ministers, "dar[ing] to love God without mediator or veil." Following Emerson's remarks, a powerful Boston theologian named Andrews Norton called the event "the latest form of infidelity"—not only because Emerson criticized the fundamentals of Protestant belief but also because he did so in the most inappropriate of venues, the Divinity School itself. Norton's criticism inaugurated a vigorous debate now referred to as the Transcendental Controversy.

Emerson's lecture "The Transcendentalist," first given in December 1841 as part of series called "The Times," resembles the addresses in that it responds to timely interest in the Transcendental group. As the purported leader of the movement, a designation that made him uncomfortable (he insisted in the lecture that "there is no such thing as a Transcendental *party*"), Emerson was expected to define the term. Intellectually, he claimed, Transcendentalism was "Idealism as it appears in 1842," an assertion of the consciousness, inspiration, individual culture, and "the power of Thought and of Will." He opposed Idealism to "Materialism," with its emphasis on facts, experience, the senses, and "the animal wants of man." The Transcendentalists were easily caricatured; but instead of countering these stereotypes, Emerson grants them: they are in fact solitary, demanding, "not good citizens," critics, complainers, and extremists. But, he concludes pointedly, they perform a valuable social role, speaking out for "thoughts and principles not marketable or perishable" in a world obsessed with things.

While Emerson's public engagement with issues of social injustice reached its peak later in his career, even in his most "transcendental" early period he was keenly aware of the plight of oppressed Americans and was writing about them. His 1838 letter to President Martin Van Buren, for instance, revealed his opposition to the treatment of the Cherokee Nation, in particular, and Native Americans generally. His wife, Lidian, and friends like Margaret Fuller sensitized him to the plight of women. As with many of his generation, however, the kindling issue for Emerson was opposition to slavery. Nowhere is his commitment more clearly revealed than in his "Address . . . on . . . the Emancipation of the Negroes in the British West Indies," delivered in Concord, Massachusetts, on 1 August 1844, the tenth anniversary of the event. While largely given over to a history of British abolitionism, the address shows Emerson at his most passionately idealistic. He discounts the influence of politics and the economic and commercial benefits of freeing slaves (i.e., the creation of a new class of consumers) to stress instead the "moral revolution" of emancipation, a revolution fired by "the repentance of the tyrant" rather than the action of the oppressed. For Emerson, West Indian emancipation, contextualized in the age-old struggle between "the material and the moral nature" of humanity, represents the triumph of right and intellect and a sign of God's will at work in the world.

TOPICS FOR DISCUSSION AND RESEARCH

1. As a lecturer Emerson was popular and financially successful, though as William Charvat points out, "for some forty years he was invited everywhere, and was repeatedly invited back, by people who 'understood' (in the ordinary sense) little of what he said; who often resented not understanding him; and who frequently were offended by what they did understand." Examine Emerson's lectures in context. What were the conditions and expectations for lecturers during the Romantic age, and how was Emerson received? The studies by Mary Kupiec Cayton and Nancy Craig Simmons reveal the material conditions and rhetoric of Emerson's lecturing, as does the historical introduction to Ronald A. Bosco and Joel Myerson's edition of Emerson's *Later Lectures*. Carl Bode's classic history of the Lyceum movement, a forerunner of what would today be called "adult education," reminds us of the larger world of speaking and teaching that Emerson moved in.

2. A frequent theme in Emerson's early addresses and essays is the choice of vocation: the work we do, and how best to do it. Practically, Emerson knew that careers were distinct in their duties. The scholar, Emerson asserts in the Phi Beta Kappa address, is society's "designated intellect"; just as others build or teach or legislate, so the scholar thinks. But that easy distinction collapses in the Divinity School address, where he equates preachers and teachers, "seers" and "sayers," "priests" and poets. Choose two or three of these terms and examine their definitions to see where they overlap. What biographical and historical forces may have made vocation such an important concept to Emerson?

3. Emerson argues in the addresses for a life of originality rather than conformity. Does his definition of "originality" remain consistent, or is it redefined

by the topics of specific addresses? In what ways can one be "original" and still work "within the system," particularly on matters of social action like abolitionism, which he describes as a moral necessity in his address on West Indian emancipation? Analyze Emerson's participation in one aspect of social reform, explain his reasons for doing so, and evaluate it in light of his fierce independence from conformity. Len Gougeon analyzes the development of Emerson's thinking on these ideas in *Virtue's Hero: Emerson, Antislavery, and Reform* and traces Emerson's influence on the Civil Rights movement of the 1960s in "The Legacy of Reform." Robert D. Habich (1990) examines Emerson's "compromised optimism" in the "American Scholar."

4. "The Transcendentalist" was delivered more than three years after the Divinity School address and the Transcendental Controversy that followed it. Its main issues were theological—whether biblical miracles were necessary to legitimize a belief in Christianity, whether religious ceremonies reflected faith or distracted from it, and whether religious authority came from historical evidence or the promptings of the heart. Using the primary sources and the contemporary reactions, consider in what ways the other, more secular addresses also addressed these religious questions of morality and authority. What did "authority" mean for Emerson, and how did his ideas carry over from the religious to the civic, legal, and social realms? The main texts of the Transcendental Controversy are reproduced in Joel Myerson's authoritative anthology (2000); essays by Burkholder and Habich (1992) analyze the social and political contexts for the Divinity School address.

RESOURCES

Primary Works

An Address Delivered before the Senior Class in Divinity College, Cambridge (Boston: James Munroe, 1838).

Ronald A. Bosco and Joel Myerson, "Historical and Textual Introduction," in *The Later Lectures of Ralph Waldo Emerson*, edited by Bosco and Myerson, 2 volumes (Athens: University of Georgia Press, 2001), pp. xvii–lxii.
Discusses the material conditions of Emerson's lecture career as well as some of the main themes of his largely neglected lectures from 1843 to 1871, which are here reproduced in authoritative texts.

Myerson, ed., *Transcendentalism: A Reader* (New York: Oxford University Press, 2000).
A collection of the most important primary texts of the movement.

An Oration, Delivered before the Phi Beta Kappa Society, at Cambridge (Boston: Munroe, 1837).

"The Transcendentalist," in Nature; Addresses, and Lectures (Boston & Cambridge: James Munroe, 1849); and *An address delivered by Ralph Waldo Emerson on August 1, 1844, at the Concord Court House* (Boston: James Munroe, 1844).

Bibliography

William Charvat, "A Chronological List of Emerson's American Lecture Engagements," *Bulletin of the New York Public Library*, 64 (1960): 492–507, 551–559, 606–610, 657–663; and 65 (1961): 40–46.

Presents a nearly complete list of places and dates, with a valuable introduction.

Biography

Robert E. Burkholder, "Emerson, Kneeland, and the Divinity School Address," *American Literature: A Journal of Literary History, Criticism, and Bibliography*, 58 (March 1986): 1–14.

Discusses the intellectual and personal connections between Emerson and Abner Kneeland, the last person to be jailed for blasphemy in the Commonwealth of Massachusetts.

Len Gougeon, *Virtue's Hero: Emerson, Antislavery, and Reform* (Athens: University of Georgia Press, 1990).

Documents Emerson's continuing engagement with social causes, particularly his opposition to slavery.

Robert D. Habich, "Emerson's Reluctant Foe: Andrews Norton and the Transcendental Controversy," *New England Quarterly: A Historical Review of New England Life and Letters*, 65 (June 1992): 208–237.

Places the Divinity School address in the context of Harvard governance and the general sensitivity to antiauthoritarianism in 1838.

Oliver Wendell Holmes, *Ralph Waldo Emerson* (Boston & New York: Houghton, Mifflin, 1885).

An appreciative literary biography that downplays Emerson's reformist activities.

Criticism

Carl Bode, *The American Lyceum: Town Meeting of the Mind* (New York: Oxford University Press, 1956).

An authoritative history of the purposes and principal speakers of the forerunner to the "adult education" movement.

Mary Kupiec Cayton, "The Making of an American Prophet: Emerson, His Audiences, and the Rise of the Culture Industry in Nineteenth-Century America," in *Ralph Waldo Emerson: A Collection of Critical Essays*, edited by Lawrence Buell (Englewood Cliffs, N.J.: Prentice Hall, 1993), pp. 77–100.

Argues that through the lectures Emerson transcended the parochial concerns of the intellectual elite and discovered ways to speak to the concerns of larger, more popular audiences.

Len Gougeon, "The Legacy of Reform: Emersonian Idealism, Moorfield Storey, and the Civil Rights Movement," in *Emerson Bicentennial Essays*, edited by

Ronald A. Bosco and Joel Myerson (Boston: Massachusetts Historical Society, 2006), pp. 183–210.
Examines Emerson's effects on African American leaders in the twentieth century.

Robert D. Habich,"Emerson's Compromised Optimism in the 'American Scholar': A Source in the Poetry," *English Language Notes*, 27 (March 1990): 40–43.
Points out Emerson's doubts about introspection embedded in one of his most otherwise optimistic addresses.

Wesley T. Mott, "'The Age of the First Person Singular': Emerson and Individualism," in *A Historical Guide to Ralph Waldo Emerson*, edited by Myerson (New York: Oxford University Press, 2000), pp. 61–100.
Examines the meaning of Emerson's terms *self-reliance* and *individualism* and traces their resonance in later American culture.

Nancy Craig Simmons, "Emerson and His Audiences: The New England Lectures, 1843–1844," in *Emerson Bicentennial Essays*, edited by Bosco and Myerson (Boston: Massachusetts Historical Society, 2006), pp. 51–85.
Analyzes Emerson's experiments to reach listening audiences effectively with his "texts in performance."

⁓✖⁓

Ralph Waldo Emerson, *Nature*

(Boston: Munroe, 1836)

Emerson's slim first book, *Nature,* contains all of the supposed contradictions that make his work intellectually complex: divided into tidy sections, its argument grows and proceeds organically; exploring the sustaining realities of the natural world, it celebrates the power of individuals; beginning with an indictment of our failures, it ends with the charge to "build . . . your own world." Though it was published relatively early in his career, *Nature* is often considered Emerson's manifesto.

Ralph Waldo Emerson (1803–1882) was born in Boston to a family whose patriarchal side dated back to the earliest English settlement during the 1630s. (As an adult he preferred to be called "Waldo," after another ancestral family member on his mother's side.) Reverend William Emerson, his father, died when Waldo was seven years old, and he grew up in modest circumstances with four other surviving brothers, his mother Ruth taking in boarders to make ends meet. Waldo followed the family tradition and attended Harvard, graduating in 1821. In his early adulthood he struggled to find his vocation: he tried and abandoned school teaching; he returned to the new Divinity School at Harvard but withdrew due to vision problems and boredom; and he became associate minister at the prestigious Second Church of Boston but resigned in 1832. Eventually, in the mid 1830s, after he returned from a trip to Europe, he decided upon the career that would support him for the rest of his life: lecturing. Despite false starts, an abiding passion for communication, ideas, and powerful words was the hallmark of Emerson's struggle to find a vocation.

As a young man Emerson struggled as well with his religious and philosophical ideas. His family were mostly liberal Christians who accepted a progressive view of New England Calvinism called Unitarianism, which held that Jesus was a divine example and that human beings were improvable by their own efforts. By Emerson's time Unitarianism had become the accepted religion of New England's educated and governing classes. But Emerson and many others increasingly found Unitarian rationalism cold, elitist, and lacking spirituality, and his dissatisfaction with religious forms led to his resignation from the pulpit in 1832. Intellectual and literary influences from Europe—particularly the works of Thomas Carlyle and Samuel Taylor Coleridge, whom he met in 1833, and Johann Wolfgang von Goethe, whose works he could read in the original German—stimulated his thinking and drew him toward Romantic views of individualism. By the mid 1830s he had embraced an organic view of human and natural relationships that his age called Transcendentalism. Not a religion but a vitalizing orientation toward life that stressed the divine spirit in every human and a sustaining relationship between people and nature, Transcendentalism became the driving force behind Emerson's early writings, and he in turn became known as the movement's chief American spokesman.

In their confident promotion of individualism and self-reliance, early works like *Nature* suggest an optimism that was not borne out by the events of Emerson's life. His beloved wife Ellen died of tuberculosis, as did two brothers; his family struggled financially, and he suffered periodically from ill health and depression. By the publication of *Nature,* however, he had remarried and moved to the growing town of Concord, where he and his second wife, Lydia (he called her Lidian), began a family. He had first planned *Nature* during a tour of Europe in 1832–1833, according to his journal, when he visited the scientific collections in the Jardin des Plantes in Paris. By 1836, however, his book had progressed far beyond natural science, expressing Emerson's fervent, almost mystical, vision of life's possibilities.

Nature begins with a classic Emersonian pronouncement—"Our age is retrospective"—which is then shown to be problematic, for our tendency to "look backward" results in a failure to think for ourselves: we worship the past, write books about it, confine our lives to the paths already traveled by others, and never have the courage to explore life for ourselves. Why can we not have an "original relation" with the world around us? Emerson's narrator asks. And what does that world offer us? Those two questions, posed at the beginning of *Nature,* in fact shape the "answers" that follow. The "ends" or purposes of Nature for humans are explored in increasing order of complexity, from the most basic material "commodity" (that is, nature as consumable stuff like firewood and food) through the most rarefied mystical "Spirit" (nature as evidence of divine intentions), as Emerson systematically builds his case for our necessary connection to the world around us. The other question Emerson poses—"Why should not we also enjoy an original relation to the universe?"—is not so much answered as it is assumed. By the end of *Nature* there is no reason why we cannot, if only we will see clearly and not rely solely on the record of the past. As Emerson begins *Nature* by identifying the problem of retrospection—looking backward—so he ends with a section entitled "Prospects" in which the solution of "pro-spection"—looking forward—is celebrated and encouraged.

TOPICS FOR DISCUSSION AND RESEARCH

1. Readers have often found Emerson's prose inspiring but sometimes elliptical. Yet, even a quick look at *Nature* reveals how Emerson's ministerial training at sermon writing lent his argument a kind of linear organization and clarity. It follows a fairly conventional rhetorical structure: identifying a problem, defining terms, posing questions, and answering them. Emerson even titles and numbers his sections. Consider the sources of this type of organization in *Nature*, perhaps by comparing it to one of his early sermons or to his lectures, or to famous sermons like Jonathan Edwards's *Sinners in the Hands of an Angry God* (1741). Does it change your view of Emerson when you realize how conventional his rhetoric can sometimes be? And how do you account for the unconventional aspects, such as his reliance on unsupported aphorisms instead of "backing up" his assertions with empirical "proof"? Background information about Emerson's sources and influences can be found in Merton M. Sealts and Alfred Riggs Ferguson's casebook *Emerson's* Nature: *Origin, Growth, Meaning*.

2. The argument of *Nature* proceeds from metaphors, language that in its compression and vividness strikes us as true. One example of a characteristic Emersonian metaphor occurs in the "Language" section of *Nature*. Berating us for being too easily satisfied with everyday uses of Nature while ignoring the world's majesty and bounty, Emerson writes, "We are like travellers using the cinders of a volcano to roast their eggs." The comparison works on several levels: it is visual and suggests the foolishness of visitors ignoring nature's immense power while stooped over a hot fissure with a frying pan; but it is also visceral, in that readers can feel the heat and power of the volcanic lava smoldering dangerously below. Like his Puritan ancestors, Emerson drew upon the power of the "homely," or familiar, metaphor to impress truth upon the mind and the emotions. Consider some of the metaphors that seem particularly effective to you. Where are the sources for Emerson's metaphors? Why do they work? Buell's *Literary Transcendentalism* and B. L. Packer's *Emerson's Fall* remain valuable first stops for inquiries about the connection between "style" and "vision" in Emerson's essays.

3. *Nature* is a radical indictment of the status quo. Emerson early on identifies the subversive effects of being "original" in our thinking. By encouraging readers to have their own "works and laws and worship," Emerson challenges intellectual, civic, and religious authority by seeming to replace the wisdom of the past with an anarchic, individualistic focus on the present. Within a few years Emerson's individualism would be scorned as "the latest form of infidelity" and a dangerous form of arrogance. Consider how Emerson outlines the risks of individuality in an essay such as "Self-Reliance," and then apply those dangers to his pronouncements about originality in *Nature*. Or consider the varied

criticism of Emerson and his responses to it. For a comprehensive discussion of Emerson and individualism, see Wesley T. Mott, "The Age of the First Person Singular," in *Historical Guide to Emerson*. For information about how Emerson's views were received, see the various contextual essays in Ronald A. Bosco and Joel Myerson, *Emerson in His Time*, and Myerson and Robert E. Burkholder, *Critical Essays on Ralph Waldo Emerson*.

4. In 1835 Emerson claimed to his fiancée that he was really a poet, though his voice was husky and his writing was mostly prose. Are there themes that the essays and poems have in common? Coordinate the ideas in *Nature* with those expressed in some of Emerson's poems—poems like "Each and All," which presents a vision of the "perfect whole" between things and their surroundings, or "The Rhodora," which raises questions about the relationships among the natural, human, and divine worlds.

5. *Nature* relies heavily on definitions, often derived from opposites—the Me versus the Not-Me, art versus nature, retrospection versus prospection. Why are definitions so crucial to Emerson's argument? Consider how Emerson defines a key term, such as *nature* or *the self* or *vision* or *discipline*, and analyze the varying tools he uses to do so, such as metaphor and example. How do those definitions connect to each other to give shape to Emerson's argument?

6. Emerson kept voluminous journals, referring to them as the storehouse for his ideas. They often allow us to see the development of key terms and phrases that show up in the essays and addresses. Using Emerson's *Journals and Miscellaneous Notebooks*, trace the genesis and development of the main ideas in *Nature*.

RESOURCES

Primary Works

William H. Gilman, Ralph H. Orth, and others, eds., *The Journals and Miscellaneous Notebooks of Ralph Waldo Emerson*, 16 volumes (Cambridge, Mass.: Harvard University Press, 1960–1982).

The Works of Ralph Waldo Emerson. Website of the Ralph Waldo Emerson Institute <http://www.rwe.org>.
Includes online texts of all of Emerson's major works.

Biography

Ronald A. Bosco and Joel Myerson, eds., *Emerson in His Own Time: A Biographical Chronicle of His Life, Drawn from Recollections, Interviews, and Memoirs by Family, Friends, and Associates* (Iowa City: University of Iowa Press, 2003).

Lawrence Buell, *Emerson* (Cambridge, Mass.: Harvard University Press, 2003).
Argues for Emerson as a public intellectual.

Robert D. Richardson Jr., *Emerson: The Mind on Fire* (Berkeley: University of California Press, 1995).
An intellectual biography that shows the relationship of Emerson's ideas to his emotional life.

Ralph L. Rusk, *The Life of Ralph Waldo Emerson* (New York: Columbia University Press, 1949).
A comprehensive biography based upon an edition of Emerson's letters.

Criticism

Lawrence Buell, *Literary Transcendentalism: Style and Vision in the American Renaissance* (Ithaca, N.Y. & London: Cornell University Press, 1973).
A landmark study of Transcendentalist literary achievement in nonfiction prose, "through a combination of intellectual history, critical explication, and genre study" (Buell).

Robert E. Burkholder and Joel Myerson, eds., *Critical Essays on Ralph Waldo Emerson* (Boston: G. K. Hall, 1983).
Contemporary essays on Emerson's prose and poetry.

Myerson, ed., *Historical Guide to Ralph Waldo Emerson* (New York & Oxford: Oxford University Press, 2000).
Includes essays on Emerson's life, philosophy, and major themes.

B. L. Packer, *Emerson's Fall: A New Interpretation of the Major Essays* (New York: Continuum, 1982).
Cooordinates an interpretation of *Nature* with the history of the book's composition.

Merton M. Sealts and Alfred Riggs Ferguson, comps., *Emerson's* Nature: *Origin, Growth, Meaning,* revised edition (Carbondale: Southern Illinois University Press, 1979).
Sources and essays in criticism.

Reference

The Ralph Waldo Emerson Society <http://www.emersonsociety.org> [accessed 16 November 2009].
The official site of the Emerson Society, particularly valuable for visual images of Emerson and a useful chronology of Emerson's life.

Margaret Fuller, "The Great Lawsuit"

Dial, July 1843

Like her contemporaries Henry David Thoreau and Edgar Allan Poe, Margaret Fuller's compelling life—both real and mythic—is intimately associated with her writing and at times threatens to overshadow it. Sarah Margaret Fuller (1810–1850), the first-born child of Timothy and Margarett Crane Fuller, received an atypically rigorous education for a child of either sex, and while she bristled at being shut out of the formal schooling available to her male friends, as a self-taught learner she mastered foreign languages and read voraciously in history, mythology, art, and literature. At twenty-five, as she was anticipating a tour of Europe, her father's sudden death left her the primary financial support of her mother, sister, and five brothers. With few opportunities open to her, she gravitated toward the traditional female occupation of teaching, on her own and as an assistant in Bronson Alcott's controversial Temple School in Boston. Around this time she began a friendship with the poet and essayist Ralph Waldo Emerson, whom she often visited for weeks at a time at his home in Concord, Massachusetts. From 1840 through 1844 they collaborated on a celebrated literary magazine of the Transcendental group, the *Dial*, with Fuller editing it from 1840 to 1842. Though never a resident, Fuller became closely associated with the writers who lived in Concord in the 1830s and 1840s: Emerson, Thoreau, Bronson Alcott and his precocious daughter Louisa May Alcott, and Nathaniel Hawthorne.

Fuller was known for her passionate nature, her forthrightness, her intellectual brilliance, and increasingly for her activism. In 1839 she began conducting a series of conversations for women, lengthy programs devoted to discussions of art and culture. She was interested in women's rights, abolitionism, and other manifestations of social reform, and she was a frequent visitor at Brook Farm, the communal social experiment in West Roxbury, outside of Boston. Her writing for the *Dial*, including "The Great Lawsuit: Man versus Men, Woman versus Women" in July 1843, and a book about her western travels, *Summer on the Lakes* (1844), brought her to the attention of the newspaper editor and reformer Horace Greeley, who offered her a paid position at the *New-York Tribune*.

Fuller moved to New York City in 1844 and began an ambitious program of writing that included book reviewing, essays on the arts, and exposés of social conditions, notably in the women's prisons. Her work for the *Tribune* was collected as *Papers on Literature and Art* in 1846. After two years in New York, Fuller realized her long-delayed dream of a European tour when Greeley sent her abroad as a foreign correspondent. She went first to England and Scotland, where she met the essayist Thomas Carlyle and other literary figures, then to France, and finally to Italy, which was being drawn into the revolutionary politics that swept across Europe at mid century. In 1847 she fell in love with Giovanni Angelo d'Ossoli, an impoverished Italian nobleman fighting for the Republican cause against the papacy in the Roman Revolution.

The birth of their son Angelo in 1848 made it increasingly difficult for Fuller and Ossoli to remain in an active war zone; in 1850, after the fall of Rome, they booked passage for the United States on the freighter *Elizabeth*, Fuller carrying with her the manuscript of her magnum opus, a history of the Roman Revolution. The *Elizabeth* weathered the transatlantic passage safely, despite the death of its captain early in the voyage, but beached on a sandbar south of Long Island during a fierce storm. Fuller, Ossoli, and their child drowned within sight of shore on 19 July 1850. Though Greeley and Thoreau both searched for her, Fuller's body was never recovered. Emerson mourned that he had lost his audience.

Fuller's posthumous reputation, and almost all scholarship on her through the 1980s, were influenced by her first biography, *The Memoirs of Margaret Fuller Ossoli*

(1852), compiled by Emerson, James Freeman Clarke, and William Henry Channing, all of them her close friends. The *Memoirs* created a more conventional image of Fuller and rearranged her personal writings to disguise or minimize some of her controversial views. Yet, she remained a complicated and controversial figure due to her forthrightness and her political significance for a generation of "new women" who read "The Great Lawsuit" as an inspiration. As the title of one biography put it, Fuller existed as both "the woman and the myth." Not until the publication of her collected letters beginning in 1983 did Fuller have the chance to speak for herself and the full range of her public and private selves become available. Today she is known for her "firsts" as a female newspaper reviewer, literary critic, and foreign correspondent. She is considered a pioneering American articulator of feminism, largely due to her most famous work, "The Great Lawsuit" (expanded in 1845 to the book *Woman in the Nineteenth Century*), a defense of women's sphere as different from but complimentary to the realm of men. Though the essay begins with an exploration of "union" and marriage as a way of fostering the mutual advance of both sexes, it concludes with a radical call for female "self-centredness" that modern critics identify as Fuller's true political position on women's liberty.

Fuller's rhetoric in "The Great Lawsuit" reflects the widespread need in the early nineteenth century to accommodate reformist arguments to existing value systems, in this case contextualizing women's liberty in the relationship of women to men. Thus, Fuller begins by arguing for the "birthright" of all human beings—liberty—and then exploring how that birthright may be furthered by certain practical realities, like a proper marriage, and thwarted by certain obstructive realities, like chivalry, economic unfairness, and polarizing notions about women's intellectual and physical inferiority. Throughout the essay Fuller recognizes the need to win over a male audience by asserting the inherent generosity of men, which is perverted by the "slavery of habit." Just as antislavery activists of the time stressed how slavery victimized both races and abolition would free all Americans, so Fuller stresses the benefits to both men and women when women are allowed an equal place in personal and social relationships.

TOPICS FOR DISCUSSION AND RESEARCH

1. How much of Fuller's argument in "The Great Lawsuit" is constructed to appeal to an empowered male audience, and how much reflects a true belief in "union" as a way for women to realize themselves? Examine the reviews at the time to see whether male readers (there would have been virtually no published reviews by women) responded positively, and to which parts of Fuller's argument. For an examination of Fuller's feminist rhetoric, see Annette Kolodny, "Inventing a Feminist Discourse."

2. Fuller's treatment of the theme of marriage is of particular importance for an essay written during a time when women were typically defined in domestic terms. An often excerpted section of "The Great Lawsuit" explores the ascending levels of gender relationships—mutual dependence ("the household partnership"), mutual idolatry, intellectual companionship, religious union—that for Fuller are the hallmarks of marriage. Again, is Fuller arguing for better

marriages or pointing out the limitations of even the highest levels of companionship? Phyllis Cole's essay "The Nineteenth-Century Women's Rights Movement and the Canonization of Margaret Fuller" provides an excellent context for this discussion.

3. The identification of gender oppression with racial oppression, a common strategy in female slave narratives, is both a useful argumentative technique and a way for Fuller to enlist readers to the cause of women's rights, for the antislavery movement had sensitized large numbers of Americans, male and female, to the severity of institutionalized injustice. In fact, Fuller calls upon not only the American antislavery movement but earlier political struggles such as the French Revolution to provide a larger context for the call for women's rights: "As men become aware that all men have not had their fair chance, they are inclined to say that no women have had a fair chance." T. Gregory Garvey's study of Fuller's political intersections is a useful place to start.

4. As the essay's title suggests, Fuller sees gender distinctions in either ideal terms (man versus woman) or individual ones (men versus women). The struggle for Fuller is not between the sexes so much as it is between our ideal nature and our social one—men struggling to fulfill the promise of man, women unable to realize the potential of woman. In a famous section of the essay she explores the "great radical dualism" that seems to certify the doctrine of "separate spheres" widely used to legitimize gender inequality in the nineteenth century. Yet, Fuller finds those differences to be socially constructed, not natural. Investigate the doctrine of Separate Spheres and apply it to an analysis of "The Great Lawsuit." Consult Charles Capper's intellectual biography for the development of Fuller's ideas on gender, or watch her ideas unfold in Robert N. Hudspeth's edition of her letters.

5. In a time when thinking about women largely stresses their relationalism—legitimized, for instance, by the important late-twentieth-century work of the psychologist Carol Gilligan—Margaret Fuller's call for women to seek fulfillment through isolation sounds perhaps even more radical today than it did in the nineteenth century. Fulfilling relationships may follow independence, she argues, but they don't cause it; only truly independent people can enter into dependent relationships: "Union is only possible to those who are units," Fuller insists. Instead, she argues for "self-dependence" and "celibacy," for a spiritual journey to freedom that each woman must make alone: "Woman, self-centred, would never be absorbed by any relation; it would be only an experience to her as to man." To many people in her society, being "self-centred" surely connoted a moral failing; even reformers such as Orestes Augustus Brownson dismissed Fuller in 1845 as a spokesperson of the Transcendentalists and criticized her equation of men and women as unchristian. (See Anne C. Rose's *Transcendentalism as a Social Movement* for apt commentary on Fuller's reformist agenda as it relates to her Transcendentalism.) Examine Fuller's complicated stance toward marriage in the essay and the way it was received in her time, perhaps by reading the reviews of Fuller's "Great Lawsuit" and *Woman in the Nineteenth Century*. What were the objections to her views of marriage, and how fair is that criticism?

RESOURCES

Primary Work

Robert N. Hudspeth, editor, *Letters of Margaret Fuller*, 6 volumes (Ithaca, N.Y.: Cornell University Press, 1983–1994).
Carefully restored and annotated letters written by Fuller that show her developing ideas and relationships.

Bibliography

Margaret Fuller Society <http://mendota.english.wisc.edu/~jasteele/> [accessed 9 November 2009].
Website of the Margaret Fuller Society; includes a useful bibliography, lists of doctoral dissertations, and biographical information.

Biography

Paula Blanchard, *Margaret Fuller: From Transcendentalism to Revolution* (New York: Delacorte, 1978).
A useful brief biography.

Charles Capper, *Margaret Fuller: An American Romantic Life*, 2 volumes (New York: Oxford University Press, 1992, 2007).
The standard biography, coordinating Fuller's life and ideas.

Criticism

Phyllis Cole, "The Nineteenth-Century Women's Rights Movement and the Canonization of Margaret Fuller," *ESQ: A Journal of the American Renaissance*, 44, 1–2 (1998): 1–33.
Places Fuller's "Great Lawsuit" in context.

T. Gregory Garvey, "Margaret Fuller's *Woman in the Nineteenth Century* and the Rhetoric of Social Reform in the 1840s," *ESQ: A Journal of the American Renaissance*, 47, 2 (2001): 113–133.
Woman represents Fuller's engagement with three reform models: Transcendentalism, politics, and associationism.

Annette Kolodny, "Inventing a Feminist Discourse: Rhetoric and Resistance in Margaret Fuller's *Woman in the Nineteenth Century*," in *Nineteenth-Century American Women Writers: A Critical Reader*, edited by Karen L. Kilcup (Malden, Mass.: Blackwell, 1998), pp. 206–230.
Shows how Fuller adapted the conventions of conversation in her writing.

Joel Myerson, ed., *Critical Essays on Margaret Fuller* (Boston: G. K. Hall, 1980).
Reprints criticism and reviews, allowing one to trace Fuller's reception from 1840 through the 1970s.

⸎

Nathaniel Hawthorne,
The House of the Seven Gables, a Romance
(Boston: Ticknor, Reed & Fields, 1851)

Following the success of *The Scarlet Letter* in 1850, Nathaniel Hawthorne (1804–1864) moved his family from Salem to the western Massachusetts village of Lenox, an artists' colony. There he experienced one of the most productive periods of his career, writing *The House of the Seven Gables* and *A Wonder-book for Girls and Boys* (1851), publishing a new edition of *Twice-Told Tales* (1851), bringing out a collection of previously published stories, *The Snow-Image, and Other Twice-Told Tales* (1852), and working on *The Blithedale Romance* (1852). In Lenox he met Herman Melville, whose laudatory essay "Hawthorne and His Mosses" had appeared in 1850. Hawthorne's third child, Rose, was born in 1851, and he enjoyed a measure of financial security that had eluded him in the past.

In 1851 he returned with his family to Concord, Massachusetts, buying the former home of the Alcotts and naming it "The Wayside." For the remainder of his life he lived there and in England, where he served as United States consul in Liverpool from 1853 to 1857. Hawthorne would go on to write two more long narratives, *The Blithedale Romance* and *The Marble Faun* (1860), as well as short stories and essays. He continued to suffer bouts of depression, financial reverses, and (as he told his publisher in 1855) frustration at being outsold by a "damn'd mob of scribbling women." But as a reviewer in the *Salem Register* wrote in 1851, "Mr. Hawthorne can no longer allege that he is an obscure, unknown, or unappreciated writer." With *The House of the Seven Gables*, his reputation was secure.

The House of the Seven Gables appeared on 9 April 1851, about a year after the publication of *The Scarlet Letter*. Less somber, with a more hopeful and conventional ending, *The House of the Seven Gables* was Hawthorne's second long narrative on themes that were familiar to readers of his short stories—the impingement of the past on the present, the corrosive effects of guilt and revenge, the secrets of the human heart. It also reflects his continuing, self-conscious attempts to exemplify the genre of the romance. The romancer, Hawthorne asserted in "The Custom-House" introduction to *The Scarlet Letter*, requires a "neutral territory, somewhere between the real world and fairy-land, where the Actual and the Imaginary may meet." In the preface to *The House of the Seven Gables*, he made more explicit the difference between the novel (which requires fidelity to the probable and ordinary course of human experience) and the romance (which gives the writer latitude but must not "swerve aside from the truth of the human heart"). The moral of *The House of the Seven Gables*, Hawthorne announced in the preface—because, he claimed, all authors purport to have one—was that "the wrong-doing of one generation lives into the successive ones."

Hawthorne dramatizes this theme by developing two intersecting sets of relationships, one composed of family members tied to the past, the other comprising two young people adamantly focused on the present. The aged Hepzibah Pyncheon and her elderly brother, Clifford, recently returned to Salem after a thirty-year prison sentence for a murder he did not commit, live in genteel poverty in their decaying ancestral home, where the cash-poor Hepzibah is forced to open a "penny shop" to support herself. The house is filled with signs of the past—most notably the forbidding portrait of Colonel Pyncheon, their Puritan relative who two centuries earlier had cheated his townsman Matthew Maule of his land and life and thereby brought a curse upon successive generations of the Pyncheon family. The Colonel is represented in the present generation by his relative, the imperious Judge Jaffrey Pyncheon, who falsely accused his cousin Clifford of murder and is obsessed with the secrets of the "House of the Seven Gables"—hidden gold and a land deed believed to be concealed somewhere within its walls.

Challenging the past-orientation of this generation are two young people destined to break the curse: Phoebe Pyncheon, the vivacious "country cousin" who comes to live with Hepzibah when her widowed mother remarries, and Holgrave, a daguerreotypist who boards at the house. A "lover of the Actual," Phoebe moves comfortably in the modern world of commerce, putting Hepzibah's penny shop on firm financial ground; yet, she is emotionally warm and sensitive. Holgrave, a self-confessed rationalist and nonconformist, prefers analysis to compassion and belittles the importance of the "odious and abominable Past," which he claims "lies upon the Present like a giant's dead body."

In working out the mystery of the house and resolving the troubled relationships of those who occupy it, Hawthorne develops several significant themes:

- "New Plebianism" vs. Old Gentility, embodied in the contrast between Phoebe's ability to manage the shop vs. Hepzibah's pride that she is inept at business
- New democracy vs. Old Royalism, exemplified by Holgrave's emphasis on the power of talent and the Judge's hypocritical reliance on tradition and the past
- Appearance vs. reality—evidenced, for example, in the Judge's duplicitous smile that masks evil intentions and in his cousin Hepzibah's stern scowl, which hides the happiness in her heart
- The triumph of justice, revealed in Judge Pyncheon's demise and the revelation of Holgrave's true identity, and
- The transformative power of domesticity and love, through which Holgrave is "tamed" and the curse broken.

Critics and readers alike praised what Holgrave calls "this long drama of wrong and retribution." A reviewer in the *Southern Literary Messenger* called *The House of the Seven Gables* a "harmonious blending of the common and familiar in the outward world, with the mellows and vivid tints of [Hawthorne's] own imagination." With a printing of 6,170 copies, the book outsold *The Scarlet Letter* in its first year, though thereafter *The Scarlet Letter* was always ahead.

TOPICS FOR DISCUSSION AND RESEARCH

1. Some critics have seen parallels between the characters in *The House of the Seven Gables* and real people that Hawthorne knew. Thomas R. Mitchell, for example, calls the lovely and sensitive Phoebe a tribute to Hawthorne's wife, Sophia. Others have noted the nonconformist Holgrave's similarities to Ralph Waldo Emerson. Still others note that, like the Pyncheons, Hawthorne was haunted by a Puritan ancestor, John Hathorne, a magistrate who presided over some of the Salem witchcraft trials. How valid are these sources, and how do they inform our understanding of the text?

2. The resolution of the story, by marriage, the death of Judge Pyncheon, and the discovery of the secret land deed, while satisfying to readers of the time, has troubled modern critics. In his introduction to a 1957 reprint of *The House of the Seven Gables*, Philip Young called the ending "unspeakably awkward." Those who agree generally point to Hawthorne's need to craft a commercially successful story, which may have led him to wrap up the plot too neatly. In what ways is the ending artistically appropriate? What arguments do critics make for its artificiality?

3. If *The House of the Seven Gables* posits a domestic resolution to the hereditary curse on the Pyncheons, it is a somewhat unusual one: a family unit composed of a pair of newlyweds, two elderly siblings, and the anomalous neighbor, "Uncle Venner." For the critic Jane Tompkins, texts are "powerful examples of the way a culture thinks about itself, articulating and proposing solutions for the problems that shape a particular historical moment." In the middle of the nineteenth century reformers like Margaret Fuller explored alternative ideas about marriage, partnership, and domesticity, and Hawthorne's own experience at the Brook Farm community exposed him to alternative family organizations. In what ways does *The House of the Seven Gables* respond to changing ideas about family and domestic values in the middle of the nineteenth century? Consider whether Hawthorne might have used his own ancestral history as a source for some of the family matters in the novel.

4. As Christopher Castiglia points out, characters like Hepzibah (childless, unmarried, and a bad housekeeper) and Clifford Pyncheon (impractical, emotional, and delicate) significantly violate "proper" roles for men and women in Victorian America. In a queer reading of the text, they challenge binary gender divisions. What was the contemporary critical reaction to these characters, and in what ways does their presence complicate the reading of the novel as conventionally sentimental?

5. Neither Hepzibah nor Phoebe, good-hearted and likeable though they may be, approaches the compelling power of Hester Prynne in *The Scarlet Letter*. As Bernard Rosenthal notes, Phoebe is unique among Hawthorne's heroines in that she faces no serious moral crises. Nina Baym has recently argued that Hepzibah is the heroine of *The House of the Seven Gables*, a distinctly female protagonist who is heroically altruistic. With a working definition of hero in mind, consider who you think is the hero of the story. How can we characterize Hawthorne's depiction of women's issues in *The House of the Seven Gables*?

6. Many critics have pointed out the similarity in title between *The House of the Seven Gables* and Edgar Allan Poe's tale, "The Fall of the House of Usher," though their endings are significantly different. What similarities do you see? What views do Hawthorne and Poe share?

RESOURCES

Criticism

Nina Baym, "The Heroine of *The House of the Seven Gables;* Or, Who Killed Jaffrey Pyncheon?" *New England Quarterly,* 77, 4 (2004): 607–618.
Argues for Hepzibah as the protagonist of the story.

Christopher Castiglia, "The Marvelous Queer Interiors of *The House of the Seven Gables,*" in *Cambridge Companion to Nathaniel Hawthorne,* edited by Richard H. Millington (New York & Cambridge: Cambridge University Press, 2004), pp. 186–206.
Sees the novel as at once asserting the rule of social "laws" and representing characters who challenge socially constructed definitions of gender.

William Charvat, "Introduction" and "Textual Introduction," in *The House of the Seven Gables. Centenary Edition of the Works of Nathaniel Hawthorne,* volume 2 (Columbus: Ohio State University Press, 1965).
Carefully documented account of the publication, sales, and history of the text.

Hawthorne in Salem <http://www.hawthorneinsalem.org/Introduction.html> [accessed 9 November 2009].
Contains reliable information and pictures of buildings and locations significant to Hawthorne's life and writings, as well as activities and resources for student research.

Bruce Michelson, "Hawthorne's House of Three Stories," *New England Quarterly,* 57, 2 (June 1984): 163–183; reprinted in *Critical Essays on Hawthorne's "The House of the Seven Gables"* (New York: G. K. Hall, 1995), pp. 76–90.
Considers *House* as a ghost story, a moral tale, and "a kind of metafiction" about the writing of romance.

Thomas R. Mitchell, *Hawthorne's Fuller Mystery* (Amherst: University of Massachusetts Press, 1998).
Traces the Hawthorne-Fuller friendship and argues for its shaping power in Hawthorne's romances.

Larry J. Reynolds, ed., *Historical Guide to Nathaniel Hawthorne* (New York: Oxford University Press, 2001).
Contains a brief biography as well as essays on the influence of mesmerism, slavery, the visual arts, and children in Hawthorne's work.

Bernard Rosenthal, ed., *Critical Essays on Hawthorne's 'The House of the Seven Gables"* (New York: G. K. Hall, 1995).

Includes contemporary reviews as well as more-recent scholarly analyses; the editor's introduction is an excellent brief survey of the novel's reception, and two essays situate the book in the history of Salem. Includes an excellent annotated bibliography through 1989.

Jane P. Tompkins, *Sensational Designs: The Cultural Work of American Fiction 1790–1860* (New York: Oxford University Press, 1985).
Argues that Hawthorne's works have been venerated as "classics" because "they embody the changing interests and beliefs of those people whose place in the cultural hierarchy empowers them to decide which works deserve the name of classic and which do not."

⁊≋⁊

Nathaniel Hawthorne, *The Scarlet Letter, a Romance*
(Boston: Ticknor, Reed & Fields, 1850)

In perhaps the most famous review in American literary history, "Hawthorne and His Mosses" (1850), Herman Melville marveled at the complex moral "darkness" of Nathaniel Hawthorne's fictional world, which Melville believed could be apprehended best by the heart, not the head. Melville confessed himself unable to tell whether this "touch of Puritanic gloom" was a literary device only or whether it existed deep within the man Hawthorne himself; but it was clear to Melville that it "derives its force from its appeals to that Calvinistic sense of Innate Depravity and Original Sin, from whose visitations, in some shape or other, no deeply thinking mind is always and wholly free."

Though Melville did not comment on *The Scarlet Letter* in his review of Hawthorne's tales, the sense of moral complexity and depth of character certainly describes Hawthorne's compelling narrative of sin, revenge, persecution, and disclosure, set in Puritan Boston of the 1640s. *The Scarlet Letter* is Hawthorne's most famous work, a legitimate candidate for the greatest American novel, and one whose characters and themes, as Melville pointed out, continue to affect both "deeply thinking minds" and sensitive hearts.

In 1850 Hawthorne had not yet achieved the public recognition that *The Scarlet Letter* would soon bring him, though not for lack of trying. Born in Salem, Massachusetts, and educated at Bowdoin College in Maine, where the poet Henry Wadsworth Longfellow and the future president Franklin Pierce were among his classmates, Hawthorne (1804–1864) attained prominence in New England literary culture relatively late in life. He supported himself periodically with political patronage jobs, but by the early 1830s he had committed himself to a literary career, producing such now-famous short stories as "My Kinsman, Major Molineux" and "Roger Malvin's Burial" as well as dozens of sketches and lesser tales designed to be sold to magazines or annual "gift books" like the *Token*. In 1842, his career still unsettled, he married Sophia Peabody of Salem. The Hawthornes lived for several years in the ancestral home of Ralph Waldo Emerson, the "Old Manse" in Concord, where Hawthorne became acquainted with the Transcendental writers Emerson, Thoreau, the Alcotts, and Margaret Fuller, a frequent visitor. (The Hawthornes returned to Concord in 1851 after the success of *The Scarlet Letter* and *The House of the Seven Gables,* this time living in the Wayside house adjacent to the Alcotts.) Hawthorne invested in the Transcendental Brook Farm community, even living there for a few months before it became clear that he was ill suited to the daily regimen of farming and self-culture. Hawthorne's collections *Twice-Told Tales* (1837) and *Mosses from an Old Manse* (1846) showed great promise, but sales were sluggish; by the late 1840s, back in Salem with his wife and their two small children, Hawthorne felt his career had not yet been successful, artistically or financially. He accepted a job in 1846 as surveyor of customs in the port of Salem, only to be ejected three years later after the Whig victory of 1848 swept Democratic appointees out of office. By September 1849 he had returned to writing. The publisher James T. Fields later recalled finding Hawthorne in a deep funk—"Who would risk publishing a book for me, the most unpopular writer in America?" he supposedly complained—but within eight months he finished *The Scarlet Letter.* Published in Boston in March 1850, it was an immediate success, selling out its first printing of 2,500 copies in just ten days.

The plot of *The Scarlet Letter,* archetypal in its depiction of the corrosive power of human guilt, is deceptively easy to summarize. Hester Prynne, absent a husband, has given birth to a child, Pearl, and when pressured to reveal the identity of Pearl's father, she steadfastly refuses, facing down the demands of the Puritan magistrates and the entreaties of Rev. Arthur Dimmesdale, Boston's most revered minister and secretly the father of Pearl. Old Roger Chillingworth, her newly returned husband, enjoins her to keep his identity secret until he can expose the perfidy of the man who cuckolded him. Living with Pearl on the fringes of town, the independent Hester is forced as her penance for adultery to wear a scarlet "A," which she turns instead into an object of beauty and pride by embroidering it herself. For the next seven years, the sin "works its office" on all four characters: Pearl grows up unpredictable and contrary; Hester becomes an isolated freethinker; Chillingworth's obsessive desire for revenge turns him into a monster; and Dimmesdale's cumulative guilt over his hypocrisy weakens his body and spirit. At last, Dimmesdale frees himself by publicly confessing himself Pearl's father, then collapses and dies. The spell broken, Pearl grows to adulthood and moves into the larger world; Chillingworth dies, deprived of the object of his scrutiny, and bequeaths his sizeable fortune to Pearl; and Hester leaves Boston but returns at last to the place of her punishment. She is buried near Dimmesdale in a grave marked by a scarlet "A."

A reviewer for the London *Athenaeum* in 1850 anticipated a century and a half of varied criticism when he called Hawthorne's novel "a mixture of Puritan reserve and wild imagination, of passion and description, of the allegorical and the real." It is clear that *The Scarlet Letter,* which has already generated a wide variety of views, will continue to generate more.

TOPICS FOR DISCUSSION AND RESEARCH

1. As befits a narrative whose title is itself a symbol—and one that characters interrogate and disagree about from the beginning of the story to the
end—the plot of *The Scarlet Letter* is driven by ambiguity, mystery, secrets,
and multiple interpretations. Using the novel and the criticism of it, consider
one important symbol and how it changes. One might begin with the "A"
itself. Publicly identified with "adultery," its meaning changes throughout the
tale, standing for "Angel" (when it appears in the heavens after the death of
the governor), then for "Able" (as the community comes to respect Hester's
capabilities)—and finally, perhaps, in an ironically obvious answer to the
question of Pearl's paternity, for "Arthur." In his biocritical study of Hawthorne (1879), the novelist Henry James famously indicted the symbolism of
The Scarlet Letter: "It is overdone at times, and becomes mechanical; it ceases
to be impressive, and grazes triviality." Yet, symbolism remains an important
topic for critics. Studies by Richard H. Fogle and others are useful starting
places for the examination of symbolism in *The Scarlet Letter* and its larger
implications for the moral complexity of the narrative.

2. It is a short step from interpreting symbols to interpreting characters. Dimmesdale, Chillingworth, and even Pearl may be seen as allegorical, but Hester
Prynne is fittingly the one around whom most of the controversy centers.
Hester is both defiant and submissive, largely mute in her protest, and her
refusal to implicate Arthur suggests strength to some readers and weakness
to others. Is she a cautionary moral example (see, for instance, Darrel Abel's
study) or an exemplary heroine (according, for example, to Nina Baym).
Jamie Barlowe, in her useful survey of the approaches to Hester, concludes
that the critical tradition tends to confirm attitudes toward women by
depicting Hester as Other, a passive character rather than an active one; the
debate that followed (in *American Literary History* 9 [Summer 1997]) is a
reminder of the varying positions. Can you identify a hero or heroine in *The
Scarlet Letter,* and for what reasons?

3. Hawthorne's contemporaries, such as the literary critic Evert A. Duyckinck,
insisted that *The Scarlet Letter* was a "psychological romance," certainly not
a novel—which in mid-century America was associated with realism. Critics today continue to disagree about issues of genre. Is *The Scarlet Letter* an
allegory, as argued by Richard C. Freed? A romance, as Roy Male contends?
Both, according to Watson Branch? Find or develop a working definition
that distinguishes the novel from the romance and try to place *The Scarlet
Letter* in one category or the other.

4. Discussions of genre often involve issues of influence, particularly Hawthorne's sources and family. Joanne Felt Diehl offers a Freudian approach
to the novel as a "family romance" that mirrors the "unconscious text Hawthorne recollects in his narrative," his own longing for an absent father and
a nurturing mother. Philip Young in *Hawthorne's Secret* also argues that
Hawthorne was working out his own troubled family relations, particularly
his relationship to his sister. Recently Thomas R. Mitchell has speculated
that Hawthorne's four romances all took their inspiration from Hawthorne's

complicated friendship with Fuller. In what specific ways do characters or events in the novel reflect Hawthorne's own experience or family?

5. "The Custom-House" introduction sets up the conventional justification that the tale is based upon fact and also creates a storytelling persona in the character of the Surveyor of the Revenue, who claims to have found both the scarlet letter and an ancient manuscript among the rubbish in the Custom House's second floor. But it also raises the issue of narration. Who is the narrator of *The Scarlet Letter*? In what ways do his or her viewpoints match Hawthorne's? Using a reliable biography of Hawthorne, try to ascertain his views of women, of religion, and of the past. Consider chapters such as "Another View of Hester," in which gendered comments about Hester's womanhood may or may not represent Hawthorne's own ideas.

RESOURCES

Biography
Henry James, *Hawthorne* (London: Macmillan, 1879).
An appreciative biocritical essay that argues that Hawthorne as an American writer lacked the advantage of a usable past.

Thomas R. Mitchell, *Hawthorne's Fuller Mystery* (Amherst: University of Massachusetts Press, 1999).
Traces the Hawthorne-Fuller friendship and argues for its shaping power in Hawthorne's romances.

Brenda Wineapple, *Hawthorne: A Life* (New York: Knopf, 2003).
A detailed, reliable biography written for a general audience, with particular attention to the autobiographical elements in the fiction.

Philip Young, *Hawthorne's Secret: An Un-told Tale* (Boston: D. R. Godine, 1984).
Examines Hawthorne's relationship with his sister as a model for *The Scarlet Letter*.

Criticism
Darrel Abel, *The Moral Picturesque: Studies in Hawthorne's Fiction* (West Lafayette, Ind.: Purdue University Press, 1988).
Argues for Hester as an exemplar of immorality.

Jamie Barlowe, "Rereading Women: Hester Prynne-ism and the Scarlet Mob of Scribblers," *American Literary History*, 9, 2 (1997): 197–225.
Connects the primarily male critical view of Hester to the treatment of women in the academy.

Nina Baym, "Hester's Defiance," in *Readings on* The Scarlet Letter, edited by Eileen Morey (San Diego, Cal.: Greenhaven Press, 1998), pp. 88–98.
Sees Hester as an alienated artist forced to define herself against a repressive Puritan culture.

Baym, "Thwarted Nature: Nathaniel Hawthorne as Feminist," in *American Novelists Revisited: Essays in Feminist Criticism*, edited by Fritz Fleischmann (Boston: G. K. Hall, 1982), pp. 58–77.
Examines Hawthorne's views of women and Hester as a positive character.

Watson Branch, "From Allegory to Romance: Hawthorne's Transformation of *The Scarlet Letter*," *Modern Philology: A Journal Devoted to Research in Medieval and Modern Literature*, 80, 2 (1982): 145–160.
Examines "how *The Scarlet Letter* grew from a rather limited though carefully wrought tale into an inexhaustible though flawed romance."

Joanne Feit Diehl, "Re-reading the Letter: Hawthorne, the Fetish, and the (Family) Romance," in *The Scarlet Letter: Complete, Authoritative Text with Biographical Background and Critical History plus Essays from Five Contemporary Critical Perspectives with Introductions and Bibliographies*, edited by Ross C. Murfin (Boston: Bedford/St. Martin's Press, 2006), pp. 314–330.
A detailed Freudian approach to the text.

Evert A. Duyckinck, "Review of *The Scarlet Letter*," *Literary World*, 6 (March 30, 1850): 323–325.
A largely positive early review.

Richard H. Fogle, *Hawthorne's Imagery: The "Proper Light and Shadow" in the Major Romances* (Norman: University of Oklahoma Press, 1969).
A comprehensive study of symbol and image.

Richard C. Freed, "Hawthorne's Reflexive Imagination: *The Scarlet Letter* as Compositional Allegory," *American Transcendental Quarterly*, 56 (March 1985): 31–54.
Argues that *The Scarlet Letter* is a metafictive allegory for the writing process, "the entire range of activities beginning with the author's idea for the work and ending with the completed work of art."

Roy R. Male, *Hawthorne's Tragic Vision* (Austin: University of Texas Press, 1957).
Develops the argument for *The Scarlet Letter* as a romance.

Herman Melville, "Hawthorne and His Mosses," *Literary World*, 6 (17 and 24 August 1850): 125–127, 145–147 <http://www.eldritchpress.org/nh/hahm.html> [accessed 9 November 2009].
An enthusiastic and perceptive review, famous for its analysis of Hawthorne's "darkness."

◦�◦

Nathaniel Hawthorne, Short Fiction (1837–1852)

Although Nathaniel Hawthorne is best known as the author of *The Scarlet Letter*, his short fiction merits as much attention as his novels. Along with Washington Irving and Edgar Allan Poe, Hawthorne was one of the pioneers of the short-story genre in American literature. Many of his short stories, or "tales" as he called them, were published together in volumes, the most famous of which are *Twice-Told Tales* (1837) and *Mosses from and Old Manse* (1846). The former collection includes thirty-six stories, all previously published, including "The Minister's Black Veil" and "The May-Pole of Merry Mount." The latter volume contains twenty-three tales, including "The Birth-Mark," "Young Goodman Brown," and "Rappaccini's Daughter." In 1852 Hawthorne published a third volume of tales, *The Snow-Image, and Other Twice-Told Tales,* which includes his early story "My Kinsman, Major Molineux."

Although Hawthorne's short-story collections did not sell particularly well, most critics at the time admired his tales. However, many of the stories that earned critical acclaim are not the ones most commonly read and admired today. Some critics praised several of the stories in *Twice-Told Tales* that are lighter in tone and subject than tales like "Young Goodman Brown" and "The Minister's Black Veil," which are more familiar to today's readers. Reviewers appreciated Hawthorne's clarity of style and his celebration of domestic life in tales such as "Sunday at Home" and "Little Annie's Ramble" and preferred these to the darker tales like "Young Goodman Brown." One of the most glowing reviews was written by the famous poet Henry Wadsworth Longfellow. His review of *Twice-Told Tales* in the *North American Review* in 1837 commended Hawthorne on his style, imagination, and depictions of New England. Perhaps the most famous review of Hawthorne's work was written by Herman Melville, whose review essay "Hawthorne and His Mosses" (1850) praised Hawthorne's *Mosses from an Old Manse* as one of the best works of American literature to date. Melville asserted that Hawthorne's fiction was nearly as good as the works of Shakespeare but also argued that it was distinctly American rather than an imitation of English literature. Poe, on the other hand, expressed mixed reactions to *Twice-Told Tales* in a review published in the *Broadway Journal* in 1842. Poe objected to Hawthorne's didacticism (one of Poe's critical pet peeves) and his use of allegory but praised his style and recognized him as one of the nation's most talented authors.

One of the best sources to begin research on Hawthorne's tales is C. E. Frazer Clark's *Nathaniel Hawthorne: A Descriptive Bibliography* (1978). For biographical information about Hawthorne, students will find Arlin Turner's *Nathaniel Hawthorne: A Biography* (1980) to be useful. For critical studies of Hawthorne's short fiction, consult Albert Von Frank's *Critical Essays on Hawthorne's Short Stories* (1991) or Millicent Bell's *New Essays on Hawthorne's Major Tales* (1993).

TOPICS FOR DISCUSSION AND RESEARCH

1. The majority of Hawthorne's tales are set in colonial New England, though there are exceptions like "Rappaccini's Daughter," which takes place in Italy. Hawthorne was particularly fascinated with the Puritan settlers, and many of his tales focus on their morality, their sense of sin and guilt, their intolerance of religious diversity, their hypocrisy, and their belief in the reality of witchcraft and Satan. At times Hawthorne felt personally connected to the Puritans he wrote about in his tales. In "Young Goodman Brown," for instance, when the

protagonist's diabolical guide states that Brown's ancestors committed deeds of cruelty toward Quakers and accused witches, Hawthorne was commenting on his own grandfather and great-grandfather (he later made a similar rhetorical move in "The Custom-House" introduction to *The Scarlet Letter*). Compare Hawthorne's depictions of Puritans and their culture with Puritan texts such as William Bradford's *Of Plymouth Plantation*, Jonathan Edwards's *Personal Narrative*, or Cotton Mather's *Wonders of the Invisible World* and *Magnalia Christi Americana*. How accurately does Hawthorne represent these people and their culture, and what seems to be his attitude toward both?

2. Hawthorne's tales were influenced by several literary movements. Like Poe, Hawthorne borrowed heavily from Gothicism in his tales, many of which feature supernatural elements, insanity, deformity, ambiguity, and doppelgängers. Unlike most Gothic fiction, however, Hawthorne's tales strike many readers as moralistic and didactic, although some critics have argued that his fiction is more open-ended in moral terms than it may first appear. Hawthorne's short stories also differ from most Gothic fiction in terms of setting. His tales do not take place in the dark, forbidding castles and ruined abbeys of Europe. Instead, they often use the wilderness as a menacing backdrop to the Puritan settlements that symbolized the sinfulness of human nature. His depictions of the wilderness relied on the notion of the sublime, a feature of both Gothicism and Romanticism. Debra Johanyak's essay "Romanticism's Fallen Edens" offers an analysis of the moral qualities of nature in "Young Goodman Brown" and "The May-Pole of Merry Mount" as well as *The Scarlet Letter*. In addition to associating forests with witches and satanic worship, Hawthorne's wilderness was populated by bloodthirsty Indians. In this sense, Hawthorne differed from many American Romantic authors such as Catharine Maria Sedgwick and James Fenimore Cooper, who frequently depicted Native Americans as noble savages. In other respects, however, Hawthorne's tales were influenced by Romanticism in their emphasis on the individual, their focus on imagination and intuition rather than logic, and their antagonism toward science, an issue that is most prominent in "Rappaccini's Daughter." More specifically, his fiction may be characterized as "Dark Romanticism," a nineteenth-century literary subgenre that overlapped with Gothicism and that was characterized by pessimism toward human nature. Like the fiction of other Dark Romantics like Poe and Melville, Hawthorne's tales expressed skepticism toward Transcendentalism's belief in the limitless potential of humanity and the oneness of the universe. Students could select a Hawthorne tale such as "Young Goodman Brown" or "Rappaccini's Daughter" and analyze how he accepts or rejects Transcendentalist concepts such as self-reliance, cosmic unity, the limitless potential of human nature, and the spirituality of nature expressed in such works as Ralph Waldo Emerson's essay *Nature* or Henry David Thoreau's *Walden*.

3. Hawthorne's short fiction is strongly influenced by the historical romance, a genre popularized in the early nineteenth century by the Scottish novelist Walter Scott and used by several of Hawthorne's American contemporaries, including Irving, Sedgwick, Cooper, and William Gilmore Simms. Historical romances are fictional works set in the past that use some of the conventions

of the medieval romance genre, such as conflict between good and evil, magic and other supernatural elements, and allegory, a literary technique that relies heavily on symbolism to convey a moral message to the reader. Examples of historical romance in Hawthorne's fiction include "Young Goodman Brown" and "My Kinsman, Major Molineux." Although such works are not judged on their historical accuracy, some scholars have examined Hawthorne's portrayal of colonial America in these stories. For example, Max Autrey analyzes Hawthorne's depiction of the shift from rural to urban society in colonial America in "My Kinsman, Major Molineux," while T. Walter Herbert Jr. reads the story's depiction of conflict between a rigid class hierarchy and an anti-authoritarian democracy within the context of changes in colonial society. In addition, William Heath examines Hawthorne's use of historical documents concerning the English maypole tradition and its decline in "The May-Pole of Merry Mount," while Frederick Newberry traces historical evidence regarding a Puritan clergyman whom Hawthorne used as the model for his Reverend Hooper. Students could research the historical events that Hawthorne retells in works such as "The May-Pole" and "The Minister's Black Veil," examine how Hawthorne shapes and alters these facts, and speculate on his possible purpose in recounting and revising these events.

4. Many of Hawthorne's stories are less concerned with their historical settings than with religious issues, and many include biblical references. "Rappacini's Daughter," "The May-Pole of Merry Mount," and "Young Goodman Brown," for instance, retell the story of the fall of Adam and Eve in Genesis. Not surprisingly, many Hawthorne scholars have studied these elements of Hawthorne's tales. Jonathan Cook's essay "New Heavens, Poor Old Earth: Satirical Apocalypse in Hawthorne's *Mosses from an Old Manse*" analyzes the millennial overtones in the tales in *Mosses from an Old Manse,* while Gaye Brown's essay "Hawthorne's 'Rappaccini's Daughter': The Distaff Christ" traces the references to New Testament texts in "Rappacini's Daughter." Students writing about these stories would do well to read the story of the fall of Adam and Eve in chapters two and three of Genesis and other biblical passages to which Hawthorne alludes in order to understand his tales more fully. The aforementioned essays by Cook and Brown will help students find the relevant biblical passages.

5. Hawthorne often resorted to symbolism and allegory in developing his themes, whether they be religious or otherwise, and many critics have discussed these elements of Hawthorne's works. Students might choose an allegorical story such as "My Kinsman, Major Molineux" or "The Minister's Black Veil" and consider which ideas or questions Hawthorne is developing through his use of symbolism. Marcia Smith Marzec's essay "'My Kinsman, Major Molineux' as Theo-Political Allegory" reads this story as not just one allegory, but two: a religious allegory about humanity's innate depravity and a political allegory about colonial America depicting the overthrow of hierarchical society by a democratic social order. Two good sources focusing on the allegorical elements of "The Minister's Black Veil" are William Freedman's essay "The Artist's Symbol and Hawthorne's Veil: 'The Minister's Black Veil' Resartus"

and Frederick Newberry's article "The Biblical Veil: Sources and Typology in Hawthorne's 'The Minister's Black Veil.'"

6. More recent analyses of Hawthorne's fiction have focused on his depictions of and attitudes toward women. Although he famously complained in 1855 about the "damn'd mob of scribbling women" whose works were outselling his own, his representations of women and his notions of gender were more complex than this comment suggests. James Keil's essay on "Young Goodman Brown" relates this tale to the emerging concept that men and women had their own proper "sphere," while John Miller's article about "Rappaccini's Daughter" analyzes Hawthorne's ambiguous depiction of Beatrice and connects this character to Hawthorne's relationship with his wife, Sophia. Another critic, Leland Person Jr., discusses how Hawthorne directed his fiction toward female readers and tried to manipulate their emotional responses. Students might explore the prevailing gender ideologies of Hawthorne's time as explained in Barbara Welter's essay "The Cult of True Womanhood: 1820–1860" and read Hawthorne's characterization of women within that context.

7. Hawthorne's relationship to his reading public has also been studied in terms of his popularity and later canonical status. For example, Jane Tompkins's essay "Masterpiece Theater" demonstrates that publishers, reviewers, and critics have appreciated his fiction over several generations, but for different reasons. Meredith McGill, on the other hand, examines Hawthorne's publication history and argues that it raises questions about how readers distinguish literature from nonliterary texts. Students might read contemporary reviews and later scholarly assessments of Hawthorne's tales to see the changes in critical paradigms as well as Hawthorne's ability to win respect across several generations of critics.

RESOURCES

Primary Works
Twice-Told Tales (Boston: American Stationers, 1837).

Mosses from an Old Manse (New York: Wiley & Putnam, 1846).

The Snow-Image, and Other Twice-Told Tales (Boston: Ticknor, Reed & Fields, 1852).

Criticism
Max L. Autrey, "'My Kinsman, Major Molineux': Hawthorne's Allegory of the Urban Movement," *College Literature*, 12 (1985): 211–221.
Examines how Hawthorne's tale depicts the shift from an agrarian to an urban society in colonial America.

Gaye Brown, "Hawthorne's 'Rappaccini's Daughter': The Distaff Christ," *Nathaniel Hawthorne Review*, 22 (1996): 21–59.
Examines the story's references to the Gospel of John and other New Testament texts.

Jonathan A. Cook, "New Heavens, Poor Old Earth: Satirical Apocalypse in Hawthorne's *Mosses from an Old Manse*," *ESQ: A Journal of the American Renaissance*, 39 (1993): 209–251.
Argues that seven of Hawthorne's apocalyptic allegories both embody and critique prevailing beliefs in the coming of the millennium.

William Freedman, "The Artist's Symbol and Hawthorne's Veil: 'The Minister's Black Veil' Resartus," *Studies in Short Fiction*, 29 (1992): 353–362.
Argues that Hawthorne used the symbolism of the minister's veil to represent the use of symbols by authors and their interpretation by readers.

William Heath, "Merry Old England and Hawthorne's 'The May-Pole of Merry Mount,'" *Nathaniel Hawthorne Review*, 33 (2007): 41–71.
Examines Hawthorne's sources in writing this tale and his narrator's attitude toward England's maypole tradition and its demise.

T. Walter Herbert Jr., "Doing Cultural Work: 'My Kinsman Major Molineux' and the Construction of the Self-Made Man," *Studies in the Novel*, 23 (1991): 20–27.
Analyzes and contextualizes the conflict between antiauthoritarian self-reliance and deference to social superiors in Hawthorne's tale.

Debra Johanyak, "Romanticism's Fallen Edens: The Malignant Contribution of Hawthorne's Literary Landscapes," *CLA Journal*, 42 (1999): 353–363.
Analyzes the association of nature with moral qualities in "Young Goodman Brown," "The May-Pole of Merry Mount," and *The Scarlet Letter*.

James C. Keil, "Hawthorne's 'Young Goodman Brown': Early Nineteenth-Century and Puritan Constructions of Gender," *New England Quarterly: A Historical Review of New England Life and Letters*, 69 (1996): 33–55.
Reads Hawthorne's story within the context of the emerging gender ideology of separate spheres.

Marcia Smith Marzec, "'My Kinsman, Major Molineux' as Theo-Political Allegory," *American Transcendental Quarterly*, 1 (1987): 274–289.
Argues that Hawthorne's tale is both a theological allegory about innate depravity and a political allegory about the democratic overthrow of aristocratic rule.

Meredith L. McGill, "The Problem of Hawthorne's Popularity," in *Reciprocal Influences: Literary Production, Distribution, and Consumption in America*, edited by Steven Fink and Susan S. Williams (Columbus: Ohio State University Press, 1999), pp. 36–54.
Argues that the publication history of Hawthorne's early fiction questions common definitions of the literary.

John N. Miller, "Fideism vs. Allegory in 'Rappaccini's Daughter,'" *Nineteenth-Century Literature*, 46 (1991): 223–244.
Explores the ambiguities and contradictions in Hawthorne's depiction of Beatrice and links that depiction to his wife, Sophia.

Frederick Newberry, "The Biblical Veil: Sources and Typology in Hawthorne's 'The Minister's Black Veil,'" *Texas Studies in Literature and Language*, 31 (1989): 169–195.

Examines historical documents about a clergyman on whom Hawthorne's Reverend Hooper was modeled and analyzes the religious symbolism of the veil.

Leland S. Person Jr., "Hawthorne's Early Tales: Male Authorship, Domestic Violence, and Female Readers," in *Hawthorne and the Real: Bicentennial Essays*, edited by Millicent Bell (Columbus: Ohio State University Press, 2005).

Analyzes Hawthorne's apparent attempts to manipulate his female readers' emotional responses to his early fiction.

Jane Tompkins, "Masterpiece Theater: The Politics of Hawthorne's Literary Reputation," *American Quarterly*, 36 (1984): 617–642.

Reviews Hawthorne's critical reception over several periods and argues that while his work often received favorable reviews, various generations of critics focused on different texts and praised them for different reasons.

⟳⟐⟳

Harriet Ann Jacobs, *Incidents in the Life of a Slave Girl, Written by Herself*

as Linda Brent, edited by Lydia Maria Child
(Boston: Published for the author, 1861)

In a genre dominated by male authors, Harriet Ann Jacobs's *Incidents in the Life of a Slave Girl* is the first—and the most frequently read—slave narrative by an African American woman. Its significance lies partly in its descriptions of experiences that are largely absent in male-authored slave narratives. Harriet Jacobs was born into slavery in Edenton, North Carolina, around 1813. As a child, she was taught to read and sew by her mistress, Margaret Horniblow, who died when Jacobs was eleven and bequeathed her to Horniblow's niece, the daughter of Dr. James Norcom. He subjected the adolescent Jacobs to continuous sexual harassment for years. Rather than submit to Norcom, Jacobs had a consensual relationship with a local white lawyer, Samuel Treadwell Sawyer, who was the father of her two children, Joseph and Louisa Matilda. During this time, Jacobs received emotional support from her grandmother Molly Horniblow, a freed slave who made her living as a baker. In retaliation for Jacobs's repeated resistance to his advances, Norcom determined to separate her from her children. Jacobs realized that Norcom would sell the children if she ran away, so she decided to hide in the attic of her grandmother's house nearby, where she could secretly follow Norcom's moves and keep her children within sight. Norcom sold the children to Sawyer while Jacobs remained hiding in an attic for nearly seven years. She spent her time sewing and reading the Bible, and she wrote several letters to Dr. Norcom in which she claimed to have escaped to the North so that he would not look for her closer to home.

In 1842 Jacobs escaped to Philadelphia, then moved to Brooklyn, New York, where Louisa had been sent to live in the home of writer and publisher Nathaniel Parker Willis. Jacobs later arranged to have her son sent to live with her brother John, an antislavery speaker. Jacobs joined him in Rochester, New York, in 1849 and worked in the antislavery reading room and bookstore above Frederick Douglass's newspaper, the *North Star*. There she became involved with a group of abolitionists and women's-rights activists, including Amy Post, who encouraged Jacobs to write a personal narrative for the antislavery cause. In 1850 Jacobs returned to the Willis household in New York. The Norcoms tried to recapture her, and in early 1852 Willis's second wife, Cornelia Grinnell Willis, purchased and emancipated her. Jacobs expressed outrage that she had to be sold in order to be freed despite Mrs. Willis's good intentions.

As she struggled to write her narrative, Jacobs sought help from Harriet Beecher Stowe, author of the abolitionist bestseller *Uncle Tom's Cabin* (1852), who turned her down. She began writing her story shortly thereafter and finished in 1858 but was unable to secure a publisher. The Boston firm Phillips and Samson agreed to publish the book if Jacobs could convince Willis or Stowe to write a preface; Jacobs refused to ask Willis, and Stowe declined. In 1861 the publishing house Thayer and Eldridge agreed to print the book if it included a preface by the well-known white abolitionist Lydia Maria Child, who also edited the book. The publishers went bankrupt before publishing *Incidents in the Life of a Slave Girl*, which was eventually printed by a Boston firm along with Child's preface. Parts of it were published serially in the *New York Tribune*, edited by the abolitionist Horace Greeley, before the book was printed. Because *Incidents* included sexual material that might offend many readers, Jacobs referred to herself in the text as Linda Brent. *Incidents in the Life of a Slave Girl* was favorably received by the abolitionist press and was reprinted in Britain the following year. However, because of the outbreak of the Civil War that year, the book received little notice outside of the antislavery press in the United States. In 1862 Jacobs left New York and moved to Savannah, Georgia, where she helped slaves who fled to the Union army for protection and to raise funds for Southern blacks until 1866. She later moved to Alexandria, Virginia, and Washington, D.C., where she worked on behalf of Quaker groups in Philadelphia and New York. She also spent time in Edenton during the Reconstruction period before returning north in 1868. She lived with her daughter, Louisa, in Cambridge, Massachusetts, and by the mid 1880s relocated to Washington, D.C., where she worked to establish the National Association of Colored Women. She died there on 7 March 1897.

TOPICS FOR DISCUSSION AND RESEARCH

1. One of the earliest critical debates concerning *Incidents in the Life of a Slave Girl* centered on its authorship. For decades it was assumed that editor Lydia Maria Child, who wrote the preface to the 1861 edition, actually wrote the narrative. In 1981, however, Jean Fagan Yellin published an essay that examined evidence

to establish Jacobs's authorship. Because the narrator/protagonist is Linda Brent, later scholars have debated whether the narrative is strictly autobiographical or is a blend of autobiography and novel in which Jacobs differentiates herself from Linda, as Mark Edelman Boren has argued. Students are encouraged to consult Yellin's *Harriet Jacobs: A Life* (2004) and compare events described in *Incidents in the Life of a Slave Girl* to the biographical facts in Yellin's book. What evidence is there that the narrative is autobiographical or that it is not?

2. *Incidents in the Life of a Slave Girl* differs from most slave narratives in that it contains relatively few descriptions of physical violence; instead, it places more emphasis on the psychological suffering endured by slave women who are constantly persecuted by the threat of sexual violence. Although the rape of enslaved women by their masters and other white men was a common feature of American slavery, and while abolitionists often referred to it as an argument against slavery, the Northern white women whom Jacobs hoped to persuade might have found an open discussion of the topic to be too shocking. Jacobs realized that her readers knew little about the experiences of slave women but also recognized the pervasiveness of a set of gender ideologies that Barbara Welter later termed the "Cult of True Womanhood." Many nineteenth-century Americans (both women and men) believed that a "true woman" must be pious, pure, domestic, and submissive to men. While it would be difficult for most white women to live according to these gender expectations, it was impossible for slave women, who could not submit to the commands of their lecherous masters without giving up their sexual purity. If Linda Brent had simply resisted Flint, she could have maintained the respect of white female readers while also pointing out one of the evils of slavery. On the other hand, had she submitted, she could have portrayed herself as merely a passive victim of the slaveholder's lechery in order to win the pity of her audience. Instead, she admits to having a tryst with Sands that results in her two children being born out of wedlock. This admission made it more difficult for Jacobs to keep the respect of her white female readers, and in a direct-narratorial aside, she both admits her mistake and argues that slavery confuses the moral sensibility of its young victims. Despite her apologetic tone, however, some recent critics, including Stephanie Li, emphasize Linda Brent's agency in her decision to have an affair with Sands; by doing so, she uses her sexuality as a weapon over her tormentor. Students would benefit from researching the expectations regarding women's sexual behavior of Jacobs's time in order to grasp the significance of her interactions with Dr. Flint and Mr. Sands as well as her descriptions of these events in *Incidents in the Life of a Slave Girl*. Sharon Block's "Early American Sexuality: Race, Colonialism, Power, and Culture" in *Radical History Review*, 82 (Winter 2002): 159–169 is a starting point for researching this topic.

3. In addition to depicting the tribulations and dilemmas of a female slave threatened with sexual violence, Jacobs's narrative provides a closer look at enslaved mothers' relationship to domesticity. According to the "separate spheres" ideology that prevailed in nineteenth-century America, women belonged in the domestic sphere and were expected to stay at home and raise their children. Ideally, the home would provide a safe haven from the often ruthless outer world. As a slave mother, however, Linda Brent does not have her own home.

Despite her love for her children, she realizes that the Flints are using them to solidify their power over her, and decides to leave them while she hides in the garret of her grandmother's house nearby. While she sews, reads the Bible, and keeps an eye on her children through a peephole, the domestic space she inhabits is a travesty on the ideal home, one that emphasizes how slavery separates mothers from children and prevents them from enjoying the comforts of home. At the end of the narrative, Linda Brent and her children are free, but she laments that she does not have her own home. This subject of domesticity in *Incidents in the Life of a Slave Girl* has attracted the attention of Mark Rifkin and several other Jacobs scholars, and students might compare Jacobs's depictions of domesticity with those found in domestic fiction featuring white women such as Susan Warner's *The Wide, Wide World* or Stowe's *Uncle Tom's Cabin*.

4. Given Jacobs's emphasis on the domestic sphere and slavery's power to destroy it, it is fitting that her narrative uses some of the conventions of domestic fiction. Compared to most other slave narratives, *Incidents in the Life of a Slave Girl* reads more like a novel in its extensive use of dialogue (much of which was probably invented or embellished from memory), characterization, and plot. More specifically, Jacobs often uses the sentimental style of domestic fiction; in doing so, she follows the example of Stowe, whose novel *Uncle Tom's Cabin* also depicts slavery as a threat to domestic values. Moreover, Jacobs's descriptions of Dr. Flint's relentless sexual harassment resemble the struggles faced by the young heroines of domestic fiction. In most of these novels, the heroine gives in to temptation, becomes a "fallen woman," and suffers an early, ignominious death or resists temptation and marries a virtuous man. In a sense, by having an affair with Sands, Linda Brent becomes a "fallen woman." Unlike these fallen women, however, Jacobs describes her efforts to reunite with her children and to free them as well as herself. She also distinguishes her narrative from domestic fiction by stating near the end, "Reader, my story ends in freedom, not in the usual way with marriage." Compare *Incidents in the Life of a Slave Girl* to male-authored slave narratives such as those by Douglass or William Wells Brown and analyze their similarities and differences in depicting family relationships among slaves and sexual exploitation of slaves.

RESOURCES

Biography
Jean Fagan Yellin, *Harriet Jacobs: A Life* (New York: Basic Civitas, 2004).
The definitive Jacobs biography.

Criticism
Mark Edelman Boren, "Slipping the Shackles of Subjectivity: The Narrator as Runaway in *Incidents in the Life of a Slave Girl*," *Genre: Forms of Discourse and Culture*, 34, 1–2 (2001): 33–62.
Analyzes how Jacobs disassociates herself from the narrator and protagonist of *Incidents*.

Virginia H. Cope, "'I Verily Believed Myself to Be a Free Woman': Harriet Jacobs's Journey into Capitalism," *African American Review,* 38, 1 (2004): 5–20.
Analyzes Jacobs's ambivalence toward Northern capitalism in *Incidents* after her emancipation.

Martha J. Cutter, "Dismantling 'The Master's House': Critical Literacy in Harriet Jacobs' *Incidents in the Life of a Slave Girl,*" *Callaloo,* 19, 1 (1996): 209–225.
Examines Jacobs's struggle to use language to liberate herself and how it was used to oppress her.

Deborah H. Garfield and Rafia Zafar, eds., *Harriet Jacobs and* Incidents in the Life of a Slave Girl: *New Critical Essays* (Cambridge, England: Cambridge University Press, 1996).
Contains fifteen essays on Jacobs and her narrative as well as abolitionism and nineteenth-century notions of black female sexuality.

Stephanie Li, "Motherhood as Resistance in Harriet Jacobs's *Incidents in the Life of a Slave Girl,*" *Legacy: A Journal of American Women Writers,* 23, 1 (2006): 14–29.
Analyzes how maternity is a means of empowerment for the slave woman Linda Brent.

Franny Nudelman, "Harriet Jacobs and the Sentimental Politics of Female Suffering," *ELH,* 59, 4 (1992): 939–964.
Examines Jacobs's use of abolitionist conventions in describing her sexual exploitation.

Mark Rifkin, "'A Home Made Sacred by Protecting Laws': Black Activist Homemaking and Geographies of Citizenship in *Incidents in the Life of a Slave Girl,*" *Differences: A Journal of Feminist Cultural Studies,* 18, 2 (2007): 72–102.
Examines how Jacobs links the black home to federal laws endorsing racial discrimination and contrasts her arguments with those of black male activists of her time.

Daneen Wardrop, "'I Stuck the Gimlet in and Waited for Evening': Writing and *Incidents in the Life of a Slave Girl,*" *Texas Studies in Literature and Language,* 49, 3 (2007): 209–229.
Analyzes the hole that Linda Brent punched in her garret wall during her seven years of hiding in *Incidents* as a symbol of the author's self-empowerment through writing.

Jean Fagan Yellin, "Written by Herself: Harriet Jacobs' Slave Narrative," *American Literature: A Journal of Literary History, Criticism, and Bibliography,* 53, 3 (1981): 479–486.
Provides conclusive evidence that *Incidents* was written by Jacobs and not by her editor Lydia Maria Child, as was previously believed.

Herman Melville, "Bartleby, the Scrivener"

November–December, 1853, *Putnam's Monthly*, collected in *The Piazza Tales*
(New York: Dix & Edwards/London: Sampson Low, 1856)

"Bartleby, the Scrivener: A Story of Wall Street" was published anonymously and serially in *Putnam's Monthly Magazine* in late 1853 and was later included in Melville's collection of stories *The Piazza Tales* in 1856 as simply "Bartleby." This story differs from most of Melville's fiction, which focuses on seafaring life. The narrator of "Bartleby" exhibits a genial complacency that prevents him from understanding the absurdity and despair he encounters. Melville may have used this narrator to represent and indirectly mock the smug superiority that he believed characterized many of his readers. The narrator is an elderly lawyer who has achieved prosperity through legal business with wealthy clients, and he emphasizes his indulgence toward Bartleby and his two other clerks. Because the narrator expects obedience from his employees, he cannot understand Bartleby's mild refusals to carry out his commands or leave the office. Bartleby poses a quiet threat to the capitalist notions of class hierarchy, deference, and private property in which the narrator implicitly believes. The narrator reveals these proprietary values by indignantly asking Bartleby, "What earthly right have you to stay here? Do you pay any rent? Do you pay my taxes? Or is this property yours?" At the end of the story, when the narrator learns of Bartleby's former position in the Dead Letter Office, he fails to realize that this soul-destroying, meaningless job resembles the absurdity of copying legal documents. The fact that this is the only information that the narrator has gleaned about Bartleby's past life, combined with the narrator's blinkered capitalist perspective, makes it inevitable that a metaphorical "wall" (symbolized by the recurring wall imagery throughout the story) stands between him and the clerk. Yet, underneath the obvious differences between Bartleby and the narrator lie deeper similarities, which may explain why the narrator retains the scrivener after he refuses to obey orders. Like Bartleby, the narrator has lost a job as a result of political changes, and both characters are physically enclosed by walls. The narrator even finds himself using Bartleby's favorite verb, "prefer." The possibility that the narrator and Bartleby are doubles is suggested by the relationship between the clerk Turkey, who is mild in the morning but uncontrollable during the afternoon, and his fellow clerk Nippers, whose behavior during the day is the exact opposite of Turkey's.

Daniel Wells suggests that Melville may have used his conventional, obtuse narrator to satirize Evert Duyckinck, a prominent editor and critic and Melville's former mentor. Duyckinck, editor of the *Literary World*, had warned Melville against expressing religious and moral skepticism in his fiction, and his magazine published a damning review of Melville's novel *Pierre* (1852). Duyckinck was often described as conventional and prudent, and Melville may have felt that he made his living off the literary labors of others in much the same way that the narrator sponges off the work of his clerks. David Kuebrich speculates that Melville was probably recalling his own youthful experiences as a clerk in a bank and in his brother's fur store while writing "Bartleby."

TOPICS FOR DISCUSSION AND RESEARCH

1. In his essay "*Bartleby, the Scrivener* and *Bleak House:* Melville's Debt To Dickens," David Jaffé points out that some elements of this story resemble the two chapters focusing on the law-stationer Mr. Snagsby in Charles Dickens's novel *Bleak House,* which was serially published in *Harper's* magazine about a year before Melville's story appeared and which Melville likely read. These chapters, "The Law-Writer" and "Our Dear Brother," describe the meaningless existence of a London clerk. Melville's bleak description of the meaningless life of an office clerk would be echoed in Franz Kafka's 1912 story "The Metamorphosis," though it is unknown whether Kafka had read "Bartleby." Students may wish to analyze "Bartleby" alongside "The Metamorphosis" or *Bleak House* in their representations of the dreary existence of low-status clerks in bureaucratic occupations.

2. "Bartleby" was written twelve years after Ralph Waldo Emerson published his essay "Self-Reliance." Examine how Melville echoes Emerson's celebration of nonconformity and his critique of social conventions through his title character and narrator. Francine Puk's essay "'Bartleby the Scrivener': A Study in Self-Reliance" (1978) is a useful resource in exploring this topic; it can be found online at <http://web.ku.edu/~zeke/bartleby/puk.htm>.

3. "Bartleby, the Scrivener" may be read as a critique of the crushing forces of capitalist society. Students may be interested in researching the structures of capitalism and the social beliefs surrounding it in nineteenth-century America and analyzing Melville's response to them in "Bartleby." Two helpful sources for this topic are Barbara Foley's essay "From Wall Street to Astor Place: Historicizing Melville's 'Bartleby'" (2000), which reads "Bartleby" within the context of class conflicts in mid-nineteenth-century America, and Naomi Reed's essay "The Specter of Wall Street: 'Bartleby, the Scrivener' and the Language of Commodities" (2004), which links the story to Marx's theories of industrial capitalism.

RESOURCES

Criticism

Barbara Foley, "From Wall Street to Astor Place: Historicizing Melville's 'Bartleby,'" *American Literature,* 72, 1 (March 2000): 87–116.
Places "Bartleby" within the context of class struggles in mid-nineteenth-century America, including the 1849 Astor Place riot.

David Jaffé, "*Bartleby, the Scrivener* and *Bleak House:* Melville's Debt To Dickens" <http://web.ku.edu/~zeke/bartleby/jaffe.html> [accessed 5 February 2009].
Traces parallels between the two texts in depicting the alienation experienced by legal copyists.

David Kuebrich, "Melville's Doctrine of Assumptions: The Hidden Ideology of Capitalist Production in 'Bartleby,'" *New England Quarterly,* 69 (September 1996): 381–405.

Analyzes how "Bartleby" reflects Melville's frustrations in seeking meaningful employment and the ideological conflicts between capitalism and labor of the early 1850s.

Naomi C. Reed, "The Specter of Wall Street: 'Bartleby, the Scrivener' and the Language of Commodities," *American Literature: A Journal of Literary History, Criticism, and Bibliography*, 76 (June 2004): 247–273.
Argues that Marx's theories about capitalism can be reread through "Bartleby" and compares the ghostliness of Bartleby to the spectral imagery in Marx's analysis of capitalism.

Jeffrey Andrew Weinstock, "Doing Justice to Bartleby," *American Transcendental Quarterly*, 17 (March 2003): 23–42.
Analyzes the narrator's lack of knowledge about Bartleby and argues that the story raises the question of how one should act justly toward others when one cannot understand them.

Daniel A. Wells, "'Bartleby the Scrivener,' Poe, and the Duyckinck Circle," *Emerson Society Quarterly*, 21 (1975): 35–39.
Argues that Melville satirized his former mentor Evert Duyckinck, Edgar Allan Poe, and the author Cornelius Mathews through his characterizations of Bartleby's employer and the clerks Nippers and Turkey.

⚬◯∞◯⚬

Herman Melville, "Benito Cereno"
October–November 1855, *Putnam's Monthly*, collected in *The Piazza Tales* (New York: Dix & Edwards/London: Sampson Low, 1856)

This novella, like "Bartleby," was published over two issues of *Putnam's* magazine in October and November 1855 and was republished in *The Piazza Tales*. The story is based on Amasa Delano's 1817 *Narrative of Voyages and Travels, in the Northern and Southern Hemispheres*, which narrates the encounter between Delano, captain of the *Perseverance*, and Benito Cereno's slave ship *Tryal* off the coast of Chile in 1805. Eric Sundquist argues that by shifting the date of the incident to 1799 and changing the name of Cereno's ship to *San Dominick*, Melville perhaps sought to tie the slave insurrection on board the ship to the Haitian slave revolt of 1791–1804 led by Toussaint L'Ouverture. (Haiti was then called Santo Domingo.) Melville's story also shares similarities with two more recent slave mutinies: one on board the Spanish ship *Amistad* in 1839 and the other on the *Creole* in 1841.

"Benito Cereno" exploits Gothic conventions in describing Delano's experiences on board the *San Dominick:* the ship is shrouded in mystery, Delano is periodically afraid that Cereno is plotting against his life, and near the end of the story Alexandro Aranda's skeleton is revealed and we learn that the Africans had slaughtered most of the Spanish officers and crew during the revolt. There is also the doppelgänger motif with Babo constantly shadowing Cereno, and the opening scene uses Gothic imagery of shrouded monks in a monastery. Unlike most Gothic fiction, however, "Benito Cereno" uses these features to comment indirectly on race and slavery.

Delano's racism, combined with his innocence, prevents him from realizing the true situation on board the *San Dominick,* but it also saves him, because Babo would have killed him if he had revealed any sign of recognition. Because of the story's point of view, some readers miss Melville's irony and mistakenly believe that he shared Delano's racist views of Africans as simple, docile, and good-natured, perceptions that are completely undercut by the final quarter of the story. "Benito Cereno" reveals Delano's racism and emphasizes the intelligence of Babo and the other Africans, including their clever use of Spanish as well as African languages, a subject analyzed by Gavin Jones. However, it is debatable whether it also depicts them as murderous savages or as freedom fighters. Cereno's deposition in the final fifth of the text portrays the Spanish as victims of bloodthirsty Africans rather than as men complicit in an atrocious traffic in humans, and the story never shifts to Babo or any African or narrates the brutalities they endured before the revolt. Indeed, Babo's mute, impaled head—that "curious hive of subtlety"—at the end of the story emphasizes his intelligence but also his lack of voice in the text.

Melville's choice of symbolism is perhaps less ambiguous than in his choice of narrative viewpoint. In addition to Babo's severed, impaled head, Melville replaced the *San Dominick*'s figurehead of Christopher Colon (Columbus) with the skeleton of Cereno's friend Aranda, who had purchased the slaves. One might infer that Columbus's discovery of the New World led to the Atlantic slave trade symbolized by Aranda. The story also uses several symbols dealing with mysteries and their solutions: Atufal's chains are secured by a lock that can only be opened by a key held by Cereno, and a Spanish sailor tosses Delano an intricate knot and tells him to cut it. Both the lock and the knot symbolize the mystery regarding the true status of the ship, and both Delano and the readers are urged to open or undo them. Because the Africans on board the *San Dominick* are hiding from Delano the fact that they have taken command of the ship, it is not surprising that the story contains several mask symbols, most notably in the sternpiece of the *San Dominick* near the beginning of the story and the "removal" of the mask after Cereno and Babo leap into Delano's boat toward the end of the story. A potentially fruitful topic of discussion and research might be analyzing the connections among the various symbols in the story and how they function—for example, as communication, deception, foreshadowing, thematic development, etc.

TOPICS FOR DISCUSSION AND RESEARCH

1. One major problem encountered by readers of "Bartleby, the Scrivener" and "Benito Cereno" is Melville's use of point of view. The former story is narrated by a prosperous lawyer who fails to understand Bartleby, while the latter story is told by a third-person narrator who tells the story from Delano's perspective.

Choose one story and analyze Melville's use of an unreliable narrator to tell the story, or compare the two stories in their ironic use of point of view. Cathy Davidson's essay "Courting God and Mammon: The Biographer's Impasse in Melville's 'Bartleby the Scrivener' (1978; available online at <http://web.ku.edu/~zeke/bartleby/davidson1.htm>) and Mary Rohrberger's article "Point of View in Benito Cereno: Machinations and Deceptions" (1965) are helpful guides regarding this topic.

2. In "Benito Cereno," Delano's perceptions of Babo and the other Africans are filtered through the lens of "romantic racialism," a term coined by George Fredrickson in *The Black Image in the White Mind* (1971) to describe white Northern stereotypes of African Americans as happy, comical, religious, and musical. These stereotypes were common in Melville's time, both in the discourses surrounding slavery and in minstrel shows. Students might research the racial assumptions about Africans that prevailed in Melville's day and analyze Melville's depictions of Africans as well as Delano's perceptions of them. Consult Jason Richards's essay "Melville's (Inter)national Burlesque: Whiteface, Blackface, and 'Benito Cereno'" (2007), which discusses the role of minstrel stereotypes in the story, or Gloria Horsley-Meacham's essay "Bull of the Nile: Symbol, History, and Racial Myth in 'Benito Cereno'" (1991), which argues that these stereotypes are balanced by the text's references to Ethiopian and Egyptian civilization.

3. Melville based "Benito Cereno" on Delano's 1817 *Narrative of Voyages and Travels,* though his depiction of the slave mutiny is based partly on the slave revolt on board the *Amistad* in 1839. Compare Melville's story to Delano's text or to the *Amistad* incident and point out how Melville departs from the historical facts. What might be Melville's intentions in doing so? What effects are produced by these alterations? One good historical study of the *Amistad* incident is Howard Jones's book *Mutiny on the Amistad* (1987). For help in examining Melville's use and revision of historical facts in "Benito Cereno," see Eric Sundquist's chapter "Melville, Delany, and New World Slavery" in his book *To Wake the Nations* (1993).

RESOURCES

Criticism

Gloria Horsley-Meacham, "Bull of the Nile: Symbol, History, and Racial Myth in 'Benito Cereno,'" *New England Quarterly,* 64 (June 1991): 225–242.

Argues that while Melville's depictions of Africans sometimes conform to racial stereotypes, he also uses references to Egyptian and Ethiopian civilizations to subvert those stereotypes.

Gavin Jones, "Dusky Comments of Silence: Language, Race, and Herman Melville's 'Benito Cereno,'" *Studies in Short Fiction,* 32 (Winter 1995): 39–50.

Argues that the story reveals how the Africans on board the *San Dominick* manipulate the Spanish language as well as African languages to their advantage against Delano and the Spaniards.

Jason Richards, "Melville's (Inter)national Burlesque: Whiteface, Blackface, and
    'Benito Cereno,'" *American Transcendental Quarterly*, 21, 2 (2007): 73–94.
Analyzes Babo's use of blackface minstrel stereotypes as well as his use of Benito
Cereno's body as a white mask of colonial authority to deceive Delano.

Eric J. Sundquist, *To Wake the Nations: Race in the Making of American Literature*
    (Cambridge, Mass.: Harvard University Press, 1993).
The chapter "Melville, Delany, and New World Slavery" analyzes "Benito Cereno"
in light of discussions about slavery as well as the Haitian Revolt of 1791–1804.

⌒◈◈◈◈◈◈⌒

Herman Melville, Early Novels (1846–1850)

Although Herman Melville is known most for his novel *Moby-Dick*, that novel
marked a downward turn in his literary reception. Ironically, some of his earlier
novels, which have long been eclipsed by *Moby-Dick*, were his most successful
commercially. Like *Moby-Dick*, his first five novels—*Typee: A Peep at Polynesian
Life* (1846), *Omoo: A Narrative of Adventures in the South Seas* (1847), *Mardi: and a
Voyage Thither* (1849), *Redburn: His First Voyage* (1849), and *White-Jacket: or, The
World in a Man-of-War* (1850)—reflect his experiences as a sailor during the early
1840s. Melville differed from most seamen in his respectable class origins. Both
his parents belonged to prestigious families; in fact, his maternal grandfather, Peter
Gransevoort, was a colonel in the Revolutionary War who fought at Saratoga, and
his paternal grandfather participated in the Boston Tea Party. The family's fortunes
suffered when his father went bankrupt and died in 1831. Melville was forced to
drop out of the Albany Academy the next year and in the next few years, he worked
several jobs—a bank clerk, a clerk in his brother's fur store, a farm hand, and a
teacher. He also studied surveying with the hope of getting work on the Erie Canal
project, but this scheme failed. Melville's first seafaring experience came in 1839
when he sailed to Liverpool and back on the *St. Lawrence* as a cabin boy. Without
hope for adequate employment on land, he again turned to the sea in 1841 by sign-
ing on with the whaler *Acushnet*. In July of the next year he and a fellow sailor, tired
of their brutal treatment, deserted in the Marquesas Islands in the South Pacific
and lived with the Typee people—an episode that he dramatized in his first novel.
Melville was surprised at the kindly treatment he received and saw the Typee as
superior to most white Christians. He was picked up by the Australian whaler *Lucy
Ann* and after he became involved in a mutiny, he was imprisoned in Tahiti with
another shipmate—an experience which he described in *Omoo*. He was picked up
by the whaler *Charles and Henry*, landed in Hawaii, and in August 1843 embarked
on the warship *United States*, which discharged him in Boston in October 1844.
This cruise formed the plot of his novel *White-Jacket*. In general, his seafaring experiences led him to draw parallels between slaves and sailors, who were severely disci-
plined and suffered horrific working conditions. He was also horrified by the brutal
treatment of natives by whites and recognized the ethnocentric narrowmindedness

of missionaries. His often romanticized depictions of the natives he encountered in the Pacific were influenced by the tradition of the Noble Savage.

Within a year after his return to America, Melville had completed his first novel, *Typee*, but publishers pressured him to cut several passages that criticized missionaries. It was eventually published in London in 1846 and became an instant success. An American edition later appeared in which the controversial passages were omitted, a fact that frustrated Melville. Although his next novel, *Omoo*, did not sell as well or win as much critical praise as *Typee*, it was successful enough to encourage Melville to become a professional writer. A few months after *Omoo* was published, he married Elizabeth Shaw, whose father, Lemuel Shaw, was Chief Justice of the Massachusetts Supreme Court. After Melville's allegorical novel *Mardi* sold poorly, he reluctantly returned to realistic adventure stories with *Redburn* and *White-Jacket*.

Critical sources focusing on Melville's early novels can be found in Joel Myerson's *Melville Dissertations: An Annotated Directory* (1972) and Brian Higgins's *Herman Melville, An Annotated Bibliography* (1979). Hershel Parker's *Herman Melville: A Biography* (1966) is one of the best sources of information about Melville's life. Howard C. Horsforth and Lynn Horth's edition of Melville's journals (volume 15 of *The Writings of Herman Melville*, 1989) provides a glimpse into Melville's life from his own perspective.

TOPICS FOR DISCUSSION AND RESEARCH

1. Melville's first five novels, like much of his later fiction, often expose injustice and prejudice as well as the ideological formations that endorse them. These novels also reveal the hypocrisy of individuals, classes, and nations that profess noble ideals but subvert them in practice. *Redburn*, for instance, includes chapters in which the narrator encounters dying paupers in Liverpool who are ignored by the police as well as harrowing descriptions of the living conditions of poor Irish immigrants traveling in steerage, where an epidemic kills about thirty passengers. *White-Jacket* often depicts the cruel treatment of sailors on an American frigate by captains and officers, including the practice of flogging, and contains a denunciation of the Articles of War. In fact, the narrator implicitly compares the oppression of sailors to that of African American slaves. The novel was sent to every member of Congress, which later outlawed flogging in the American navy partly as a result of reading *White-Jacket*. Students might compare the flogging scenes in this novel to whipping scenes in slave narratives such as Frederick Douglass's 1845 *Narrative* and consider how Melville borrows the imagery and emotional appeal of slave narratives in his depictions of flogging. Alternatively, students may research the practice of flogging in the U.S. Navy and the role of *White-Jacket* in abolishing it by consulting the Navy Department Library website "Flogging in the US Navy" <http://www.history.navy.mil/library/online/flogging.htm>.

2. In addition to depicting the suffering of paupers, Irish immigrants, and sailors and denouncing those who oppress or neglect them, Melville's early novels also challenged the racist views of his audience, exposed the barbarity of white men toward Polynesians, and attacked the ethnocentrism of Western mission-

aries. Unlike most of his literary contemporaries, who either ignored African Americans or resorted to caricature in depicting them, Melville portrays black sailors either neutrally or sympathetically. His depictions of Polynesians in his first three novels are even more positive, and they refute the colonialist discourse that portrayed Polynesians as murderous cannibals, though they are limited by his reliance on the Noble Savage motif. Samuel Otter argues that while these depictions were shaped by the scientific discourse of race, they also reveal Melville's manipulations of that discourse. In contrast to his Polynesian characters, Melville portrays white missionaries in *Typee* and *Omoo* as misguided at best, and often reveals the unfortunate results of their intervention in native society. In addition, John Samson argues that *Omoo* parodies missionary texts by comparing his wandering sailors to missionaries. In this respect, these novels went against colonialist discourse. However, as Douglas Ivison and Malini Johar Schueller have demonstrated, Melville also participated in this discourse through his use of noble-savage characterizations, his descriptions of the South Sea Islands as an exotic paradise, and the travel-narrative genre in which he wrote. Students might explore Melville's relationship to colonialist discourse, including its racial assumptions and its justification for domination, in any of his early novels.

3. Melville's depictions of Polynesians as noble savages emphasize their innocence, a recurring theme in much of his fiction. In *Redburn*, however, Melville satirically portrays his narrator/protagonist as more naive and pretentious than innocent. Redburn foolishly assumes that the captain and crew of the *Highlander* will treat him favorably because of his family's genteel background, and he becomes disillusioned after suffering constant ridicule and abuse for his lack of nautical skills. His illusions are again shattered when he learns that his friend Harry is not as kind and honest as he had initially believed. More generally, his belief in human decency is shaken by the treatment of poor people on the ship and in Liverpool as well as the vicious behavior of sailors and officers. Marvin Fisher argues that Melville uses his protagonist to critique American anti-intellectualism and ethnocentrism, while Jonathan Hall examines the narrator's relationship to his younger self. More generally, students might consider what Melville's implied attitudes are toward Redburn's assumptions about class status and the human potential for evil. Another topic for students writing about *Redburn* would be a comparison of the narrator with the narrator of "Bartleby, the Scrivener" or "Benito Cereno" that analyzes the limitations of each narrator's perspective. In what ways does Melville subtly criticize the narrator's assumptions regarding class, race, or humanity in general that causes his failure to understand others?

4. While Melville was able to make his social critiques clear to the public with a straightforward narrative style in *Redburn* as well as *Typee*, *Omoo*, and *White-Jacket*, few critics appreciated or understood his allegorical novel *Mardi*, which foreshadowed the philosophical style of his later novels *Moby-Dick*, *Pierre* (1852), and *The Confidence-Man* (1857). Melville's departure from the travel-narrative genre early in the novel disappointed readers who expected *Mardi* to resemble *Typee* and *Omoo*, and his use of other genres (including the captivity narrative, quest narrative, and political and literary satire) also confused his audience. John Evelev analyzes Melville's combination of narrative genres, and

Cindy Weinstein examines why Melville's reviewers reacted negatively to his characterization and use of allegory in *Mardi*. The negative reception of *Mardi* anticipated the critical and commercial failures of his later experimental novels, which in many ways resemble the innovations of twentieth-century modernist fiction. Readers of *Mardi* might consider Melville's disruption of his readers' expectations of narrative and the effects of such disruptions.

RESOURCES

Primary Works

Typee: A Peep at Polynesian Life. During a Four Months' Residence in a Valley of the Marquesas (New York: Wiley & Putnam, 1846).

Omoo: A Narrative of Adventures in the South Seas; Being a Sequel to the "Residence in the Marquesas Islands" (London: John Murray, 1847).

Mardi: and A Voyage Thither (New York: Harper, 1849).

Redburn: His First Voyage. Being the Sailor-Boy Confessions and Reminiscences of the Son-of-a-Gentleman, in the Merchant Service (New York: Harper, 1849).

White-Jacket; or, The World in a Man-of-War (New York: Harper, 1850).

Criticism

Jill Barnum, Wyn Kelley, and Christopher Sten, eds., *"Whole Oceans Away": Melville and the Pacific* (Kent, Ohio: Kent State University Press, 2007).
Contains ten articles focusing on Melville's early seafaring novels.

John Evelev, "'Every One to His Trade': *Mardi*, Literary Form, and Professional Ideology," *American Literature: A Journal of Literary History, Criticism, and Bibliography*, 75 (June 2003): 305–333.
Analyzes how the mix of narrative genres in *Mardi* reflects Melville's negotiations with changing and conflicting notions of professional authorship.

Marvin Fisher, "The American Character, the American Imagination, and the Test of International Travel in *Redburn*," in *Melville "Among the Nations,"* edited by Sanford E. Marovitz and A. C. Christodoulou (Kent, Ohio: Kent State University Press, 2001), pp. 49–60.
Discusses how Melville uses his ignorant, provincial narrator/protagonist to critique American ethnocentrism and skepticism toward imagination and artistic refinement.

Jonathan L. Hall, "'Every Man of Them Almost Was a Volume of Voyages': Writing the Self in Melville's *Redburn*," *American Transcendental Quarterly*, 5, 4 (1991): 259–271.
Argues that the reflections of the narrator upon his younger self in *Redburn* contradict nineteenth-century and modern assumptions about the relationship between our past and present selves.

Douglas Ivison, "'I Saw Everything but Could Comprehend Nothing': Melville's
    Typee, Travel Narrative, and Colonial Discourse," *American Transcendental
    Quarterly*, 16, 2 (2002): 115–130.
Argues that Melville's critique of European civilization in *Typee* fails to transcend
imperialist ideology because it uses the colonialist literary genre of the travel
narrative.

James L. Machor, "Reading the 'Rinsings of the Cup': The Antebellum Recep-
    tion of Melville's *Omoo*," *Nineteenth-Century Literature*, 59, 1 (2004):
    53–77.
Compares the receptions of *Omoo* and *Typee* and argues that the less favorable
reception of *Omoo* altered Melville's notion of his relationship to his audience in
ways that shaped *Mardi*.

Samuel Otter, "'Race' in *Typee* and *White-Jacket*," in *The Cambridge Companion to
    Herman Melville*, edited by Robert S. Levine (Cambridge, England: Cam-
    bridge University Press, 1998), pp. 12–36.
Analyzes how scientific studies of race influenced Melville's depictions of human
bodies and racial difference in two of his early novels.

John Samson, "Profaning the Sacred: Melville's *Omoo* and Missionary Narratives,"
    American Literature: A Journal of Literary History, Criticism, and Bibliography,
    56 (1984): 496–509.
Analyzes how Melville parodies Calvinist missionary narratives in *Omoo* by drawing parallels between his vagabond protagonists and the missionaries of these
narratives.

Malini Johar Schueller, "Indians, Polynesians, and Empire Making: The Case of
    Herman Melville," in *Genealogy and Literature*, edited by Lee Quinby (Min-
    neapolis: University of Minnesota Press, 1995), pp. 48–67.
Argues that while Melville criticizes white colonial domination of Polynesians
in *Typee*, *Omoo*, and *Mardi*, he participates in colonialist discourse through his
emphasis on racial differences.

G. R. Thompson, ed., "ESQ Special Issue: Actuality of Place in *Typee* and Other
    Island Writings," *ESQ: A Journal of the American Renaissance*, 51, 1–3 (2005).
Special issue containing twelve articles focusing on *Typee*.

Cindy Weinstein, "The Calm before the Storm: Laboring through *Mardi*,"
    American Literature: A Journal of Literary History, Criticism, and Bibliography,
    65, 2 (1993): 239–253.
Argues that Melville's two-dimensional characterization and use of allegory in
Mardi disrupted middle-class notions of individuality and resembled the mecha-
nization of industrial society.

Herman Melville, *Moby-Dick; or, The Whale*

(New York: Harper, 1851)

Moby-Dick; or The Whale, arguably the greatest American novel, matches its title character in immensity, uniqueness, and elusiveness. The novel, by making references to Biblical scripture, Homeric epic, Shakespearean tragedy, Milton's *Paradise Lost* (1667), and other canonical works, and by combining an adventure tale with a myriad of other genres (including allegory, scientific essay, polemic, philosophical treatise, and drama, to name a few) is one of the most allusive and complex texts in American literature. It also elevated the occupation of whaling, then regarded with contempt by most Americans, to epic stature.

Although *Moby-Dick* has been firmly entrenched in the canon of American literature for nearly a century, its initial reviews were mixed. The novel proved to be controversial soon after its publication as *The Whale* by Richard Bentley in London in October 1851 and as *Moby-Dick; or, The Whale* by Harper and Brothers in the United States a month later. Although some reviewers were impressed by the novel's style and the power of Melville's imagination, other critics objected to the vulgarity of the forecastle scenes and Melville's sympathetic treatment of paganism. In addition, while Melville's knowledge of whales and whaling was often praised, several critics remarked that the more abstract, philosophical sections detracted from the interest of the adventures described, and disliked the novel's mixture of genres. Many English reviewers also criticized the novel's ending, in which the narrator's apparent death violates the plausibility of his telling the tale (due to a printer's error, the English edition did not include the epilogue in which Ishmael describes his rescue). The best sources regarding the novel's critical reception are Hershel Parker and Harrison Hayford's Moby-Dick *As Doubloon* and Kevin J. Hayes's *The Critical Response to Herman Melville's* Moby-Dick. During his lifetime, Melville and his American publishers failed to sell the initial run of three thousand copies (by comparison, over three hundred thousand copies of *Uncle Tom's Cabin* were sold during the first year after its publication). It was ignored by later generations of critics until the 1920s, when it was praised as a precursor to Modernism's interest in literary experimentation and narrative fragmentation.

In writing *Moby-Dick*, Melville drew upon his eighteen-month voyage aboard the whaler *Acushnet* during the early 1840s. In addition, he was inspired by the disaster suffered by the whaler *Essex*, which in 1820 was rammed by a sperm whale. Melville read the harrowing account of this incident by first mate Owen Chase, one of eight men who survived the shipwreck. A similar catastrophe struck the whaler *Ann Alexander* when it was staved by a sperm whale in August 1851 (news of the event reached the United States in October), a coincidence that made the publication of *Moby-Dick* especially timely. The novel was also influenced by reports of a ferocious albino sperm whale named Mocha Dick that was reportedly killed during the late 1830s.

Melville's depictions of whales and the sea were heavily indebted to both Romanticism and Gothicism and are in many ways characteristic of romance literature. Like other Romantic texts, *Moby-Dick* emphasizes the beauty and power of nature, and depicts both the ocean and the whales as sublime—i.e., beautiful, awe-inspiring, and menacing. He also emphasizes the individual uniqueness of his characters, particularly the tragic hero, Ahab, who may be compared to Satan of *Paradise Lost* as a powerful figure who tries and fails to defeat an omnipotent adversary. Melville also introduces the doppelgänger motif of Gothicism in Ishmael's relationship with Queequeg and more significantly in Ahab's conflict with Moby Dick, who, like his adversary, is scarred and mutilated. The Gothic emphasis on supernaturalism is also evident in the whale itself, which has a remarkable, ghostly-white color and is preternaturally intelligent and malicious in its attacks on whalers. Moreover, the Gothic interest in insanity is pronounced in Ahab's monomania and Pip's derangement. Melville once described the novel thus: "It is not a piece of fine feminine Spitalfields silk—but it is of the horrible texture of a fabric that should be woven of ships' cables and hausers. A polar wind blows through it, & birds of prey hover over it."

TOPICS FOR DISCUSSION AND RESEARCH

1. One of the more prominent features of *Moby-Dick* is its frequent allusion to the Bible. The narrator's biblical namesake appears in Genesis as Abram's first son, and fittingly, both Ishmaels are social outcasts. Ahab's biblical counterpart was a wicked king of Israel mentioned in 1 Kings, though King Ahab does not share the monomanical lust for vengeance that Melville's character does. Ishmael is warned about Ahab by a mysterious man named Elijah, whose biblical namesake is a prophet who urges King Ahab to renounce his evil ways. Another allusion appears in the ship *Rachel,* whose captain is searching for his lost son. Rachel is one of Jacob's wives in Genesis who for many years is unable to bear children; she is mentioned in Jeremiah 31:15 and Matthew 2:18 as "weeping for her children, and would not be comforted, because they are not." Perhaps the most central biblical reference is to the book of Jonah, which features a reluctant prophet who is thrown overboard during a storm at sea and is swallowed by a whale. Another biblical passage that mentions whales is in Job 41, in which God compares himself to the leviathan (whale) in might. Other characters and ships whose names have biblical counterparts are the ship *Jeroboam* (a king of ancient Israel), Gabriel (an angel in Judaism, Christianity, and Islam), and Captains Peleg (a descendent of Noah) and Bildad (one of Job's counselors). Although not all of these characters correspond precisely with their biblical equivalents, these names resonated with meaning for American and British readers, many of whom were familiar with the Bible. Students may be interested in consulting Melville's biblical references and analyzing the ways in which he uses and changes biblical stories and characters.

2. More recent *Moby-Dick* scholarship has frequently discussed the novel's depictions of race. Although Melville was not immune to the racialist thinking of his day or the notion of the noble savage, *Moby-Dick* relies less on popular, often pernicious racial ideologies than many other texts of its time. Melville's depiction of the harpooners Queequeg, Tashtego, and Daggoo, as well as the black cabin boy Pip and the black cook Fleece, are largely sympathetic, and Ishmael's

close bond with Queequeg suggests a similarity that transcends notions of innate racial difference. Ishmael recognizes Queequeg's humanity and even joins him in worshiping the god Yojo, a scene that was sharply criticized by several reviewers as a rejection of Christianity in favor of paganism. Students might research the scientific study of race in nineteenth-century America and examine whether Melville's treatment of race in *Moby-Dick* may be shaped by these notions in some ways or departs from them in others. One starting point is Stephen Jay Gould's *The Mismeasure of Man* (1981). Another useful source is Thomas Gossett's *Race: The History of an Idea in America* (1963); in particular, see chapter three, "Nineteenth Century Anthropology."

3. Another controversial topic in *Moby-Dick* scholarship has been the novel's homoeroticism, a theme which scholars interested in sexuality have also analyzed in his posthumously published novella *Billy Budd*. This theme emerges most obviously in "The Counterpane" chapter in which Ishmael wakes up in the arms of his bedmate Queequeg in the Spouter's Inn and refers to himself as Queequeg's bride, and in the chapter "A Squeeze of the Hand," in which Ishmael describes how he and his shipmates enjoy squeezing each other's fingers while breaking up lumps of congealed sperm oil. Some scholars have speculated that these scenes may reveal hints about Melville's sexual orientation, though biographers have not found evidence of this. Students may wish to examine nineteenth-century notions regarding same-sex desire and analyze these elements of *Moby-Dick* within this context.

4. This issue of same-sex affection in *Moby-Dick* also brings up the concept of gender, and more particularly, masculinity, issues that have been analyzed by scholars in gender studies. For instance, while Ahab embodies the traditional masculine qualities of fearlessness and determination in his quest of Moby-Dick, his severed leg may be read as a castration that has "unmanned" and "unmasted" him. More specifically, Queequeg is feminized in the "Cistern and Buckets" chapter when he acts as a figurative midwife and rescues Tashtego, who had fallen into the cavity of a dead sperm whale's head, which the narrator compares to a womb. At the same time, the novel is rife with phallic imagery, such as Ahab's prosthetic ivory leg or the harpoons used in hunting whales. Not surprisingly, Melville's depiction of an all-male world has attracted the attention of many scholars; for an example, see Leland Person's essay "Melville's Cassock," which analyzes the variety of masculinities depicted in the novel. Students might better understand Melville's treatment of masculinity by comparing *Moby-Dick* to other literature of the time (including seafaring literature) or to contemporary popular notions of masculinity.

5. Aside from its allusive nature and thematic content, much scholarship has focused on Melville's mixture of genres and the novel's unusual narrative structure, issues that have often baffled his readers and reviewers. Some scholars such as Carolyn Karcher have argued that the chapters in *Moby-Dick* that digress from the main plot (such as the classification of whales in the "Cetology" chapter) should not be ignored or dismissed as structural weaknesses, and that the text should be seen as more than a story about

Ahab and Moby-Dick. In this sense, scholars argue, *Moby-Dick* should not be read simply as a novel but as an encyclopedic and experimental text that problematizes common assumptions about textual genres. One possible essay or discussion topic might be the ways that *Moby-Dick* challenges readers' expectations regarding literary genres, and what Melville may have gained with his experimental approach.

RESOURCES

In addition to the sources listed below, the journal *Leviathan: A Journal of Melville Studies* often includes articles on *Moby-Dick* and has devoted several issues to the novel.

Primary Work

Herman Melville, *Moby-Dick: An Authoritative Text, Reviews and Letters by Melville, Analogues and Sources, Criticism,* edited by Harrison Hayford and Hershel Parker (New York: Norton, 2001).
A definitive edition of the novel combined with various contextual documents and critical analyses of the text.

Biography

Hershel Parker, *Herman Melville: A Biography,* 2 volumes (Baltimore: Johns Hopkins University Press, 1996).
One of the most recent and thorough Melville biographies.

Criticism

Jill Barnum, Wyn Kelley, and Christopher Sten, eds., *"Whole Oceans Away": Melville and the Pacific* (Kent, Ohio: Kent State University Press, 2007).
Essay collection containing two articles on representations of Japan and Asia in *Moby-Dick* and another essay comparing the novel to America's "war on terror" of the early 2000s.

Fred V. Bernard, "The Question of Race in *Moby-Dick," Massachusetts Review: A Quarterly of Literature, the Arts and Public Affairs,* 43, 3 (2002): 383–404.
Analyzes textual evidence suggesting the possibility that the narrator Ishmael is a mulatto.

Harold Bloom, ed., *Herman Melville's* Moby-Dick (New York: Chelsea, 1986).
Includes eight essays about the novel.

John Bryant, Mary K. Bercaw Edwards, and Timothy Marr, eds., *Ungraspable Phantom: Essays on* Moby-Dick (Kent, Ohio: Kent State University Press, 2006).
A collection of twenty-one essays on *Moby-Dick* presented at an international conference in 2001.

Andrew Delbanco, *Melville: His World and Work* (New York: Knopf, 2005).
Analyzes *Moby-Dick* and Melville's other works within the context of his life and cultural milieu.

Kevin J. Hayes, ed., *The Critical Response to Herman Melville's* Moby-Dick (Westport, Conn.: Greenwood Press, 1994).
Includes a more selective sample of contemporary reviews than Moby-Dick as *Doubloon* and more recent scholarly essays about the novel.

Carolyn L. Karcher, "The Pleasures of Reading *Moby-Dick*," *Leviathan: A Journal of Melville Studies*, 10 (June 2008): 104–116.
Suggests ways of appreciating the mixture of genres in the novel.

Hershel Parker and Harrison Hayford, eds., Moby-Dick *As Doubloon: Essays and Extracts (1851–1970)* (New York: Norton, 1970).
A collection of contemporary English and American reviews of the novel as well as later critical essays.

Eyal Peretz, *Literature, Disaster, and the Enigma of Power: A Reading of* Moby-Dick (Stanford, Cal.: Stanford University Press, 2003).
Argues that *Moby-Dick* challenges traditional notions of what constitutes literature and reads the novel within the context of later theorists who also question such notions.

Leland S. Person Jr., "Melville's Cassock: Putting on Masculinity in *Moby-Dick*," *ESQ: A Journal of the American Renaissance*, 40 (First quarter 1994): 1–26.
Argues that Melville depicts an all-male world to question prevailing notions of masculinity and explore alternative masculine identities.

Clare L. Spark, *Hunting Captain Ahab: Psychological Warfare and the Melville Revival* (Kent, Ohio: Kent State University Press, 2006).
Analyzes the cultural forces that shaped the Melville Revival among literary critics during the early and middle twentieth century.

Robert T. Tally Jr., "Anti-Ishmael: Novel Beginnings in *Moby-Dick*," *Literature Interpretation Theory*, 18 (January–March 2007): 1–19.
Argues that focusing on Ishmael tends to construct *Moby-Dick* as a nationalist narrative, and offers a transnational reading of the novel by analyzing the earlier sections "Etymology" and "Extracts."

Shawn Thomson, *The Romantic Architecture of Herman Melville's* Moby-Dick (London: Associated University Presses, 2001).
Examines *Moby-Dick* as a Romantic text in which Ahab's idealism conflicts with Ishmael's individual consciousness.

The Poems of Edgar Allan Poe

edited by Floyd Stovall

(Charlottesville: University Press of Virginia, 1965)

In the preface to his 1845 collection *The Raven and Other Poems*, Edgar Allan Poe (1809–1849) wrote, "With me poetry has been not a purpose, but a passion." Though Poe was undeservedly negative about the quality of his writing, telling James Russell Lowell in 1844 that all of his poetry was "hurried & unconsidered," his own theories of deliberate composition and his continuing revision of his verse show the great importance he placed upon poetry as an art. With tales Poe could pay the bills, and with criticism he could debate the literati of his day. But true poetry, he believed, elevated the soul and put its readers in touch with the sublime.

Most of Poe's poetic activity was concentrated in his very early and very late careers. Born in Boston in 1809 and orphaned as a young child (his mother died when he was three years old; his father disappeared or died around the same time), Poe was taken in by a prosperous Virginia merchant, John Allan, and his wife, Frances. Poe experienced a turbulent youth that included the financial and emotional instability that was to mark his entire life; the exotic and dreamlike world of poetry may have offered him some respite. Still in his teens, while stationed with the U.S. Army in Boston harbor, he published a slim volume titled *Tamerlane and Other Poems* (Boston, 1827). Two years later he expanded that work as *Al Aaraaf, Tamerlane, and Minor Poems* (Baltimore, 1829). (The title poem refers to the Muslim limbo world of Al Aaraaf, populated in the poem by poets and their dreams.) Shortly after his dismissal from the U.S. Military Academy at West Point and with the help of donations from his fellow cadets, Poe brought out *Poems; Second Edition* (New York, 1831), which included extensively revised versions of "Tamerlane" and "Al Aaraaf" as well as notable new poems such as "Israfel," "Irene" (later called "The Sleeper"), and an early version of "The City in the Sea." By the mid 1830s, Poe was increasingly saddled with the burdens of adulthood—including his marriage in 1836 to his young cousin Virginia Clemm—and for the remainder of his life he struggled to support himself as a fiction writer, an editor, a literary critic, a book reviewer, and other occupations in America's burgeoning magazine culture that paid better than poetry did. But the publication in 1845 of *The Raven and Other Poems* brought renewed attention to his recent poems, among them "A Dream within Dream" (revised 1839) and "Dream-Land" (1844). During his last years he published some of his most notable verse: "Ulalume—A Ballad" (1847), "The Bells" (1848, revised 1849), a second poem titled "To Helen" (1848), and "Annabel Lee" (1849). Poe died in Baltimore in 1849 at age forty.

Poe's theoretical and critical writing about poetry was in part animated by his campaign to expose the literati of his day, whom he accused of self-promotion and artistic close-mindedness. He objected to the puffery of second-rate verse in the guise of moralism and nationalism and was merciless in exposing the artistic flaws of his more-popular competitors—most of whom, as he said in a scathing review of the poet Joseph Rodman Drake (1836), lacked the "Poetic Sentiment" ("the sense of the beautiful, of the sublime, and of the mystical") and substituted mere ingenuity for true imagination. While Poe could be fearless, personal, and bitingly sarcastic in exposing the pedestrian and unpoetic in the work of his contemporaries, on theoretical grounds his aesthetic was coherent and text-centered: a poem must be brief, achieve a unity of effect, stimulate readers' sense of the beautiful, transport us to the sublime, and avoid what Poe called "the heresy of the Didactic." His critical theory of poetry, discussed in detail elsewhere in this volume, may be deduced from "The Philosophy of Composition" (his supposed explanation in 1846 of how he composed "The Raven"), "The Poetic Principle" (1850), and his many review essays, especially a lengthy 1842 review of *Ballads and Other Poems* by Henry Wadsworth Longfellow. All are conveniently reprinted with annotations in *The Selected Writings of Edgar Allan Poe*, edited by G. R. Thompson (New York: Norton, 2004).

TOPICS FOR DISCUSSION AND RESEARCH.

1. Just as Poe's achievements as a short-story writer can be too hastily reduced to dramatizations of the macabre and supernatural, so too it is unwise to limit the thematic range of his poetry to psychological aberrations or to a formulaic obsession (as he famously phrases it in "The Philosophy of Composition") with "the death of a beautiful woman." Though his fascination with subconscious responses to reality remains a constant, in fact Poe's poetic themes are broader than mere madness: the temptations and dangers of solitude (as in "Dream-Land" and "Al Aaraaf"), the plight of the artistic temperament ("Sonnet—To Science"), the dangers of imagination and self-indulgence ("The Raven"), and the passions of love ("To Helen") and loss ("Annabel Lee"). If Poe did at times write hastily and under financial pressure, his best poems reveal a mastery of style and a considered attention to the ways music, rhyme, and form contribute to the stimulation of the poetic sensibility that was his goal as a poet and his benchmark as a critic. For all his innovation, Poe illustrated in his verse great skill in conventional poetic forms like the elegy or in poetic devices such as onomatopoeia in "The Bells."

2. Due in part to his mercurial personality and the exaggerations of his vices into a distorted "Poe myth," Poe's critical reputation has always been difficult to separate from his biographical reputation. In his *Fable for Critics* (1848), for instance, James Russell Lowell referred to Poe's work ambivalently as three-fifths genius and "two-fifths sheer fudge." Compare and contrast appraisals of Poe today with those in his lifetime by consulting both reviews and the letters or journals of other writers. Chronological collections such as Eric W. Carlson's *Recognition of Edgar Allan Poe* or I. M. Walker's *Edgar Allan Poe: The Critical Heritage* offer selections of early criticism; compilations like those by Graham Clarke help to chart Poe's reputation today. A similar area of research is Poe's reputation outside the United States. Lois Davis Vines's *Poe Abroad* contains detailed historical discussions organized by country. Essays in the Modern Language Association's annual *American Literary Scholarship* evaluate the voluminous scholarly and critical attention to Poe and his work.

3. Readers often note the parallels between Poe's life and his poetic subjects. Sometimes those connections are fairly transparent, as in poems such as "Annabel Lee" (likely occasioned by the death of Virginia Clemm) and the autobiographical "Alone" ("From childhood's hour I have not been / As others were"). At other times the connections are far more speculative. Examine some of the ways critics have seen Poe's life manifested in his works. In what ways are these biographical readings satisfying, and in what ways do they depend upon faulty assumptions and the "Poe myth"? Marie Bonaparte's Freudian approach and the sometimes indiscriminate conflating of author and work on internet postings offer examples of both extremes. Scott Peeples's *Edgar Allan Poe Revisited* is a reliable guide to separating the man from the myth, as is the website of the Edgar Allan Poe Society of Baltimore. Heywood Ehrlich's *Poe Webliography* provides a useful entrée to Poe's online presence.

4. The theoretical similarities between poetry and fiction—both limited in extent, for example, and each aimed at a unifying effect—raise other comparisons between the two genres for Poe. Consider the thematic similarities between, for example, the narrators' destructive curiosity in "Descent into the Maelstrom" and "The Raven" or the prevalence of what John Paul Eakin has called the "Lazarus plot" in the tales and the poems.

5. Poe's reliance on psychology is implicit in his poetic theory and sometimes explicit in his works. (In "Imp of the Perverse," for instance, the narrator contrasts his explanation of "perversity" with the faulty work of phrenologists and other psychologists of the time.) Investigate Poe's psychological understandings in light of nineteenth-century science and apply it to an understanding of his poetic theory or of poems like "Dream-Land" that dramatize the unconscious mind at work.

6. Poe's writing has enjoyed popular incarnations in films, television, and recordings, from Roger Corman's B-movie versions of the tales to the animated send-up of "The Raven" on *The Simpsons*. Investigate the ways in which the written texts are modified for visual and audio adaptations. For useful starting places, see the filmography by Don G. Smith, the study of media adaptations by Ronald L. Smith, Steve Hockensmith's interview with Corman, and Burton R. Pollin's periodic checklists of Poe and music in *Poe Studies/Dark Romanticism*.

RESOURCES

Biography

Marie Bonaparte, *Edgar Poe, Étude Psychanalytique* (Paris, 1933), translated as *The Life and Works of Edgar Allan Poe: a Psychoanalytique Interpretation*, 2 volumes (New York: Humanities Press, 1949).
A classic study with a foreword by Freud.

The Edgar Allan Poe Society of Baltimore <http://www.eapoe.org/index.htm> [accessed 4 November 2009].

A valuable miscellany of criticism, biography, and images; includes under "General Topics" reliable discussions of frequently raised biographical issues, such as Poe and alcohol/drug use and Poe's death, and valuable (if incomplete) information about Poe's finances, his family, and his reputation.

Heywood Ehrlich, *A Poe Webliography: Edgar Allan Poe on the Internet* <http://andromeda.rutgers.edu/~ehrlich/poesites.html> [accessed 4 November 2009].
A critical guide to web resources, "including electronic texts, HTML-encoded texts, hypertexts, secondary works, commentaries, and indexes."

Jeffrey Meyers, *Edgar Allan Poe: His Life and Legacy* (New York: Scribners, 1992).
A readable and accurate biography that emphasizes Poe's legacy for later writers.

Scott Peeples, *Edgar Allan Poe Revisited* (New York: Twayne, 1998).
A biocritical study that corrects many of the popular misconceptions of Poe's life.

Arthur Hobson Quinn, *Edgar Allan Poe: A Critical Biography* (New York: Appleton-Century, 1941).
A groundbreaking study that debunks some of the persistent myths surrounding Poe's life.

Bibliography
Burton R. Pollin, "Music and Edgar Allan Poe: A Fourth Annotated Checklist," *Poe Studies/Dark Romanticism: History, Theory, Interpretation,* 36 (2003): 77–100.
A guide to recorded adaptations of Poe's work.

Criticism
Eric W. Carlson, ed., *The Recognition of Edgar Allan Poe: Selected Criticism since 1829* (Ann Arbor: University of Michigan Press, 1970).
Includes reviews and critical essays.

Graham Clarke, ed., *Edgar Allan Poe: Critical Assessments*, 4 volumes (London: Routledge, 1992).
A massive collection of essays, ranging from Poe's biography to contemporary theoretical approaches.

Frederick S. Frank and Anthony Magistrale, *The Poe Encyclopedia* (Westport, Conn.: Greenwood Press, 1997).
A useful guide to themes, topics, people, and titles, organized alphabetically.

Kevin J. Hayes, ed., *The Cambridge Companion to Edgar Allan Poe* (Cambridge & New York: Cambridge University Press, 2002).
Includes "The Poet as Critic" by Kent Ljungquist (pp. 7–20) and "Two Verse Masterworks: 'The Raven' and 'Ulalume'" by Richard Kopley and Kevin J. Hayes (pp. 191–204).

J. Gerald Kennedy, ed., *Historical Guide to Edgar Allan Poe* (New York: Oxford
  University Press, 2001).
Essays place Poe in his sociohistorical contexts, including discussions of the pub-
lishing industry, sensationalism, and gender issues.

Scott Peeples, *The Afterlife of Edgar Allan Poe* (Rochester, N.Y.: Camden House,
  2004).
Surveys various theoretical approaches to Poe, from psychoanalysis to
post-structuralism.

Don G. Smith, *The Poe Cinema: A Critical Filmography* (Jefferson, N.C.: McFar-
  land, 1998).
Provides information on eighty-one film adaptations of Poe's work.

Ronald L. Smith, *Poe in the Media: Screen, Songs, and Spoken Word Recordings*
  (New York & London: Garland, 1990).
Lively and detailed commentary on adaptations of Poe's work, organized by title
and genre.

Lois Davis Vines, ed., *Poe Abroad: Influence, Reputation, Affinities* (Iowa City:
  University of Iowa Press, 1999).
Seventeen essays trace Poe's presence in European, South American, and Asian
countries.

I. M. Walker, ed., *Edgar Allan Poe: The Critical Heritage* (London: Routledge,
  1986).
Selections of criticism and reviews.

Jeffrey Andrew Weinstock and Tony Magistrale, eds., *Approaches to Teaching Poe's
  Prose and Poetry* (New York: Modern Language Association, 2008).
A valuable collection of interpretive/pedagogical essays, though weighted toward
the fiction. Includes "Teaching Poe's 'The Raven' and 'Annabel Lee' as Elegies"
by Philip Edward Phillips (pp. 76-80) and "Mourning and Eve(ning): Teaching
Poe's Poetry" by Benjamin F. Fisher (pp. 81–87).

⸎

Edgar Allan Poe, *Tales of the Grotesque and Arabesque*
2 volumes (Philadelphia: Lea & Blanchard, 1840);
Tales
(New York & London: Wiley & Putnam, 1845)

Few American authors fascinated readers as much as Edgar Allan Poe, and
few have been as misunderstood. This misunderstanding is partly due to the
earliest biography of Poe, which painted him as nearly indistinguishable from
the insane, drug-addled narrators and protagonists of his Gothic fiction. Today
Poe is known mostly for writing "The Raven" as well as dozens of Gothic tales
such as "The Tell-Tale Heart" and "The Fall of the House of Usher." However,

he was a remarkably versatile writer, and his other literary and critical work has attracted much less public recognition. Although he rose to fame after the publication of "The Raven" in 1845, he was known in his time as a literary critic and editor of literary magazines; he was also a prolific writer of Romantic poetry and one of the pioneers of what is now called detective fiction. He was one of few American writers to make a living as an author, a difficult goal at a time when literary works were not protected by copyright laws.

Poe was born in Boston on 19 January 1809. His father abandoned the family soon after Poe's birth, and his mother died when Poe was two years old. He was taken in by John and Frances Allan of Richmond, Virginia. When he was six, the Allans moved with Poe to England, where he attended school, and returned to Richmond five years later. Poe attended the University of Virginia but went to Boston in 1827 after a quarrel with John Allan over financial support. After a two-year career in the army and a six-month stint at the United States Military Academy at West Point, New York, Poe moved to New York City in 1831 and later to Baltimore, where he published his first story, "MS Found in a Bottle," in the *Saturday Visitor* in 1833. This publication attracted the literary establishment and was one of the first successes of his literary career.

In 1835 Poe secretly married his thirteen-year-old cousin Virginia Clemm. That next year he began publishing his stories and reviews in *The Southern Literary Messenger* in Richmond and later was hired as an editor by the magazine. Poe's reviews in the *Messenger* earned him a reputation as a ruthless critic. His disagreements with the owner and his excessive drinking led to his forced resignation two years later, and in 1838 his only novel, *The Narrative of Arthur Gordon Pym*, was published. A year later, he moved to Philadelphia and became editor of *Burton's Gentleman's Magazine*, which published many of his stories and reviews. That same year, Poe published *Tales of the Grotesque and Arabesque*, which received mixed reviews and sold few copies. He stayed one year at *Burton's*, which was bought by George Rex Graham in December 1840, and in 1841 he continued to work for the magazine after it was renamed *Graham's Lady's and Gentleman's Magazine*. During his tenure at *Graham's*, Virginia became severely ill, and Poe's own illness led *Graham's* to replace him. Poe tried unsuccessfully to secure a government appointment and also tried to make a living by giving lectures. In 1844 he and his family moved to New York City, where he found work at the *Evening Mirror* and later the *Broadway Journal*. The *Evening Mirror* published his poem "The Raven" in January 1845, an event that made Poe a literary celebrity, and in July of that year *Tales*, his second collection of stories, was published. Poe also created waves in literary circles by publicly accusing the American poet Henry Wadsworth Longfellow of plagiarism, one of several literary controversies that marked Poe's career. Around this time Poe's life and career began to collapse. The *Broadway Journal*, of which he was editor and part owner, folded in 1846, and despite Poe's attempt to improve Virginia's health and his own career by moving to Fordham, New York, Virginia died of tuberculosis in January 1847 after a five-year illness. During the late 1840s Poe continued to write and publish poems, tales, and reviews and also gave lectures on poetic theory. In 1849 he pledged himself off alcohol and became engaged, but on Election Day he was found delirious on the streets of Baltimore and died soon thereafter.

Tales of the Grotesque and Arabesque and Tales contain most of Poe's best-known short stories, and most of these stories are heavily influenced by Gothicism. The "Gothicism" study guide in section II of this volume may be useful to students who are unfamiliar with this genre. Students looking for critical sources focusing on stories in these two collections may consult Leona Rasmussen Phillips's Edgar Allan Poe: An Annotated Bibliography (1978). Eric Carlson's Critical Essays on Edgar Allan Poe (1987) is also a helpful resource, as is Kevin J. Hayes's collection of essays The Cambridge Companion to Edgar Allan Poe (2002).

TOPICS FOR DISCUSSION AND RESEARCH

1. Unlike many American fiction writers who set their stories in the present or in the colonial past, Poe often used exotic locations in the more distant past in his Gothic tales. These fantastic settings allowed Poe to create characters and describe events that would have been inappropriate and implausible in more realistic settings. His detailed descriptions of settings and his narrators' psychological state created an intense emotional atmosphere and was typical of much Gothic literature. However, there was enough demand from the American reading public for Gothic fiction, and many of Poe's tales fulfilled that interest. Students interested in Gothic literature might research the popularity of this genre in Poe's day and examine how he adopted, manipulated, and revised its conventions. David Stevens's The Gothic Tradition (2000) provides historical information about Gothic literature, and Robert Martin and Eric Savoy's American Gothic: New Interventions in a National Narrative (2009) includes essays on Poe's Gothic fiction as well as that of other American Gothic authors.

2. Poe's Gothic tales include many of the themes characteristic of the genre. One of the most prominent themes is insanity, as in "The Fall of the House of Usher." In many cases, such as "The Tell-Tale Heart," "Ligeia," and "The Cask of Amontillado," the narrator is insane, which makes the entire narration unreliable. Poe's insane narrators have also led many readers to conclude erroneously that Poe himself shared these delusions. Overlapping with the theme of madness is the emphasis on perversity. Poe approaches this notion most directly in "The Imp of the Perverse," in which the narrator commits murder with a poisoned candle and his crime goes undetected for years until he voluntarily confesses. The narrator's confession is motivated not by a sense of guilt but by an irrational, self-destructive impulse. Poe's exploration of such perversity in this and other Gothic tales such as "The Tell-Tale Heart" and "The Black Cat" suggests that such absurd and disturbing thoughts and behaviors may not be limited to madmen but may be part of human psychology. One possible topic for a research paper might be the discourse of abnormal human psychology of Poe's day and tracing the influences of that discourse on Poe's tales. David Punter's essay "Narrative and Psychology in Gothic Fiction" in

Gothic Fictions: Prohibition/Transgression (1989) is a helpful source with regard to this topic.

3. The insane narrators and characters of Poe's Gothic stories are tormented by various fears, some of them due to paranoia and others that are well founded. While some of these characters fear death, others are afraid of the dead returning to life. "The Premature Burial" and "The Mask of the Red Death" explore the former fear, while the latter fear is dramatized in "The Fall of the House of Usher," "Ligeia," and "Morella," in which dead women come back to life. The fear of death in Poe's fiction is explored by J. Gerald Kennedy in *Poe, Death, and the Life of Writing,* which also examines popular attitudes toward death in nineteenth-century America. Consult Kennedy's book and consider whether Poe's representations of the fear of death in stories like "The Premature Burial" were typical of American attitudes at the time.

4. In several of Poe's Gothic works the theme of death is combined with the male narrator's love for a woman who inevitably dies. The recurring motif of beautiful, dead women in Poe's fiction should not be surprising to readers of his essay "The Philosophy of Composition," in which he asserts, "the death, then, of a beautiful woman is, unquestionably, the most poetical topic in the world." Examples of this motif include "Ligeia," "Morella," "Berenice," and "The Oval Portrait." Some critics have traced this pattern in Poe's fiction to the deaths of several women in Poe's life, including his wife, Virginia. Although several feminist critics have seen Poe's apparent obsession with beautiful, dead women as misogynistic, Joan Dayan complicates this notion in her essay "Poe's Women." Peter Coviello comments on the sexual elements of these works and links them to his racial fears. Choose several stories by Poe that depict the death of a female character. What traits are attributed to these characters? Do you see a pattern throughout these stories, and if so, does that pattern suggest Poe's attitudes toward women or death? Do these characters and their deaths illustrate Poe's idea about the death of a beautiful woman that he expresses in "The Philosophy of Composition"?

5. Although most of Poe's short stories may be categorized as Gothic, he was also a pioneer of detective fiction. Four stories in *Tales*—"The Gold-Bug," "The Purloined Letter," "The Murders in the Rue Morgue," and "The Mystery of Marie Roget"—are some of the earliest examples of this genre. Unlike the morbid and deranged characters and narrators of his Gothic fiction, the latter three stories feature C. Auguste Dupin, the eccentric, hyperrational detective who uses unusual logical methods to solve mysteries. "The Gold-Bug" features the odd and brilliant William Legrand, whose sanity is doubted by the narrator until Legrand cracks the code that leads him to the treasure of the legendary pirate Captain Kidd. Lawrence Frank's chapter on Poe's detective fiction is a good place to start for those doing research on these stories. Students might also compare Poe's detective stories to his Gothic tales and examine how he represents the human mind. For example, are there significant differences between Dupin in "The Purloined Letter" and Roderick Usher of "The Fall of the House of Usher" in how their minds operate, and if so, what are they? Are there any similarities?

6. "The Gold-Bug" is one of few Poe tales that features an African American (Legrand's dim-witted servant Jupiter), but recently scholars have examined racial themes and indirect representations of slavery in Poe's fiction generally. For instance, Joan Dayan's "Romance and Race" and J. Gerald Kennedy and Lilianne Weisberg's essay collection *Romancing the Shadow* connect Poe's support for slavery and his racial anxieties to his fiction, and Dayan examines the connections between his attitudes toward slavery to his depictions of pure, white women in her essay "Amorous Bondage." Students might analyze Poe's depiction of Jupiter in "The Gold-Bug" and consider his role in the story with regard to Legrand's superior intellect. Alternatively, students might examine the racialized elements of Poe's depiction of the murderer in "The Murders in the Rue Morgue"; the essays by Lindon Barrett and Elsie Lemire in *Romancing the Shadow* that analyze this story are particularly helpful.

RESOURCES

Bibliography

This bibliography does not include sources that focus only on one or a few of Poe's fictional works. Aside from these sources, two journals devoted to critical analyses of Poe's works are *The Edgar Allan Poe Review* and *Poe Studies/Dark Romanticism: History, Theory, Interpretation.*

Criticism

Graham Clarke, ed., *Edgar Allan Poe: Critical Assessments* (East Sussex, U.K.: Helm Information, 1991).
The four volumes in this series include *Life and Works; Poe in the Nineteenth Century; Poe the Writer: Poems, Criticism and Short Stories;* and *Poe in the Twentieth Century.*

Peter Coviello, "Poe in Love: Pedophilia, Morbidity, and the Logic of Slavery," *ELH,* 70 (Fall 2003): 875–901.
Argues that analyses of the sexual elements of Poe's works should not be separated from his expressions of racial anxiety, and argues that Poe's distinctive narratorial style and his emphasis on morbidity link these two elements of his works.

Joan Dayan, "Amorous Bondage: Poe, Ladies, and Slaves," *American Literature: A Journal of Literary History, Criticism, and Bibliography,* 66 (June 1994): 239–273.
Connects Poe's idealization of white women with his support for slavery.

Dayan, "Poe's Women: A Feminist Poe?" *Poe Studies/Dark Romanticism: History, Theory, Interpretation,* 26 (June–December 1993): 1–12.
Analyzes how Poe's works question prevailing gender definitions.

Dayan, "Romance and Race," in *The Columbia History of the American Novel,* edited by Emory Elliott (New York: Columbia University Press, 1991), pp. 89–109.

Examines Poe's attitudes toward slavery and African Americans in connection with several of his fictional works.

The Edgar Allan Poe Society of Baltimore <http://www.eapoe.org/index.htm> [accessed 24 February 2009].
Includes links to the complete works of Poe, to articles published between 1968 and 1979 in the journal *Poe Studies/Dark Romanticism,* and to lectures and articles about Poe and his works dating back to 1829.

Lawrence Frank, *Victorian Detective Fiction and the Nature of Evidence: The Scientific Investigations of Poe, Dickens, and Doyle* (Basingstoke, U.K.: Palgrave Macmillan, 2003).
Part one of this book discusses Poe's detective stories.

J. Gerald Kennedy, *Poe, Death, and the Life of Writing* (New Haven, Conn.: Yale University Press, 1987).
Situates Poe's works within nineteenth-century attitudes toward death and examines the connections between writing and death in his works.

Kennedy and Liliane Weissberg, eds., *Romancing the Shadow: Poe and Race* (Oxford, England: Oxford University Press, 2001).
Contains nine essays about Poe's attitudes toward and depictions of African Americans and racial mixing in his fiction and "The Raven."

The Poe Studies Association <http://www2.lv.psu.edu/PSA> [accessed 5 February 2009].
Includes links to each issue of *The Edgar Allan Poe Review* (dating back to 2000) and to the Poe Studies Association newsletters (dating back to 1973), links to other websites related to Poe, and information about the annual Poe Studies Association conference.

Catharine Maria Sedgwick, *Hope Leslie; or Early Times in the Massachusetts*
(New York: White, Gallaher & White, 1827; revised edition, New York: Harper, 1842)

Although Catharine Maria Sedgwick may not be as familiar to readers of American literature as James Fenimore Cooper, their works share several similarities, and her novels deserve as much critical attention as his. Like Cooper, Sedgwick wrote historical novels about America's colonial past at a time when the nation was struggling to create its own identity through literature. Both authors depicted the encounters between English settlers and Native Americans in New England, and both were heavily influenced by Romanticism, particularly the glorification of nature and the use of the noble-savage motif in portraying Native Americans.

Sedgwick was born in Stockbridge, Massachusetts, in 1789 to Theodore and Pamela Dwight Sedgwick. Her father was a prominent Federalist lawyer and politician who was elected to the Senate in 1796, became Speaker of the House of Representatives in 1799, and was appointed to the Massachusetts Supreme Court in 1802. As a result of her father's political success and her family's wealth (her mother's grandfather, Ephraim Williams, was the founder of Williams College), Catharine was given a better formal education than most young women of her age received, although it was not comparable to that which her brothers received and did not prepare her for a public career. Sedgwick suffered another handicap in the lack of strong female role models in her home during her childhood—her mother was often ill and depressed, and her two older sisters married and left home during Sedgwick's childhood. However, she received emotional support from her four brothers, even after they married and left home, and they encouraged her studies and gave her moral and practical support in her literary endeavors. Sedgwick maintained strong relationships with her brothers and their children.

These relationships were particularly important to Sedgwick because she never married. She told her niece, "So many I have loved have made a shipwreck of happiness in marriage or have found it a dreary joyless condition." Her attitude may have been influenced by the struggles of her two married sisters. She explored the issue of marriage in her last novel, *Married or Single?* (1857), which argues that women should not wed if doing so jeopardized their sense of self-worth. In one sense, Sedgwick's heroines were more conventional than their creator in that most of them end up marrying, but most of them also show an independent spirit that reflected their author and that was unusual among fictional heroines of Sedgwick's time.

Aside from her decision to remain single, Sedgwick went against convention in other ways as well. Although she was strongly influenced by her patrician father, she eventually rejected his distrust of democracy and his disdain for common people. In addition, she was raised in the Calvinist religion but converted to Unitarianism in 1821, an action that led her to write a pamphlet criticizing religious intolerance. She expanded upon these ideas in her first novel, *A New-England Tale* (1822), which features a Quaker protagonist, and she later wrote about a Shaker village in her second novel, *Redwood* (1824), without denouncing their faith. This attitude was linked to her sympathy that she often revealed through her fiction for other oppressed groups, such as Native Americans and African Americans, and it extended toward her opposition to slavery, a sentiment that she expressed in some of her novels, although she did not belong to an abolitionist organization. However, she did join the Women's Prison Association late in life and revealed her opposition to the penal system in *The Linwoods* (1835) and *Married or Single?*

A female author of the time who questioned the status quo regarding marriage, religion, slavery, and women's "proper" behavior would not expect recognition for her literary accomplishments. However, Sedgwick's work was well received in her day, and she was often compared to other Romantic authors such as Cooper, Washington Irving, and the poet William Cullen Bryant as a creator of an indigenous American literary tradition. In the preface to *A New-England Tale*, she wrote that she made a "humble effort to add something to the scanty stock of Native American Literature." Unfortunately, her works were devalued for their sentimentality or entirely neglected by American literary scholars during most of the twentieth century and have only recently been rediscovered. She followed *Hope Leslie* with numerous short stories and essays (some of which were written for young readers) that were published in respected literary magazines such as *Graham's* and *Godey's Lady's Book,* as well as several other historical romances.

TOPICS FOR DISCUSSION AND RESEARCH

1. *Hope Leslie; or Early Times in the Massachusetts* is one of four historical romances written by Sedgwick. Like Cooper, Irving, and Nathaniel Hawthorne, Sedgwick used this genre to construct a narrative of America's origins. In doing so, she contributed to the development of both a distinctly American literary tradition and a literary definition of American identity, as Maria Karafilis, Gustavus Stadler, and Susanne Opfermann have discussed. While her depictions of some Puritan characters are positive, Sedgwick points out the racism and brutality of the English settlers in taking lands from the Pequot tribe. *Hope Leslie* is set during the 1630s and 1640s, and the novel begins shortly after the Pequot War of 1636–1637. This war consisted of attacks and counterattacks between Pequots and English settlers and culminated in the massacre of hundreds of Pequots—mostly women and children—by a combination of English and Narragansett forces in Mystic in present-day southeastern Connecticut. The fact that Sedgwick wrote about conflicts between English settlers and Native Americans during the 1820s is historically significant because during that decade white Americans were expanding aggressively into Native American territories, and Congress passed the Indian Removal Act three years after the novel was published. Sedgwick's positive portrayal of the Pequots and her criticism of anti-Indian prejudice is therefore timely, although she invoked the popular motif of the vanishing Indian near the end of the novel, and Maureen Tuthill argues that the novel condones Indian removal and justifies Puritan violence against the Pequots. Nevertheless, Sedgwick's depiction of Magawisca, daughter of the Pequot sachem (chief) Mononotto, is especially positive. Magawisca is wise, independent, and justly proud of her Pequot heritage. She also acts as a peacemaker between the Pequots and English early in the novel by sacrificing her body to save Everell's life—a scene reminiscent of the story of Pocahontas, the daughter of the Algonquian chief Powhatan who physically defended the English explorer John Smith from his executioners. According to Jeffrey Insko, this scene exemplifies Sedgwick's creative alteration of historical facts for literary effect. Taking this background into account, students might compare this scene in *Hope Leslie* to John Smith's account of Pocahontas saving his life in his *General History of Virginia*.

2. Sedgwick's relatively enlightened racial attitudes are reflected in her depiction of interracial marriage in the novel. When Magawisca tells Hope that her

sister Faith marries Magawisca's brother Oneco, Hope is shocked by the act of miscegenation, and Magawisca takes offense at Hope's reaction by suggesting that her family's blood is superior to that of Hope's family. The narrator makes no moral judgment on the marriage, but the fact that Sedgwick brings up this issue without condemning it is noteworthy during a time when most white Americans frowned upon interracial marriage. Her glowing portrayal of the Pequots makes the idea of Pequot/Puritan marriages more palatable to her audience, and may have been inspired by a relative who married a Native American. This family connection would make for an interesting research topic in light of Sedgwick's depictions of Pequots in *Hope Leslie*. Information on this topic may be found in Karen Woods Weierman's essay "Reading and Writing *Hope Leslie:* Catharine Maria Sedgwick's Indian 'Connections'" (2002).

3. Sedgwick's flattering portrayal of Native Americans may be seen as part of the noble-savage theme that appears in much Romantic literature. Many European and white American authors depicted the noble savage as a non-European who embodies many of the traits that civilized Europeans and European Americans lack, such as honestly, loyalty, generosity, physical health, courage, and most of all, a close relationship with nature. This image countered the popular stereotype of deceitful, murderous Indians. Because Sedgwick, like many white authors of the Romantic period, celebrated nature in *Hope Leslie*, it should not be surprising that she also glorified those whom she saw as living harmoniously with nature. Although Sedgwick's romanticized depictions of Native Americans were not unique, her research into Mohawk customs allowed her to portray Native Americans more accurately than most authors of her time. Students may wish to compare Sedgwick's depictions of Native Americans to Lydia Maria Child's *Hobomok* (1824), James Fenimore Cooper's *The Last of the Mohicans* (1826), and William Gilmore Simms's *The Yemassee* (1835).

4. Sedgwick's sympathy for oppressed groups was not only revealed in her depictions of the Pequots but in her female characters as well. Sedgwick's title character is an intelligent and independent young woman growing up in a Puritan society that expected women to obey all male authority figures without fail. She disobeys the magistrates of her settlement in liberating from jail the Pequot woman Nelema, who is convicted of witchcraft. Later, she and Magawisca make a plan for Hope's reunion with her sister Faith, even though this would break colonial law. Hope also goes against the sentiments of her Puritan community in her friendships with Magawisca and Nelema as well as her admiration for the Pequots and their culture. These interracial friendships and their limitations are examined by Ivy Schweitzer. Hope's friend Magawisca also reveals her moral and physical courage by going against her father's authority and saving Everell from execution. Later, during her trial, her proud defense of her own people against Puritan racism allows Sedgwick to combine her feminism with her admiration for Native Americans. Several scholars, including Amanda Emerson and Judith Fetterly, have analyzed Sedgwick's treatment of the subjugation of women in Puritan colonial society, and Amy Dunham Strand has discussed how

the novel offers a model for women's political activism. One might research the social condition of women in Puritan colonial history and examine how Sedgwick represents the subjugation of such women and imagines how they might revolt against it. The thirty-three-reel microfilm collection *New England Women and Their Families in the 18th and 19th Centuries: Personal Papers, Letters, and Diaries* provides excellent research opportunities. If that collection is not available, *American Women: a Library of Congress Guide to the Study of Women's History and Culture in the United States*, edited by Sheridan Harvey et al. (Washington, D.C.: University Press of New England, 2001), provides a reliable guide to other resources; and Deirdre Beddoe, *Discovering Women's History: A Practical Guide To Researching the Lives of Women Since 1800*, third edition (White Plains, N.Y.: Longman: 1998), provides advice about research strategies.

RESOURCES

Criticism

Amanda Emerson, "History, Memory, and the Echoes of Equivalence in Catharine Maria Sedgwick's *Hope Leslie*," *Legacy: A Journal of American Women Writers*, 24, 1 (2007): 24–49.
Analyzes Sedgwick's critique of the subjugation of women in a purportedly democratic nation in *Hope Leslie*.

Judith Fetterley, "'My Sister! My Sister!': The Rhetoric of Catharine Sedgwick's *Hope Leslie*," in *Catharine Maria Sedgwick: Critical Perspectives*, edited by Lucinda L. Damon-Bach and Victoria Clements (Boston: Northeastern University Press, 2003), pp. 78–99.
Argues that the novel is unable to resolve the problems of gender inequality. Preceded by excerpts of four contemporary reviews.

Jeffrey Insko, "Anachronistic Imaginings: *Hope Leslie*'s Challenge to Historicism," *American Literary History*, 16 (Summer 2004): 179–207.
Argues that Sedgwick's novel offers an alternative understanding of history and creatively takes historical events out of their original context.

Maria Karafilis, "Catharine Maria Sedgwick's *Hope Leslie:* The Crisis between Ethical Political Action and U.S. Literary Nationalism in the New Republic," *American Transcendental Quarterly*, 12 (1998): 327–344.
Examines the conflict between Sedgwick's promotion of democratic values in her novel and her desire to create a distinctively national literature.

Susanne Opfermann, "Lydia Maria Child, James Fenimore Cooper, and Catharine Maria Sedgwick: A Dialogue on Race, Culture, and Gender," in *Soft Canons: American Women Writers and Masculine Tradition*, edited by Karen L. Kilcup (Iowa City: University of Iowa Press, 1999), pp. 27–47.
Examines the "dialogue" between *Hope Leslie* and Child's and Cooper's "Indian" novels regarding issues of national identity, power, and cultural hierarchy.

Ivy Schweitzer, *Perfecting Friendship: Politics and Affiliation in Early American Literature* (Chapel Hill: University of North Carolina Press, 2006).
Chapter five, "The Ethical Horizon of American Friendship in Catharine Maria Sedgwick's *Hope Leslie*," analyzes the strengths and limitations of Hope Leslie's friendship with Magawisca.

Gustavus Stadler, "Magawisca's Body of Knowledge: Nation-Building in *Hope Leslie*," *Yale Journal of Criticism: Interpretation in the Humanities,* 12 (Spring 1999): 41–56.
Connects the corporeality of American Indians in Sedgwick's novel to the development of private subjectivity and American nationalism.

Amy Dunham Strand, "Interpositions: *Hope Leslie,* Women's Petitions, and Historical Fiction in Jacksonian America," *Studies in American Fiction,* 32 (Autumn 2004): 131–164.
Argues that Sedgwick's depictions of characters interceding on behalf of the powerless offered a model for women's petition campaigns.

Maureen Tuthill, "Land and the Narrative Site in Sedgwick's *Hope Leslie*," *American Transcendental Quarterly,* 19 (June 2005): 95–113.
Argues that Sedgwick's novel endorses Indian removal and exonerates Puritan violence against the Pequots.

Karen Woods Weierman, "Reading and Writing *Hope Leslie:* Catharine Maria Sedgwick's Indian 'Connections,'" *New England Quarterly: A Historical Review of New England Life and Letters,* 75 (September 2002): 415–443.
Reads Sedgwick's depictions of Pequots in the context of her family's relationships to Native Americans.

⟋⟍⟋⟍

William Gilmore Simms, *The Sword and the Distaff; or "Fair, Fat and Forty," A Story of the South, at the Close of the Revolution*

(Charleston, S.C.: Walker, Richards & Co., 1852; republished as *Woodcraft; or, Hawks about the Dovecote, A Story of the South at the Close of the Revolution* (New York: Redfield, 1854)

Judging from most American literature course syllabi and anthologies, one might get the impression that the only American author who lived south of the Mason-Dixon line before 1865 was Edgar Allan Poe, although he spent much of his life outside the South and is not generally seen as Southern. One might also get the idea that every American who wrote about slavery during this period opposed it. Although the number of antislavery texts from this period exceeds the number of proslavery texts, this imbalance is explained by the fact that antislavery literature was the product of a highly organized movement, whereas most proslavery literature was written in reaction to abolitionist propaganda in general and to Harriet Beecher Stowe's antislavery novel *Uncle Tom's Cabin* in particular. The neglect of Southern and proslavery American literature helps to explain why the novels and poems of William Gilmore Simms are usually not included in American literature survey courses and anthologies. Nevertheless, Simms was one of the more prolific American authors during this period, and some scholars feel that his work merits more attention, even though his views regarding race offend most readers today.

Simms was born in Charleston, South Carolina, in 1806. His mother died in 1808, and that same year his father fled Charleston for the frontier after his business failed, leaving his son in the care of the boy's maternal grandmother. Simms's formal education ended at age twelve; as a result, he was largely self-taught. His grandmother inspired his imagination by telling ghost stories and war tales, and while he served as an apothecary's apprentice during his adolescence, he read obsessively and began writing poems for local newspapers. In 1824 he reunited with his father in Mississippi, and while touring the countryside with him, Simms listened to stories and learned about frontier life and indigenous communities. Shortly thereafter, Simms returned to Charleston, gave up the apothecary trade, began studying law, and started a literary magazine called *The Album*. The magazine lasted only a year but presaged Simms's career as an author and literary editor. He included poems on Southern topics, stories about South Carolina during the Revolutionary War, and travel letters. He also published a monody for General John Cotesworth Pinckney in 1825, and his collections of poems *Lyrical and Other Poems* and *Early Lays* appeared in 1827. That year he was admitted to the Charleston bar, but he soon abandoned his legal practice to pursue his literary career. During the previous year he had married Anna Malcolm Giles, who died six years later. In 1828, Simms became an editor of the *Southern Literary Gazette;* in 1830 he began editing the *City Gazette*, which folded in 1832. After expressing his opposition to Nullification (South Carolina's attempt to nullify a federal law) in the *City Gazette*, he was attacked by a pro-Nullification mob. That year he visited the North and made contacts in the literary world that would later aid his career.

During this period Simms began writing in earnest, publishing three volumes of verse: *The Vision of Cortes* (1829), *The Tricolor, or Three Days of Blood in Paris* (1830), and *Atalantis, a Tale of the Sea* (1832), which established his literary reputation. Simms later published *Poems: Descriptive, Dramatic, Legendary, and Contemplative* (1853) along with a history and geography of South Carolina and several biographies. He also served as editor of the proslavery *Southern Quarterly Review* from 1849 to 1854 as well as *Magnolia* in 1842–1843.

Simms turned his attention to fiction in 1833 when he wrote and published his novel *Martin Faber, the Story of a Criminal*, with which he first reached a national audience. Although some of his Southern contemporaries such as George Washington Harris and Augustus Baldwin Longstreet wrote sketches of so-called Southwestern humor, Simms chose instead to write historical romances of the South. These works show the influence of Sir Walter Scott and James Fenimore

Cooper and formed the basis of his literary reputation. Two of his best-known romances are *The Yemassee: A Romance of Carolina* (1835) and *The Partisan: A Tale of the Revolution* (1835). After *Uncle Tom's Cabin* appeared in 1852, Simms condemned it in several reviews and wrote *The Sword and the Distaff; or "Fair, Fat and Forty," A Story of the South, at the Close of the Revolution*, which some critics see as a response to Stowe's novel. The novel was published serially in Charleston's *Southern Literary Gazette* between 28 February and 6 November 1852 before being published as a book that same year. Simms republished the book in 1854 under the title *Woodcraft; or, Hawks about the Dovecote, A Story of the South at the Close of the Revolution*. Simms wrote more than twenty other novels, many of them "border romances" about the contemporary Southern frontier as well as historical romances set in the South during the colonial and Revolutionary periods. Those set during the Revolutionary War allowed Simms to compare colonial rebellion against Britain with Southern resistance to the North. Despite his sectional views, Simms was compared by several Northern critics to Cooper, and in 1845 Poe called him "[t]he best novelist which this country has, on the whole, produced" and "immeasurably the greatest writer of fiction in America."

Despite the considerable energy that Simms devoted to his novels and periodicals, he found time to get involved in state politics. During the mid 1840s, he served two years in the South Carolina legislature, and later was defeated by one vote while running for lieutenant governor. Although Simms opposed Nullification in 1832, he later became a staunch Secessionist before and during the Civil War, and in 1856 he went on a disastrous lecture tour of the North in which he offended many of his listeners with divisive sectional rhetoric. His bitterness toward the North increased after his home and library, which included many Revolutionary War manuscripts, were burned by General William Tecumseh Sherman's army in 1865. He died in 1870.

The Sword and the Distaff is arguably the most historically significant of Simms's novels because of its role in the literary controversy surrounding slavery that broke out in the wake of *Uncle Tom's Cabin*. Although the novel counters Stowe's attacks on slavery by depicting the institution favorably, its action takes place during the years immediately following the Revolutionary War rather than the mid nineteenth century. *The Sword and the Distaff* features Captain Porgy, a portly, convivial gentleman and slaveholder of South Carolina who appears in some of Simms's earlier novels. Much of the novel describes the struggles of Porgy and his neighbors to restore social order in the aftermath of the war. Simms indirectly treats the theme of Southern secession through the struggle of South Carolinians for independence from Great Britain.

The Sword and the Distaff, along with many other of Simms's works, can often be better understood by learning about the author's life and beliefs. For biographical information about Simms, turn to John Caldwell Guilds's *Simms: A Literary Life* (1992). Guilds has also edited two useful collections of critical essays about *The Sword and the Distaff* and Simms's other works: *Long Years of Neglect: The Work and Reputation of William Gilmore Simms* (1988) and *William Gilmore Simms and the American Frontier* (1997).

TOPICS FOR DISCUSSION AND RESEARCH

1. One central issue in Simms scholarship has been the neglect of his work in the canon of nineteenth-century American literature, which has been dominated by authors who were later associated with the American Renaissance, most of whom were from New England or New York. Much of this neglect stems from ideological and regional factors, and it began late in Simms's life. Mary Ann Wimsatt points out that it resulted from his support for the Confederacy during the Civil War, and John Caldwell Guilds, Phebe Davidson, and Debra Reddin van Tuyll blame his support for slavery and Southern secession. Students might analyze *The Sword and the Distaff* along with other proslavery novels such as John Pendleton Kennedy's *Swallow Barn* (1832) and Caroline Lee Hentz's *The Planter's Northern Bride* (1854) as responses to abolitionist attacks on slavery. For those interested in Simms's reaction to *Uncle Tom's Cabin,* consult Charles Watson's essay "Simms's Review of *Uncle Tom's Cabin*" (1976).

2. Simms's difficult relationship with the northeastern publishing establishment led him to consider the importance of Southern literary magazines in forming a Southern identity for authors and readers. His decision to publish *The Sword and the Distaff* in the *Southern Literary Gazette* was part of this strategy, which Patricia Okker discusses in her article "Serial Politics in William Gilmore Simms's *Woodcraft*." In this essay Okker studies the relationship between *The Sword and the Distaff* (*Woodcraft*) and the *Southern Literary Messenger.* Although serialized novels have until recently been studied less than novels published as books, they were popular in Simms's time, and they often helped build a sense of community among readers. Students might consult Okker's article and write about Simms's decision to publish the novel in this periodical as part his effort to create a Southern literary audience that would sustain Southern authors.

3. Despite the unpopularity of his views, in several ways Simms was in step with his literary contemporaries such as Lydia Maria Child, James Fenimore Cooper, Catharine Maria Sedgwick, and Nathaniel Hawthorne, all authors of historical romances who tried to make their works distinctively American. Consider Simms's purpose in turning to America's past in writing *The Sword and the Distaff* and compare it to Child's *Hobomok*, Sedgwick's *Hope Leslie*, Hawthorne's *The Scarlet Letter*, or one of Cooper's "Leather-Stocking" novels such as *The Last of the Mohicans* and compare Simms's representations of America's past with those found in any of these other novels. Guilds's biography of Simms may provide some insight into Simms's motivation in writing about the post–Revolutionary War South in his novel.

4. The Southern culture that Simms celebrated was shaped largely by gender ideologies, a subject addressed by several recent scholars. For example, Saranne Weller focuses on how Porgy in *The Sword and the Distaff* offers a sensible male response to the antislavery rhetoric of *Uncle Tom's Cabin*. Students might examine how Simms's treatment of gender in *The Sword and the Distaff* engages with his construction and representation of Southern identity. In particular, one could examine Simms's depiction of Porgy's masculine

identity, or analyze how Simms portrays the character Widow Eveleigh as an example of Southern women. One might also compare *The Sword and the Distaff* to Stowe's *Uncle Tom's Cabin* in their treatment of Southern gender identities.

5. Simms was in many ways a literary spokesman of the South, and all of his novels take place in the South. On the other hand, *The Sword and the Distaff* and several of his other novels take place around the time of the Revolutionary War, an event that united South and North into a nation. Consider to what extent *The Sword and the Distaff* is specifically about the South and in what ways it is about the nation as a whole. Students may also wish to take into account Simms's support for secession, a subject that is explained in Guilds's biography. Another source to consider is L. Moffitt Cecil's article "Simms's Porgy as National Hero" (1965).

RESOURCES

Primary Work

John Caldwell Guilds and Charles Hudson, eds., *An Early and Strong Sympathy: The Indian Writings of William Gilmore Simms* (Columbia: University of South Carolina Press for the South Caroliniana Library, 2003).
An anthology of Simms's letters, essays, poems, and stories that comment on or depict Native Americans, often in a positive light.

Biography

John Caldwell Guilds, *Simms: A Literary Life* (Fayetteville: University of Arkansas Press, 1992).
The definitive Simms biography.

Mary Ann Wimsatt, "The Professional Author in the South: William Gilmore Simms and Antebellum Literary Publishing," in *The Professions of Authorship: Essays in Honor of Matthew J. Bruccoli*, edited by Richard Layman and Joel Myerson (Columbia: University of South Carolina Press, 1996), pp. 121–134.
Discusses the cultural forces that prevented Simms from achieving further success as a Southern professional author.

Criticism

Thomas M. Allen, "South of the American Renaissance," *American Literary History*, 16 (Fall 2004): 496–508.
A review essay of three collections of Simms's writings that discusses his work in connection to the American Renaissance.

Matthew C. Brennan, "The Nature of Simms's Southern Ecology," *South Carolina Review*, 39 (Spring 2007): 52–60.
Examines environmentalist and agrarian themes in Simms's essays and poetry.

Kevin Collins, "Experiments in Realism: Doubling in Simms's *The Cassique of Kiawah,*" *Southern Literary Journal,* 34 (Spring 2002): 1–13.
Examines how Simms moves from Romanticism toward Realism in this novel by using two characters to perform the same role.

Phebe Davidson and Debra Reddin van Tuyll, "William Gilmore Simms: A Literary Casualty of the Civil War," in *Memory and Myth: The Civil War in Fiction and Film from* Uncle Tom's Cabin *to* Cold Mountain, edited by David B. Sachsman, S. Kittrell Rushing, and Roy Morris Jr. (West Lafayette, Ind.: Purdue University Press, 2007), pp. 95–103.
Connects the neglect of Simms's works to his advocacy of slavery and Southern secession.

John Caldwell Guilds, *William Gilmore Simms and the American Frontier* (Athens: University of Georgia Press, 1997).
Includes seventeen essays focusing on Simms's depictions of the Southern frontier.

Guilds, ed., *Long Years of Neglect: The Work and Reputation of William Gilmore Simms* (Fayetteville: University of Arkansas Press, 1988).
A collection of essays examining Simms's works and literary career.

Debra Johanyak, "William Gilmore Simms: Deviant Paradigms of Southern Womanhood?" *Mississippi Quarterly,* 46 (Fall 1993): 573–588.
Analyzes Simms's depictions of women in his fiction.

Patricia Okker, "Gender and Secession in Simms's *Katharine Walton,*" *Southern Literary Journal,* 29 (Spring 1997): 17–31.
Argues that Simms's depictions of women in this novel masked the conflict between his secessionist views and the pro-Union stance of *Godey's Lady's Book,* which published the novel.

Okker, "Serial Politics in William Gilmore Simms's *Woodcraft,*" in *Periodical Literature in Nineteenth-Century America,* edited by Kenneth M. Price and Susan Belasco Smith (Charlottesville: University Press of Virginia, 1995), pp. 150–165.
Analyzes Simms's decision to publish his proslavery novel in a Southern periodical in order to reach a Southern audience.

Joseph V. Ridgely, *William Gilmore Simms* (New Haven, Conn.: College and University Press, 1962).
A critical overview of Simms's work.

Saranne Weller, "'To Create and Cherish a True Southern Literature': Genre, Gender and Authorship in William Gilmore Simms's Answer to *Uncle Tom's Cabin,*" *Literature Compass,* 2 (2005).
Analyzes how Simms depicts the "sensible" South in his novel *Woodcraft* as a response to the dichotomy between the male public sphere and the female domestic sphere in Stowe's novel.

⌒◇◇◇◇◇◇

Harriet Beecher Stowe, *Uncle Tom's Cabin; or, Life among the Lowly*

(Boston: Jewett / Cleveland: Jewett, Proctor & Worthington, 1852)

Harriet Beecher Stowe is best known as the author of the best-selling antislavery novel *Uncle Tom's Cabin,* and rightly so. It was the most controversial book of its time, and it spawned scores of literary imitations and refutations, stage productions, songs, and even a children's game. It also contributed to the conflicts over slavery that culminated in the Civil War; when President Abraham Lincoln met Stowe, he allegedly said, "So you're the little lady who wrote the book that made this big war!" It has given us the phrases "Uncle Tom" and "Simon Legree" as terms for submissive African Americans and cruel taskmasters. Nevertheless, many readers of this novel know little about Stowe's life and other literary achievements.

Harriet Elizabeth Beecher was born 14 June 1811, in Litchfield, Connecticut, to Reverend Lyman Beecher, a well-known Calvinist minister, and Roxana Foote Beecher, who died when Harriet was five years old. Harriet had eleven siblings, two of whom later became prominent in their own right: Catharine, a leader in women's education, and Henry Ward, an antislavery theologian. In 1832 the family moved to Cincinnati, Ohio, where Reverend Beecher accepted a position as president of the Lane Theological Seminary. Because Cincinnati shares a border with Kentucky, a slaveholding state, many fugitive slaves came through that city on their way north, and as a result, slavery was a prominent issue there. While in Cincinnati the Beechers, including Harriet, joined the abolitionist movement that was beginning to gain momentum. Four years later, Harriet married Calvin Ellis Stowe, a biblical scholar and teacher; they eventually had seven children. In 1850 when Calvin accepted a teaching position at Bowdoin College, the Stowes moved to Brunswick, Maine.

That same year, Congress passed the Fugitive Slave Act as a compromise between Northern and Southern congressmen. This new law gave slaveholders more power to capture fugitive slaves and made it illegal for citizens to harbor fugitives or refuse help to those attempting to catch them. The legislation outraged many Northerners, even those who previously did not consider themselves abolitionists. About this law, Stowe wrote, "the time is come when even a woman or a child who can speak a word for freedom and humanity is bound to speak." She was inspired to write an antislavery novel after experiencing a vision in church that made her imagine a slave being beaten to death. She also saw writing as a way of supplementing her husband's income and had already written and published the temperance story "Let Every Man Mind His Own Business" in 1839. She began working on a novel that was published in forty weekly installments in the Free Soil periodical *The National Era* beginning in 5 June 1851. With weekly deadlines looming, Stowe finished the novel in such haste that later she allegedly claimed, "God wrote it." The serialized novel was so popular that the *National Era* editor proposed publishing it as a book. *Uncle Tom's Cabin; or, Life among the Lowly* was released on 20 March 1852, and soon sold out; it eventually sold over three hundred thousand copies and made Stowe a celebrity. When *Uncle Tom's Cabin* became popular in Britain, where abolitionism was mainstream, Stowe made a triumphant tour of the nation that she later described in *Sunny Memories of Foreign Lands* (1854). The novel was translated into numerous foreign languages and inspired several imitations. Predictably, it was attacked by proslavery Southerners, and the backlash produced a spate of "anti-Tom" novels and plays. Because Stowe spent little time in the South, she felt compelled to authenticate her depictions of slavery, and to that end she compiled supporting documents and testimonies and published them as *A Key to Uncle Tom's Cabin* in 1853.

While Stowe never joined an abolitionist organization, she stayed committed to the movement through her writing and activism. In 1856 Stowe wrote the novel *Dred, a Tale of the Great Dismal Swamp*, which features the antislavery Southerner Nina Gordon and a Nat Turner–like slave rebel. In 1863 she wrote an essay for *Atlantic Monthly* titled "Sojourner Truth, the Libyan Sibyl," a tribute to the famous former slave turned abolitionist, feminist, and evangelist whom she had met years before. A year earlier, Stowe visited President Lincoln to urge him to abolish slavery quickly.

Despite her abolitionist commitments, many of Stowe's later works such as the historical novel *The Minister's Wooing* (1859), the local-color novels *The Pearl of Orr's Island* (1862) and *Oldtown Folks* (1869), and the domestic novel *Pink and White Tyranny* (1871) focused more on New England life. She moved to Hartford, Connecticut, in 1873 and died there in 1896 at age eighty-five.

TOPICS FOR DISCUSSION AND RESEARCH

1. *Uncle Tom's Cabin* combines elements of abolitionist literature, sentimental fiction, melodrama, and Christianity in its scathing depictions of slavery. The antislavery movement had been active for two decades before the novel was written, and Stowe's eighteen years in Cincinnati had put her in contact with fugitive slaves and abolitionists. She borrowed many arguments from the movement, such as the heartrending portrayals of separated slave families and the criticism of Christian hypocrites who used scripture to defend slavery. The novel was also influenced by the growing number of slave narratives, which combined abolitionist rhetoric with exciting tales of the adventures of fugitive slaves. As Robin Winks points out, many readers believed that Stowe had modeled Uncle Tom after Josiah Henson, a slave who escaped to Canada and published a personal narrative in 1849. Moreover, the character George Harris bears a striking resemblance in appearance and rhetorical flourish to Frederick Douglass, whose famous *Narrative of the Life of Frederick H. Douglass* was published six years before Stowe began writing her novel. An interesting research project is to compare Stowe's fictional account with what is known about the historical reality. Was her portrayal of slave life historically accurate? How did she shape her account for maximal effect? The composition and publishing

history of the novel should be taken into account in such a project. Books by E. Bruce Kirkham and Claire Parfait listed below will provide necessary information.

2. Stowe's novel also relied heavily on the conventions of sentimental fiction by focusing on domestic settings and issues, as Myra Jehlen argues in her essay "The Family Militant." Nowhere is this feature more prominent than in the chapter describing the home of the Hallidays, a matriarchal Quaker family in rural Indiana who help Eliza and Harry reunite with George Harris and help them escape to Canada. In her influential study *Sensational Designs,* Jane Tompkins analyzes the Halliday home as a utopian alternative to the corrupt, male-dominated world that condones slavery. In depicting women in these domestic refuges, Stowe relies in some ways on conventional notions of femininity while going against others. Like most of her readers, Stowe believed that women are naturally pious and virtuous and that they belong in the home. However, she rejected the notion that women should avoid involvement in public issues like politics and slavery. Rather, she suggests that they should be like the wife of the Ohio senator Bird, who not only helps Eliza escape but also uses her moral influence over her husband and urges him to outlaw slavery. As Tompkins points out, Stowe's narrator promotes "feminine" over "masculine" values with regard to slavery by implying that we should follow our hearts rather than our heads. Students interested in gender issues might begin with Tompkins's book to explore the novel's representation of female empowerment in the context of gender ideologies in Stowe's day or in connection with its attitudes toward religion, race, and slavery.

3. Stowe's Calvinist upbringing is evident throughout much of the novel, which argues that it is every Christian's duty to God to work toward the abolition of slavery. Stowe also relied on Christian imagery by depicting Eva St. Clare as a little angel, Uncle Tom as a black Christ figure who saves sinners through his death, and Simon Legree as Satan incarnate. The novel concludes with warnings of an apocalypse for a sin-stained nation and a corrupt church if it continues to allow slavery. While these elements may strike readers today as "preachy," Stowe's didactic tone and her unwavering belief in Christianity as the only true religion were more commonplace in her day. The combination of abolitionism and religious zeal was also familiar to her audience, since the antislavery movement was deeply imbued with Protestant evangelicalism. A possible research topic is the use of Christian theology and scripture on both sides of the slavery controversy and Stowe's contribution to that debate. Patricia Hill's "Uncle Tom's Cabin as a Religious Text" <http://utc.iath.virginia.edu/interpret/exhibits/hill/hill.html> is a useful resource for this study.

4. Although *Uncle Tom's Cabin* did more than any other novel to promote abolition, its depictions of African Americans have often been criticized. Marva Banks notes that reactions among African Americans were mixed when the novel first appeared and became more negative during the twentieth century. Stowe makes several sweeping generalizations about "the Negro mind" and often relied on stereotypes of black people as naturally musical, patient,

comical, or religious. Many scholars such as Arthur Riss have analyzed Stowe's racial views as examples of "romantic racialism," a term coined by twentieth-century historian George Fredrickson to describe the racial prejudices of Northern whites in Stowe's time (see Fredrickson's essay "Uncle Tom and the Anglo-Saxons" in the Norton critical edition of the novel). Sarah Meer has also pointed out that Stowe's use of racist humor was borrowed from black-face minstrel shows, particularly in her portrayal of the unruly slave girl Topsy. These studies provide an excellent foundation for a study of racial attitudes within the abolitionist movement to understand Stowe's romantic racialism and its connection to her antislavery message.

5. Many twentieth-century critics dismissed *Uncle Tom's Cabin* because of its didactic nature as well as its popularity. Their arguments were that true literature cannot make moral arguments and try to alter the world and that if a text is immensely popular, it is therefore not ahead of its time and not great. This elitist assumption was often combined with disdain among male scholars for women writers and sentimental literature. However, in the late twentieth century many scholars, most notably Jane Tompkins, rediscovered the quality, significance, and emotional power of the novel and have helped to move it into the American literary canon. Students might explore how literary critics of Stowe's day felt toward didactic literature and how those attitudes helped shape the commercial success and critical reception of her novel. A selection of early reviews of the novel is available at <http://chnm.gmu.edu/lostmuseum/searchlm.php?function=find&exhibit=uncletom&browse=uncletom>.

RESOURCES

Primary Work

Harriet Beecher Stowe, *Uncle Tom's Cabin. Authoritative Text, Backgrounds and Contexts, Criticism,* edited by Elizabeth Ammons (New York: Norton, 1994).

Includes contextual documents, contemporary reviews, and more recent essays about the novel.

Biography

Joan D. Hedrick, *Harriet Beecher Stowe: A Life* (New York: Oxford University Press, 1994).

The definitive Stowe biography.

Criticism

Elizabeth Ammons, ed., *Critical Essays on Harriet Beecher Stowe* (Boston: G. K. Hall, 1980).

Contains several nineteenth-century reviews and more recent essays on *Uncle Tom's Cabin* (some of which are reprinted in Ammons's 1994 Norton edition listed above).

Marva Banks, "*Uncle Tom's Cabin* and Antebellum Black Response," in *Readers in History: Nineteenth-Century American Literature and the Contexts of Response,* edited by James L. Machor (Baltimore: Johns Hopkins University Press, 1993), pp. 209–227.
Reveals that African Americans praised Stowe's antislavery message but often objected to her use of racial stereotypes and her endorsement of colonization schemes for blacks.

Myra Jehlen, "The Family Militant: Domesticity versus Slavery in *Uncle Tom's Cabin,*" *Criticism: A Quarterly for Literature and the Arts,* 31, 4 (1989): 383–400.
Examines how female characters and domestic values encourage male characters to achieve self-possession and live up to their ideals.

E. Bruce Kirkham, *The Building of* Uncle Tom's Cabin (Knoxville: University of Tennessee Press, 1977).
Explains the composition, serialization, and publication history of Stowe's novel.

Sarah Meer, *Uncle Tom Mania: Slavery, Minstrelsy and Transatlantic Culture in the 1850s* (Athens: University of Georgia Press, 2005).
Analyzes the connections among *Uncle Tom's Cabin,* stage productions of the novel, and minstrel shows in both the United States and Britain.

Claire Parfait, *The Publishing History of* Uncle Tom's Cabin, *1852–2002* (Aldershot, U.K.: Ashgate, 2007).
Provides information about the novel's composition and publication.

Arthur Riss, "Racial Essentialism and Family Values in *Uncle Tom's Cabin,*" *American Quarterly,* 46, 4 (1994): 513–544.
Examines Stowe's use of romantic racialism for antislavery purposes and analyzes how her depictions of separated slave families countered proslavery depictions of the plantation as a family unit.

Eric J. Sundquist, ed., *New Essays on* Uncle Tom's Cabin (Cambridge, England: Cambridge University Press, 1986).
A collection of five essays focusing on female abolitionists, Gothic imagery, Stowe's characterizations of African Americans, her correspondence with authors of slave narratives, and nineteenth-century American women's literature.

Jane P. Tompkins, *Sensational Designs: The Cultural Work of American Fiction, 1790–1860* (New York: Oxford University Press, 1985).
The chapter "Sentimental Power: *Uncle Tom's Cabin* and the Politics of Literary History" analyzes Stowe's use of domesticity, sentimentality, and religion to effect social change in her novel.

Robin W. Winks, "The Making of a Fugitive Slave Narrative: Josiah Henson and Uncle Tom—A Case Study," in *The Slave's Narrative,* edited by Charles T. Davis and Henry Louis Gates Jr. (New York: Oxford University Press, 1985), pp. 112–146.

Examines the connections between Stowe's novel and the narrative of Josiah Henson, whom many saw as the model for Uncle Tom.

⌒◯◯◯ ∘

Henry David Thoreau, Political Essays (1849–1860)

In late July 1846 Henry David Thoreau spent a night in Concord jail for refusing to pay six years' worth of poll taxes that he owed because he did not wish to support a government that supported the Mexican American War and legalized slavery. Thoreau was also not alone in his opposition to the Mexican-American War, which some Americans saw as an aggressive act justified by the notion of Manifest Destiny. In addition, many Northern Whigs and abolitionists opposed the war because it was promoted by Southern Democrats who wanted to increase the amount of land onto which slaveholders could settle and thereby increase their power in Congress through the representatives elected in these new lands. Thoreau differed from most critics of the war by peaceably breaking the law. Aside from his two-year stay near Walden Pond, Thoreau is best known for this morally based act of disobedience. He recounted this experience in an 1848 lecture, which was later published in May 1849 in Elizabeth Peabody's journal *Aesthetic Papers* as "Resistance to Civil Government," an essay that is better known as "Civil Disobedience." Thoreau wrote two other essays—"Slavery in Massachusetts" (1854) and "A Plea for Captain John Brown" (1860)—that overlap with this text in arguing for the right of individuals to protest against a corrupted government and to provoke the opprobrium of a morally weakened community by criticizing the status quo.

Civil disobedience is often defined as a nonviolent act performed by a person or group that violates a law that the violator believes is immoral. Many also believe that a person committing civil disobedience should not resist any attempt by legal authorities to detain or punish that person. Interestingly, Thoreau does not offer an explicit definition of civil disobedience in any of these essays, nor does he clarify whether it should avoid violence. While his own act of civil disobedience was nonviolent, he later suggested in "A Plea for Captain John Brown" that violence can be justifiable if it is used against oppressive regimes, such as those condoning chattel slavery.

Thoreau's notion of civil disobedience may be traced back to the concept of a "higher law" in the Declaration of Independence and ultimately to John Locke's philosophy of natural rights—a subject discussed in Deak Nabers's essay "Thoreau's Natural Constitution." In Locke's *Second Treatise on Government* (1689), he argues that people not only have a right but also a duty to rebel against an immoral government. The Founding Fathers committed a collective act of disobedience against what they viewed as a corrupt government; Thoreau extended that principle to the individual. For Thoreau, while the divine right of kings was rejected in the United States in the name of democracy, democracy itself has been transformed into the rule of the majority. In this respect, Thoreau's concept of civil disobedience conforms to both Romanticism and Transcendentalism by privileging the nonconformist individual over a materialistic, amoral society that preserves the status quo.

Thoreau's opposition to slavery was also typical of many New England intellectuals, including William Lloyd Garrison, editor of the abolitionist newspaper *The Liberator*, who publicly burned a copy of the U.S. Constitution because he believed that it supported slavery. As James Duban notes, both men were influenced by the moral philosophy of Jonathan Dymond. Despite the overlap in beliefs between Thoreau and abolitionists, however, he did not belong to an anti-slavery society, perhaps because he believed that such groups had their own form of "groupthink" and did not share his commitment to individualism.

"Resistance to Civil Government" also invokes the notion that government is a necessary evil whose power must be contained. This concept was popular among Democratic Republicans during the early nineteenth century, particularly Thomas Jefferson. This idea has recurred throughout American political thought, most notably in the conservative wing of the Republican Party commonly associated with Ronald Reagan during the late twentieth century. The opening quotation in "Resistance to Civil Government," "That government is best which governs least," encapsulates the Democratic-Republican laissez-faire ideal of government, and appeared on the masthead of the periodical *The Democratic Review*. However, Thoreau's point was not to endorse the "small government" ideology of the Democratic Party; rather, he argued that justice could only come about through the exertion of the individual's conscience, not through majority consensus.

Though "Slavery in Massachusetts" features some of the same ideas that Thoreau expressed in "Resistance to Civil Government," its context was different. Thoreau delivered "Slavery in Massachusetts" at an abolitionist rally in Framingham, Massachusetts on 4 July 1854, soon after the rendition of Anthony Burns, a fugitive slave, in Massachusetts. A crowd of abolitionists attacked the federal courthouse in Boston where Burns was being tried by Justice Edward G. Loring, and thirteen were arrested. Thoreau, like many abolitionists, was outraged by this incident and by the 1850 Fugitive Slave Law that enabled Burns to be caught and returned to his owner, Charles Suttle of Virginia. A similar incident had occurred three years earlier, when Thomas Sims, a fugitive slave from Georgia, was arrested and tried in Boston and returned to his master. Although the slaveholders won both cases, these events galvanized the abolitionist movement in New England. Thoreau's speech was based on his journal notes written during the Sims case, and Sandra Harbert Petrulionis observes that he left out some inflammatory passages from his notes in order to win over the audience. In addition to mentioning the Burns and Sims cases, Thoreau refers to the Kansas-Nebraska Act, which ruled that the question of whether slavery would be legal in this territory would be determined by the settlers, an idea that was called "popular sovereignty." Thoreau argues that the violation of human rights in Massachusetts is at least as important as the future of the Kansas-Nebraska territory. This essay differs from "Resistance to Civil Government" in that he shows greater confidence in the moral judgment of the community. Unlike his refusal to pay a poll tax—an individual act of civil disobedience—this incident was a communal act of civil disobedience against an immoral law. Students may wish to research the Sims and Burns incidents and the reactions of New England abolitionists to attain a better understanding of Thoreau's situation, audience, and purpose in this essay.

Thoreau's antislavery commitments extended to admiration for John Brown, an ardent abolitionist who led a raid on a federal arsenal at Harpers Ferry, Virginia, on 16 October 1859. Brown had become impatient with nonviolent attempts to abolish slavery, and this was not the first time he used force for anti-slavery purposes. In 1856 he led an armed antislavery militia (including several of his sons) against pro-slavery settlers in "Bleeding Kansas." While Brown was in Concord raising funds to buy arms for his militia, Thoreau met him twice and was deeply impressed by him. Brown later devised a plan for arming slaves and eventually bringing slavery to an end, and he appealed to wealthy abolitionists for financial support while organizing a band of soldiers for an attack on Harpers Ferry. The band included three of his sons as well as five African Americans. The raid resulted in the deaths of twelve of his twenty-one men, one U.S. Marine, and several local men. Brown and his surviving followers were captured two days later and were executed on 2 December 1859. As a violent incident that further divided the nation over slavery, Brown's raid was one of several events that led to the Civil War.

Thoreau read "A Plea for Captain John Brown" in Concord two weeks after Brown's assault, and the speech was later published in February 1860 in an anthology titled *Echoes of Harper's Ferry*, edited by the abolitionist James Redpath. Thoreau openly endorsed Brown's actions. As in his other essays discussed here, Thoreau implied that the North was as guilty as the South for slavery's existence because few Northerners took a stand against it. He expressed his anger toward the criticisms leveled against Brown by newspapers, Republicans, and abolitionists; Thoreau depicted him as sane, morally upright, and valiant, and compared him to Puritan settlers and the heroes of the Revolutionary War. Most notably, he depicted Brown as a Christ figure who sacrificed his life for humankind. For Thoreau, Brown epitomized the Emersonian ideal of individualism even more than Thoreau himself did, and as James Donahue argues, he saw Brown's raid as an act of civil disobedience, one which had a much more profound impact on American society with regard to slavery than Thoreau's refusal to pay a poll tax. Partly because of "A Plea for Captain John Brown," Brown was later celebrated by abolitionists during the Civil War.

Students looking for sources on Thoreau's essays will find Raymond Borst's *Henry David Thoreau: A Descriptive Bibliography* (1982) to be helpful. For those interested in Thoreau's life, one of the best biographies of Thoreau is Robert Richardson's *Henry Thoreau: A Life of the Mind* (1988). Students might also consult Barry Kritzberg's essay "Thoreau, Slavery, and Resistance to Civil Government" which focuses on the three essays covered in this study guide.

TOPICS FOR DISCUSSION AND RESEARCH

1. "Resistance to Civil Government" has had a profound impact on how later generations protested against government-sanctioned oppression in India, the United States, and throughout the world, as Evan Carton points out in his

essay "The Price of Privilege: 'Civil Disobedience' at 150." Thoreau's concept of civil disobedience was promoted by Mohandas Gandhi, the leader of the Indian independence movement against British colonial rule during the 1940s, and by Reverend Martin Luther King Jr. in his protest against racial discrimination and poverty in the United States during the 1950s and 1960s. Students might trace the impact of Thoreau's concept on such movements and assess the importance of this concept in struggles against oppression throughout history. Two helpful sources for this topic are Manfred Steger's "Mahatma Gandhi and the Anarchist Legacy of Henry David Thoreau" (1993) and King's "Letter from Birmingham Jail" (1863), available online at <http://www.africa.upenn. edu/Articles_Gen/Letter_Birmingham.html>.

2. Although Thoreau portrays himself as a lone conscientious objector to slavery and the Mexican War in "Resistance to Civil Government," he was joined by many New England abolitionists in his feelings of outrage regarding the Burns case. Consider Thoreau as a member of an antislavery community rather than an outsider, and explore the impact of his "Slavery in Massachusetts" essay on the New England abolitionist community. Richardson's biography of Thoreau and Robert C. Albrecht's essay "Conflict and Resolution: 'Slavery in Massachusetts'" (1973) will be helpful in researching this topic.

3. While Thoreau is credited with originating the concept of civil disobedience, he was able to develop the concept from John Locke's theory of natural law, Jonathan Dymond's theory of conscientious nonviolent resistance, and Unitarian beliefs about the importance of conscience. Choose one of Thoreau's political essays and analyze its statements about conscience and justice in light of the concepts of these earlier philosophers and theologians. To get started, consult James Duban's essay "Conscience and Consciousness: The Liberal Christian Context of Thoreau's Political Ethics" regarding the influence of Unitarian theology on "Resistance to Civil Government" or his essay "Thoreau, Garrison, and Dymond: Unbending Firmness of the Mind," which explains how Dymond's *Essays on the Principles of Morality* influenced Thoreau's belief in nonviolent protest against slavery. For information about the influence of natural law theory on Thoreau's political essays, see Deak Nabers's article "Thoreau's Natural Constitution."

4. After Brown's raid at Harpers Ferry, newspaper editors denounced him, and most leaders of the new Republican party distanced themselves from him. Many abolitionists also criticized Brown's actions; in fact, Garrison stated in *The Liberator* that the raid was "a misguided, wild, and apparently insane . . . effort." Robert Albrecht points out in his essay "Conflict and Resolution: 'Slavery in Massachusetts'" that Thoreau's audience did not support Brown, nor did most Northerners. One possible research topic is to compare the denunciations of Brown's raid with Thoreau's approval and to examine the reasons for both. David Reynolds's biography *John Brown, Abolitionist: The Man Who Killed Slavery, Sparked the Civil War, and Seeded Civil Rights* (2006) provides information about the reactions to Brown's raid.

5. "A Plea for Captain John Brown" emphasizes Brown's manhood, a theme that Thoreau had earlier stressed in "Resistance to Civil Government." Thoreau's

sense of manhood in these essays has less to do with physical strength than with courage and moral conviction. This connection between masculinity and virtue echoes the rhetoric of Thomas Paine's *Common Sense* (1776) and *The Crisis* (1776–1783); both are available online at <http://www.ushistory.org/PAINE>. Compare either Thoreau essay to one of Paine's essays in how they associate resistance to oppression with masculinity. One might also compare the historical contexts of both authors. In what ways is the controversy surrounding slavery similar to the American colonists' quest for national independence? Are these contexts different in any significant way?

REFERENCES

Primary Works
"Resistance to Civil Government," *Aesthetic Papers* (1849).

"Slavery in Massachusetts," *Liberator*, 24 (1854).

"A Plea for Captain John Brown," in *Echoes of Harper's Ferry*, edited by James Redpath (Boston: Thayer & Eldridge, 1860).

Criticism
Robert C. Albrecht, "Conflict and Resolution: 'Slavery in Massachusetts,'" *ESQ: A Journal of the American Renaissance*, 19, 72 (1973): 179–188.
Places Thoreau's 1854 address within the context of historical events and Thoreau's other political writing.

Albrecht, "Thoreau and His Audience: 'A Plea for Captain John Brown'," *American Literature: A Journal of Literary History, Criticism, and Bibliography*, 32 (January 1961): 393–402.
Examines the rhetorical devices Thoreau used in his defense of Brown to persuade a skeptical audience.

Evan Carton, "The Price of Privilege: 'Civil Disobedience' at 150," *American Scholar*, 67, 4 (Autumn 1998): 105–112.
Examines the ideological legacy of Thoreau's essay in the twentieth century.

James J. Donahue, "'Hardly the Voice of the Same Man': 'Civil Disobedience' and Thoreau's Response to John Brown," *Midwest Quarterly: A Journal of Contemporary Thought*, 48 (Winter 2007): 247–265.
Argues that Thoreau takes the abstract principles of his "Resistance" essay to a political level in his defense of Brown.

James Duban, "Conscience and Consciousness: The Liberal Christian Context of Thoreau's Political Ethics," *New England Quarterly: A Historical Review of New England Life and Letters*, 60, 2 (June 1987): 208–222.
Examines the influence of Unitarian beliefs regarding conscience on "Resistance to Civil Government."

Duban, "Thoreau, Garrison, and Dymond: Unbending Firmness of the Mind," *American Literature: A Journal of Literary History, Criticism, and Bibliography*, 57 (May 1985): 309–317.
Traces the influence of Jonathan Dymond's *Essays on the Principles of Morality* on Thoreau's and William Lloyd Garrison's belief in nonviolent protest against slavery.

Jason Haslam, "'They Locked the Door on My Meditations': Thoreau and the Prison House of Identity," *Genre: Forms of Discourse and Culture*, 35 (Fall–Winter 2002): 449–478.
Examines "Civil Disobedience" within the context of the American prison system and its effects on reform, society, and the individual.

Barry Kritzberg, "Thoreau, Slavery, and Resistance to Civil Government," *Massachusetts Review: A Quarterly of Literature, the Arts and Public Affairs*, 30 (Winter 1989): 535–565.
Discusses Thoreau's political essays in connection to his conflicts with government.

Deak Nabers, "Thoreau's Natural Constitution," *American Literary History*, 19 (Winter 2007): 824–848.
Analyzes Thoreau's use of natural law in his political writings to argue against slavery and his recognition of its limitations.

Sandra Harbert Petrulionis, "Editorial Savoir Faire: Thoreau Transforms His Journal into 'Slavery in Massachusetts,'" *Resources for American Literary Study*, 25, 2 (1999): 206–231.
Describes how Thoreau revised his journal notes into the speech "Slavery in Massachusetts" and deleted incendiary passages in order to appeal to his listeners and create a potential audience for the forthcoming *Walden*.

Manfred Steger, "Mahatma Gandhi and the Anarchist Legacy of Henry David Thoreau," *Southern Humanities Review*, 27, 3 (Summer 1993): 201–215.
An extended comparative analysis between the political ideals of Thoreau and Gandhi.

Barry Wood, "Thoreau's Narrative Art in 'Civil Disobedience,'" *Philological Quarterly*, 60 (Winter 1981): 105–115.
Examines Thoreau's artistic and narrative skill in his famous essay.

⸙

Henry David Thoreau, *Walden; or, Life in the Woods*
(Boston: Ticknor & Fields, 1854)

One of the major Transcendental writers, with Ralph Waldo Emerson and Margaret Fuller, Henry David Thoreau (1817–1862) was the only member of the group to be born in Concord, Massachusetts, and he will probably always be most closely associated with his birthplace because of his most famous book, *Walden* (1854), an imaginative version of his two-year stay at the shores of nearby Walden Pond. Although it is often thought of as an autobiography, *Walden* is more properly a rumination on some major Romantic themes, including our relationship to Nature, the importance of individualism, and our proper (and improper) debts to society.

Thoreau was raised in a family that valued nonconformity (his mother and aunts were active in Concord's antislavery efforts); he attended Harvard College, and after his graduation in 1837 he returned to Concord, where he spent several restive years teaching school, working in his family's pencil-making business, and surveying the nearby countryside as he puzzled over his role in a newly commercialized town. He became a protégé of Emerson, who inspired him to pursue the independent spirit already latent in him, and he was likely the one who encouraged Thoreau to begin keeping a journal of his thoughts and observations.

The reasons for Thoreau's decision to live by himself on the shores of Walden Pond will probably never be known for certain—it may have been grief over his brother John's sudden death from lockjaw in 1842, pressure to fit into society, a desire to test his notions of economic independence, or plans to write a book memorializing his brother. But in 1845 Thoreau borrowed an ax from his neighbor Bronson Alcott, cleared some trees on land that Emerson had purchased as a wood lot, and for little more than $28 built a snug 10 ft. x 15 ft. house on the shore of Walden Pond, scarcely a mile from the center of Concord. There, Thoreau conducted his experiment in "living deliberately," as he called it, from July 1845 until September 1847.

Thoreau's life at Walden is clouded by persistent myths and misconceptions. He was no hermit; he walked to town frequently to check on his parents, see friends, and conduct business, and he often enjoyed company in his Walden house. He famously claims in *Walden* to have had three chairs: one for solitude, two for friendship, and three for society. While at the pond he kept an attentive eye on the social causes most important to him, abolitionism and the war with Mexico. (During one of his trips to Concord, in July 1846, he was arrested for nonpayment of taxes as a war protest; there, he spent the night in jail that resulted in his famous essay "Resistance to Civil Government.") Nor was he a loafer; during his two years at Walden he kept voluminous notes on his observations of natural life at the pond, grew beans as a cash crop to pay for the needs he could not supply for himself, and took occasional jobs as a surveyor and handyman. He did write a book at the pond, though not intentionally the book *Walden;* instead, it was *A Week on the Concord and Merrimack Rivers* (1849), a hybrid of travel narrative and philosophy that was one of the great commercial flops in American publishing history. Though he explains in *Walden* his reason for leaving the pond—"I had several more lives to live, and could not spare any more time for that one"—some readers persist in seeing his departure as a sign of failure.

Had Thoreau succeeded in nothing else, his book *Walden,* now undisputedly one of the classics of American Romantic literature, would alone justify his sojourn at the pond. *Walden* records and dramatizes Thoreau's efforts to live richly (the financial irony runs throughout the book), purposefully, and simply, all the while appreciating and celebrating the natural environment. The book begins in rhetorically conventional ways: in a long chapter entitled "Economy," Thoreau establishes a problem, analyzes its cause, and proposes a solution. "The mass of men," Thoreau memorably declares, "lead lives of quiet desperation" and see no way out of the economic and philosophical rat race that makes them unhappy. For Thoreau as a writer the problem itself is problematic, for at least two reasons: first, because it assumes a "meanness" in his audience's lives that they might not perceive, and second, because the causes of unhappiness for Thoreau—affluence, social esteem, conventionality, respectability—would for most of his readers constitute social goods. We accept mediocrity in life only at our peril, Thoreau writes at the end of *Walden:* "There is an incessant influx of novelty into the world, and yet we tolerate incredible dullness." *Walden* chronicles, by way of example, Thoreau's own struggle to live economically, simply, and originally.

By the time *Walden* was published in 1854, Thoreau's life had changed in significant ways. He embraced abolitionism as the only solution to the evil of slavery, coming at last to admire the radical abolitionist John Brown. His scientific interest in natural history increasingly occupied his time and writings. His friendship with Emerson had cooled. What remained was his insistence on principle and a stubborn independence. By the late 1850s tuberculosis had begun to weaken him; he died in Concord in 1862 at the age of 44. Asked whether he had made his peace with God, Thoreau had reportedly quipped, "I did not know that we had quarreled."

TOPICS FOR DISCUSSION AND RESEARCH

1. The notion of an economical life, which runs throughout *Walden,* is a key issue, though not an easy one for readers to define. To be economical, Thoreau argues, with a shrewd nod toward his commercially minded readers, means to balance cost and worth—to spend not just one's money wisely but also one's time and to make those decisions consciously, not in blind conformity to social values. Since the real cost of a thing is "the amount of what I will call life which is required to be exchanged for it," it is important not to overspend, life being a limited and precious commodity. In answer to those who hold that we are trapped by certain necessities, Thoreau identifies as the only true "necessaries of life" food, clothing, shelter, and fuel. Readers have always balked at Thoreau's extremism, but his purpose seems not to reduce life to bare subsistence but to distinguish what we require (something to eat, a roof over our heads, clothing to keep us warm) from what we choose (elaborate meals, impressive houses, fashionable clothing). Consider whether Thoreau means the term "economy" literally or figuratively. For an interesting alternative economic approach to *Walden,* see Robert Gross's examination of commercialism in Concord.

2. One way to measure the development of Thoreau's argument in *Walden* is to chart how his vocabulary changes in regard to certain major themes. For instance, he begins by counseling economical living; that is, the avoidance of financially costly temptations. By chapter 11, "Higher Laws," he is examin-

ing appetite and lust, and he recommends "some new austerity" that redirects us to matters of the spirit instead of the body. Similarly, in chapter 2, "Where I Lived, and What I Lived For," he makes his famous plea, "Simplicity, simplicity, simplicity! I say, let your affairs be as two or three, and not a hundred or a thousand; instead of a million count half a dozen, and keep your accounts on your thumb-nail." Yet, he concludes *Walden* by recommending "Extravagance," not only in our expression but also in our lives. Trace Thoreau's use of certain key words, and investigate the etymology of terms like "extravagance," which means not self-indulgence but walking beyond bounds. Has Thoreau abandoned key themes like economy or simplicity by the end of *Walden*, or has he redefined them?

3. Thoreau's originality of expression can easily blind us to his extensive reading and use of sources, from Hindu scriptures to horticultural manuals. Investigate some of his sources and their effects on his thinking, distinguishing where he accepts their ideas from where he disagrees with them. Annotated editions of *Walden* such as those by Walter Harding (1995) and Jeffrey S. Cramer (2004) will help readers sort out and identify Thoreau's many allusions. Robert D. Richardson Jr.'s intellectual biography *Henry Thoreau: A Life of the Mind* (1986) traces the sources of Thoreau's ideas in his wide reading. W. Barksdale Maynard's study of the cultural significance of Walden Pond contextualizes Thoreau's particular interest in local history and geography.

4. There are many interpretations of the organization of *Walden*. Sargent Bush Jr. points out, for instance, the catechismal nature of the book, its attempts to offer a secular alternative to Calvinistic fatalism; Sherman Paul sees its structure as organic, a chronicle of Thoreau's quest for purity and rebirth. The consummate Thoreau scholar Walter Harding once identified five ways of reading *Walden:* as a nature book, a do-it-yourself manual to the simple life, a satire of modern living, a masterpiece of literary style, and a spiritual guidebook. Using a handbook of literary terms, try to categorize *Walden* by genre or by structure: is it like a sermon, a meditation, an autobiography, a dramatic monologue?

5. *Walden* has always been a controversial book, for its message and for its form. Detractors of the book continue to cite what they see as Thoreau's self-centeredness, his gender bias, and his seeming disregard for the crushing pressures of poverty, while its admirers applaud the book as an indictment of commercialism, a guidebook for environmental consciousness, and a bracing call for freedom and responsible living. What patterns emerge from the contemporary responses to *Walden*? And how is the book received differently today? In a special issue of the *Concord Saunterer* commemorating the 150th anniversary of the publication of *Walden*, a host of Thoreau scholars offer reasons for the book's relevance to modern readers, in the United States and internationally. Essay collections edited by Richard J. Schneider, Sandra Harbert Petrulionis, and Laura Dassow Walls illustrate the wide range of scholarly approaches, from the economic to the environmental to the political.

RESOURCES

Criticism

Sargent Bush Jr., "The End and Means in *Walden:* Thoreau's Use of the Catechism," *ESQ: A Journal of the American Renaissance*, 31 (First Quarter, 1985): 1–10.
Argues that Thoreau provides a secular answer to questions about the meaning of life.

Walter Harding, "Five Ways of Looking at *Walden*," *Massachusetts Review*, 4 (Autumn 1962): 149–62. Revised version at <http://www.walden.org/Institute/thoreau/about2/H/WalterHarding/FiveWays.htm> [accessed 4 November 2009].
Discusses various genres that *Walden* fits.

W. Barksdale Maynard, *Walden Pond: A History* (New York: Oxford University Press, 2004).
Traces the pond's meaning from Thoreau's time through the present, as well as the efforts to preserve Walden Woods.

Sherman Paul, "Resolution at Walden," *Accent*, 12 (1953): 101–113.
Examines the structure of *Walden* as evidence of Thoreau's personal struggle to achieve purity.

Sandra Harbert Petrulionis and Laura Dassow Walls, eds., *More Day to Dawn: Thoreau's* Walden *for the Twenty-First Century* (Amherst: University of Massachusetts Press, 2007).
Includes essays on environmentalism, women's issues, and other topics.

Biography

Robert E. Gross, "That Terrible Thoreau," in *Historical Guide to Henry David Thoreau*, edited by William E. Cain (New York: Oxford University Press, 2000), pp. 181–241.
Presents Thoreau's decisions as a response to commercialism in nineteenth-century Concord.

Walter Harding, *The Days of Henry Thoreau*, second edition (New York: Dover, 1982).
The most reliable biography of Thoreau.

Robert D. Richardson Jr., *Henry Thoreau: A Life of the Mind* (Berkeley: University of California Press, 1986).
Coordinates Thoreau's ideas with his reading.

Reference

Walter Harding and Michael Meyer, *The New Thoreau Handbook* (New York: New York University Press, 1980).
Indispensable resource for factual information about Thoreau's life, works, ideas, and sources.

The Thoreau Society <http://www.thoreausociety.org> [accessed 4 November 2009].
The official site of the Thoreau Society, containing texts, chronologies, and links.

Meyer, *Several More Lives to Live: Thoreau's Political Reputation in America* (Westport, Conn.: Greenwood Press, 1977).
Shows how Thoreau's ideas supported various political positions in the twentieth century.

Richard J. Schneider, ed., *Thoreau's Sense of Place: Essays in American Environmental Writing* (Iowa City: University of Iowa Press, 2000).
Scholarly essays examining Thoreau's environmental ideas and comparing his work to others such as Annie Dillard, Wendell Berry, William Wordsworth, and the Hudson River Painters.

"Thoreau's *Walden* in the Twenty-First Century" and "Thoreau's *Walden* in the Global Community," *The Concord Saunterer,* Special Walden Sesquicentennial Issue, new series 12/13 (2004–2005): 7–18, 19–58.
Appreciations of Thoreau's relevance today, with excellent attention to the international appeal of *Walden.*

⟡

Susan B. Warner, *The Wide, Wide World*

as Elizabeth Wetherell
(New York: Putnam, 1851 [i.e., 1850]

Born into an affluent New York family, Susan Bogert Warner (1819–1885) enjoyed a privileged childhood quite unlike the self-sacrifice and modest circumstances of her adult life, when she became one of the most prolific novelists of the nineteenth century. Her father was a successful and ambitious lawyer, and both parents doted on Susan, their first child to survive infancy. She was a precocious and bookish child, well educated in the genteel arts of music and painting, as well as in languages, mathematics, and history. Warner's young life was marked, however, by two tragedies that are mirrored in the fictional *The Wide, Wide World.* First, her mother died in 1828, when Susan was nine years old; her father brought in his sister to raise the children and manage the household. Second, the economic Panic of 1837 devastated the family finances and set her father on a downward financial spiral of lawsuits and unpaid bills. The Warners, now including a younger sister, Anna, were forced to move from their New York City mansion to a drafty farmhouse on Constitution Island, near West Point on the Hudson River; there Susan and Anna made their home for the rest of their lives.

Around 1841, Susan Warner experienced a religious conversion, and in the succeeding years she devoted herself to supporting missionary work, distributing tracts, and proselytizing in the behind-the-scenes ways open to polite women of the time. As Jane Tompkins points out, the work of evangelical Christianity gave Warner a sense of self-worth, a respite from the crushing isolation of Constitution Island, and "a sense of purpose in a society in which unmarried women frequently had no functional place." But missionary work did not pay the bills. The family's fortunes continued to decline, and in 1848, after watching their belongings being auctioned off to pay debts, Warner began writing a novel about a motherless girl caught up in an often unwelcoming web of circumstance and forced to learn the lessons of piety, self-sacrifice, and submission. Published in 1850 under the pseudonym Elizabeth Wetherell, *The Wide, Wide World* became a runaway best seller. The novel went through fourteen American editions in two years, its sales at the time exceeded only by Harriet Beecher Stowe's *Uncle Tom's Cabin*. Reprinted in England, often in pirated editions, it was translated into French, German, and Polish. Encouraged, Warner published a second religious novel about a young girl, *Queechy* (1852), which enjoyed some success. (Alexander Cowie claims that the two novels "sold an aggregate of 104,000 copies in three years.") For the remainder of her life she diligently turned out books designed to inspire and sustain the devotional life of her readers. By the time of her death in 1885, Warner had written twenty-seven novels, four volumes of biblical history, innumerable tracts and essays (some of which were published anonymously), and collaborated with Anna on four additional novels, two collections of short stories, and a children's magazine.

The plot of *The Wide, Wide World*, which borrows from evangelical rhetoric, religious tracts, the sentimental tradition, children's stories, and (though Warner would likely have denied it) the popular novel of seduction, centers on Ellen Montgomery, a ten- or eleven-year-old orphan who moves from guardian to guardian as she learns to accept her lot, find a sustaining family situation, and subjugate her personal strivings to a perfect obedience to and love for Jesus Christ. Ellen's various displacements fall into three plot lines. In the first, she is separated from her loving mother and distracted father and sent to the country while her parents journey to Europe, ostensibly to improve her mother's health. When Mrs. Montgomery dies and Mr. Montgomery is lost at sea, Ellen is left in the care of her emotionally distant aunt, Miss Fortune Emerson, and a series of father-figures, notably the kindly farm manager Mr. Van Brunt. In the second section, Ellen ingratiates herself in country society, becoming deeply involved with a wealthy local family who treats her as a sister. The Humphreys become Ellen's measure of all things good. Alice Humphreys, motherless like Ellen, is sweet, pious, and a model of loving devotion; her brother, John Humphreys, a divinity student, is heroic, moral, and passionately committed to the spiritual life. Despite his dictatorial nature, Ellen idolizes and falls in love with John, who carefully directs her intellectual and spiritual development and insists that she strive for perfect devotion to the divine. In the third section, after Alice dies and Ellen's Aunt Fortune marries Mr. Van Brunt, Ellen is sent abroad to Scotland to live with yet another surrogate family, the socially active Lindsays, whose patriarch wants Ellen to renounce her American friends, call him father, and obey him in all things. She is finally rescued by John Humphreys, who returns her to the United States, where they are married.

TOPICS FOR DISCUSSION AND RESEARCH

1. *The Wide, Wide World* was a great popular success promoting Victorian virtues of duty, self-sacrifice, and piety but tested the patience of reviewers. *The Literary World,* for instance, called it "a very excellent example of the now common class of religious novels" but found the story too "diffuse." A reviewer for *Holden's Dollar Magazine,* while praising Warner's intentions, called the book's plot "disjointed and rickety" and its style "artificial and forced." Later evaluations were less measured; Alexander Cowie, for instance, in his influential *Rise of the American Novel* (1948), called Ellen "an impossible prissy" and complained that the novel had no plot, only an endless series of crises. Then as now, Warner's literary excesses have overshadowed some genuine artistic merits. Warner had a talent for creating narrative out of sometimes unpromising materials (an applesauce "bee," for example); she describes the homes, foods, and fashions of nineteenth-century America with journalistic attention to detail; and she could deftly reproduce dialect and capture local customs in ways worthy of the regionalist writers who came later in the century. How much has critical opinion of the novel changed? Examining nineteenth-century and modern evaluations of *The Wide, Wide World* may reveal some continuities among those who find it flawed on literary grounds. Students can locate early criticism of the novel in collections such as *Nineteenth Century Literature Criticism.* Modern critics who can look past the sentimentalism and melodrama that characterize the novel (and much of nineteenth-century fiction) tend to center their discussion instead on matters of genre, ideology, gender, and intent.

2. Debates over the appropriate genre of *The Wide, Wide World* are long-standing. Most critics in her own time and today place Warner's narrative in the category of domestic fiction, but definitions of the domestic novel vary. Edward Halsey Foster calls it "a type of didactic novel that preached the virtues of family life," while Nina Baym broadens the genre to include novels with "a setting chiefly within ordinary people's homes and a plot made up of incidents that were appropriate to such a setting." Baym also raises the possibility that *The Wide, Wide World* can be seen as a "national novel" that defined the American experience for readers abroad. For Tompkins, the novel is a "bildungsroman in reverse": "Instead of initiating her into society, the heroine's experience teaches her how to withdraw into the citadel of herself." Apply a working definition of domesticity or the initiation novel to the plot of *The Wide, Wide World* as a way of analyzing its success.

3. Discussions of gender and nationality raise other important issues of ideology and culture. Warner's novel dramatizes a host of Victorian religious and social ideals, but does it support them or subvert them? There seems little doubt that Warner sincerely wanted to promote devotion and submission to divine will. Yet, modern critics point out in Ellen's experience some of the more troubling aspects of domination and submission, particularly in a story of a young girl forced to submit to the will of older men who frequently try to kiss her. Choose some ideological component of gender construction in Victorian America—piety, or maternalism, or gracefulness—and examine whether it is confirmed or tested in the novel. Grace Ann Hovet and Theodore R. Hovet

argue, for instance, that *The Wide, Wide World* critiques the male rhetoric of vision, which exercises power by imaging women as transparent and forcing Ellen to erase her selfhood as a consequence. Catharine O'Connell finds in the novel an indictment of Victorian sexual politics, particularly through the character of John Humphreys, who—as brother, teacher, minister, and husband—is a composite of oppressive male authority figures.

4. Another critical/research issue is the extent to which Ellen Montgomery's story draws on the life of Warner herself, and to what end. Consider some of the biographical parallels, perhaps focusing on Ellen's economic situation as compared to the Warners'. How useful is it to see these parallels? For a model of this approach see the essay by Jana L. Argersinger, who connects Warner to Ellen by seeing *The Wide, Wide World* not as a bildungsroman but as a Kunstlerroman, the covert story of an artist's development. To Argersinger, Ellen's striving for recognition and affection approximates the tenuous "act of authorial seduction" between antebellum women authors like Warner and the audiences they tried to cultivate.

5. A final critical issue is the enormous appeal of *The Wide, Wide World,* a flawed and lengthy novel that continues to find readers. Baym accounts for Warner's sales as part of a vogue for domestic stories that combined didactic narratives with moral suasion. Tompkins maintains that readers continue to identify with Ellen because they share her needs and fears—a sense of undeserved misfortune, for example, or a need for love and attention and the fear of losing them. Foster attributes the continuing power of *The Wide, Wide World* to Warner's "passionate conviction," which compels the reader with its sincerity. Students might examine the various explanations and use contemporary reviews and criticism to test which of the reasons seems to apply today.

RESOURCES

Biography
Anna B. Warner, *Susan Warner* (New York: Putnam, 1909).
An affectionate portrait by Susan Warner's sister, valuable particularly for its generous quotation of journal entries and letters.

Bibliography
Dorothy Hurlbut Sanderson, *They Wrote for a Living: A Bibliography of the Works of Susan Bogert Warner and Anna Bartlett Warner* (West Point, N.Y.: Constitution Island Association, 1976).
Lists all book publications by each author; valuable for tracing reprints and foreign translations; includes a brief plot summary for each book.

Criticism

Jana L. Argersinger, "Family Embraces: The Unholy Kiss and Authorial Relations in *The Wide, Wide World*," *American Literature: A Journal of Literary History, Criticism, and Bibliography*, 74, 2 (June 2002): 251–285.
Sees the emphasis on kissing and affection as a metaphor for Warner's relationship to her audience in an untested literary marketplace.

Nina Baym, *Novels, Readers, and Reviewers: Responses to Fiction in Antebellum America* (Ithaca, N.Y.: Cornell University Press, 1984).
Considers *The Wide, Wide World* in the context of other domestic novels.

Alexander Cowie, *The Rise of the American Novel* (New York: American Book Company, 1948).
An unappreciative account of the novel as a religious "rant."

Edward Halsey Foster, *Susan and Anna Warner* (New York: Twayne, 1978).
A biographical and critical study; chapter 2 is devoted to *The Wide, Wide World*—its style, themes, readership, sales, and appeal.

Grace Ann Hovet and Theodore R. Hovet, "Tableaux Vivants: Masculine Vision and Feminine Reflections in Novels by Warner, Alcott, Stowe, and Wharton," *American Transcendental Quarterly*, 7 (December 1993): 335–356.
Interprets the novel as a critique of male rhetoric of vision, which diminished women by referring to them in metaphors of transparency.

Catharine O'Connell, "'We must sorrow': Silence, Suffering, and Sentimentality in Susan Warner's *The Wide, Wide World*," *Studies in American Fiction*, 25 (Spring 1997): 21–39.
Considers the novel's examination of gender politics, especially through the oppressive character of John Humphreys, a grotesque condensation of dominating male roles in the nineteenth century.

Review of *The Wide, Wide World*, *The Literary World*, 7 (Dec. 28, 1850): 524–525.
Praises it as a religious novel but points out the unstructured plot.

Review of *The Wide, Wide World*, *Holden's Dollar Magazine*, 7 (March 1851): 136–137.
Criticizes Warner's style and the loosely constructed plot.

Jane Tompkins, "Afterword" to *The Wide, Wide World* by Susan B. Warner (New York: Feminist Press, 1987), pp. 584–608.
Argues for the novel's continuing appeal to readers as a female initiation story.

Walt Whitman, "Song of Myself"

in *Leaves of Grass,* anonymous
(Brooklyn, N.Y.: Fowler & Wells, 1855)
revised 1856, 1860–1861, 1867, 1871, 1876, 1881–1882

Walt Whitman's "Song of Myself," the centerpiece of his groundbreaking volume of poetry *Leaves of Grass,* is perhaps the most remarkable poem of nineteenth-century America. Breaking with poetic conventions of rhyme, meter, and subject matter, this sprawling epic foreshadowed the works of later American poets such as Carl Sandburg, e. e. cummings, and Allen Ginsberg. While the poem's subject is much broader than Whitman himself, it also reflects the unique personality and varied experiences of its creator.

Whitman was born Huntington, New York, in 1819 to Walter and Louisa Van Velsor Whitman. Louisa belonged to Elias Hicks's mystical Quaker sect, while Walter Sr. was a carpenter who embraced the radical philosophy of Thomas Paine and freethinking utopian reformers Frances Wright and Robert Dale Owen. The Whitmans relocated to Brooklyn in 1823, and the family's financial struggles forced them to move several times. Although his formal education ended at age eleven after only five years, Whitman was self-educated and read widely. He became a printer's apprentice for the *Patriot,* a Long Island newspaper, and later worked for the Whig weekly *Long Island Star.* He also began attending theaters and became involved in local politics. After working as a compositor in New York City, Whitman rejoined his family in Long Island in 1836 and taught intermittently there for two years. In 1838 he returned to the newspaper world; he founded the *Long Islander* in Huntington and later edited the *Aurora* in 1842 and the Brooklyn *Daily Eagle* in 1846–1848. His opposition to the conservative wing of the Democratic party and his endorsement of the Wilmot Proviso, which proposed to prohibit the expansion of slavery into new territories, led to his dismissal from the *Daily Eagle.* He moved to New Orleans and briefly served as editor of the *Crescent;* his observations of slavery there strengthened his opposition to the institution. He returned to Brooklyn in the fall of 1848 and founded the Free-Soil newspaper *The Brooklyn Freeman.*

Whitman's journalistic work did not prevent him from following his literary impulses. He published his temperance novel, *Franklin Evans; or, The Inebriate,* in 1842, though he later dismissed this work. During the early 1850s he abandoned journalism to work as a carpenter in Brooklyn; meanwhile, he began writing poetry that later appeared in *Leaves of Grass,* which he published anonymously in June 1855 at his own expense. The book included an engraving of Whitman next to the title page and contained twelve untitled poems, and one poem of over 1,300 lines that was titled "Poem of Walt Whitman, an American" in the 1856 edition of *Leaves of Grass* and "Song of Myself" in the 1860 edition of the volume. In the 1867 edition the poem was divided into fifty-two stanzas. In this poem Whitman not only explores his own identity but also sees the profound connections between himself, other humans, and the universe, a concept associated with Transcendentalism. It includes long descriptions of battles and disasters as well as depictions of fugitive slaves, workers, and various urban and natural scenes. Part of its significance lies in its explicit descriptions of sexuality, including homoeroticism, at a time when such expressions were virtually unheard of and tacitly discouraged. "Song of Myself" and the other poems included in *Leaves of Grass* were unusual for their use of free verse instead of conventional meter and end rhyme. He sent a copy to Ralph Waldo Emerson, who responded with enthusiastic praise. Whitman included Emerson's letter in the second edition of the book in 1856, which included several new poems. He republished the book six more times throughout his life, adding new poems to each edition. Not surprisingly, several critics objected to the book's sexual explicitness, including homoerotic passages that reflected his sexual orientation.

Despite his fame after publishing *Leaves of Grass*, Whitman engaged in several other lines of work. He worked briefly for the Brooklyn *Daily Times* in the late 1850s. During the Civil War he served as a nurse in Union Army hospitals in Washington, D.C.; he later drew on this experience in many of the poems from this period, which he collected in *Drum-Taps and Sequel* (1865–1866) and in his prose work *Memoranda during the War* (1876). He stayed in Washington after the war, working for the Indian Bureau until being fired on moral grounds in 1865 when Secretary of the Interior James Harlan discovered Whitman's 1860 edition of *Leaves of Grass;* he then found a job in the Attorney General's office, where he worked until 1872. Meanwhile, he published *Passage to India*, a collection of poems, in 1870 and his political essay *Democratic Vistas* in 1871. He suffered a stroke in early 1873 that paralyzed him permanently. Later that spring he visited his dying mother in Camden, New Jersey, and stayed there for the rest of his life, living with his brother George and then in his own house. In addition to republishing expanding editions of *Leaves of Grass*, Whitman published another prose work, *Specimen Days*, in 1881. At this time his work was enjoying a favorable reception in England. He died on 26 March 1892.

Two good starting points for research on "Song of Myself" are Edwin Haviland Miller's *Walt Whitman's "Song of Myself": A Mosaic of Interpretations* (1989), which includes hundreds of reviews and essays about the poem, and Ezra Greenspan's *Song of Myself: A Sourcebook and Critical Edition* (2005), which includes contemporary reviews of the poem as well as critical essays written between 1917 and 1997. Also see Joel Myerson's *Walt Whitman: A Descriptive Bibliography* (1993). Those seeking biographical information about Whitman will want to consult Justin Kaplan's *Walt Whitman: A Life* (2003).

TOPICS FOR DISCUSSION AND RESEARCH

1. Whitman's magnum opus "Song of Myself" was as much a reflection of its time as it was ahead of its time. In some ways it exemplifies Emerson's Transcendentalist ideas. For instance, Whitman's conception of the self is comparable to that expressed by Emerson in his essay *Nature*. Like Emerson, Whitman suggests that the self is not a limited, discrete center of consciousness separate from other selves or the world: "Through me the afflatus surging and surging. . . . through me the current and index." In this sense, "Song of Myself" pro-

motes the Transcendentalist notion of cosmic unity, and erases interpersonal boundaries, including those between himself and his readers, a topic discussed in Joseph Coulson's essay "The Poem Is the Body." Despite the apparent egotism of the poem's title, Whitman is trying to escape the conventional notion of the self and reach a higher level of consciousness. This notion of the self also allows Whitman to empathize with runaway slaves, prostitutes, soldiers, and other kinds of people whose experiences differ widely from his own. The connections Whitman draws between himself and others exemplify the poem's democratic spirit, an issue explored in Herbert Levine's essay "'Song of Myself' As Whitman's American Bible." In addition, the poem's representations of lower-class people have been analyzed by Barbara Clancy, Andrew Lawson, and Dana Phillips. Students might explore Whitman's journalistic career as described in Kaplan's biography to compare his attitudes toward socially marginal people in "Song of Myself" to those he expressed as a journalist.

2. In addition to escaping traditional notions of the self and empathizing with others, Whitman's poem is shaped by Transcendentalism in other ways as well. For example, it portrays life as cyclical rather than linear, a concept also espoused by Emerson and Henry David Thoreau. Rather than seeing death as the end of life, he depicts both as part of the same ever-repeating process. Moreover, with respect to religion, "Song of Myself" shares the Transcendentalists' skepticism toward organized religion, especially Christianity. For example, section 48 expresses the pantheistic notion that God is everywhere, and section 24 includes the heretical statement "the scent of these arm-pits is aroma finer than prayer." In addition, Whitman shares the optimism of Transcendentalism by repeatedly emphasizing the beauty, power, and virtue of humans and the natural world. Finally, his poem puts into practice Emerson's argument in "The American Scholar" that American writers should not simply revere and imitate the literary masterpieces of the past but should create bold, original literature. Students might compare Whitman's development of a Transcendentalist theme such as cosmic unity or the rejection of literary convention in "Song of Myself" to Thoreau's *Walden* or Emerson's "The American Scholar" address or his essay *Nature*. In what ways can you see Emerson's or Thoreau's influence on the poem? In what ways does the poem's treatment of these themes differ from these Transcendentalist texts or take those themes further?

3. In some ways, however, "Song of Myself" departs from Transcendentalism as well as Romanticism. For example, whereas Transcendentalists rarely discussed sex explicitly, Whitman frequently and openly celebrates the beauty of both male and female sexuality. Daneen Wardrop argues that the poem celebrates the joy of pregnancy. More generally, Whitman rejects the Christian notion that equates the body with sin, and frequently glorifies the body, a topic examined by many scholars, such as Taylor Hagood, who analyzes the poem's hair and feet imagery. Even more unusual for its time is the poem's explicit homoeroticism. One interesting essay topic would be analyzing Whitman's depiction of homoeroticism within the context of the predominant attitudes toward homosexuality in Whitman's time. The poem also differs from most Romantic literature, which either neglects urban life or depicts it as a place to escape

from in order to commune with nature. In contrast, while "Song of Myself" often celebrates the beauty of nature, it also includes several extended descriptions of urban life that emphasize its vitality and its variety of humanity.

4. The formal characteristics of Whitman's poem are as innovative as its treatment of sexuality and his focus on urban life. His rejection of rhyme and regular meter in this and other poems foreshadowed the development of free verse in the twentieth century, when the term was first coined. Many readers struggle with the poem's unusual grammar and diction, a challenge addressed in Gayle Smith's essay "Reading 'Song of Myself.'" The poem also stands out in the irregular length of its lines, which sometimes continue past the right margin. The line lengths and free verse give the poem an "organic" feel and also resemble prose rather than conventional poetry. One might compare the free verse and long lines of "Song of Myself" to the works of twentieth-century American poets Carl Sandburg and Allen Ginsberg. The poem is also structured more loosely than most Romantic poetry, which often grouped lines into stanzas of regular length. The first three editions of the poem were not divided into sections, and when it was divided into sections in the 1867 edition of *Leaves of Grass*, the sections shared no patterns regarding length. However, the poem often uses parallel structures within sections that give them a sense of unity. Why might Whitman have altered the structure in his revisions?

RESOURCES

Biography
Justin Kaplan, *Walt Whitman: A Life* (New York: Simon & Schuster, 1980).
A reliable biography of Whitman.

Bibliography
Joel Myerson, *Walt Whitman: A Descriptive Bibliography* (Pittsburgh: University of Pittsburgh Press, 1993).
The definitive primary bibliography.

Criticism
Barbara M. Clancy, "'If He Be Not Himself the Age Transfigured': The Poet, the 'Cultivating Class,' and Whitman's 1855 'Song of Myself,'" *Walt Whitman Quarterly Review*, 14 (Summer 1996): 21–38.
Analyzes Whitman's depictions of the working classes and his attempts to transcend social divisions.

Joseph Coulson, "The Poem Is the Body: Pronominal Relation in 'Song of Myself,'" in *Walt Whitman of Mickle Street: A Centennial Collection*, edited by Geoffrey M. Sill (Knoxville: University of Tennessee Press, 1994), pp. 123–128.
Analyzes Whitman's use of pronouns to engage readers.

Ezra Greenspan, ed., *Walt Whitman's 'Song of Myself': A Sourcebook and Critical Edition* (New York: Routledge, 2005).
Contains contextual documents, contemporary reviews and essays, twentieth-century essays, a bibliography, and the 1881–1882 edition of the poem.

Taylor Hagood, "Hair, Feet, Body, and Connectedness in 'Song of Myself,'" *Walt Whitman Quarterly Review*, 21 (Summer 2003): 25–34.
Examines how Whitman uses images of hair and feet to resolve the tensions between celebrating individuality and promoting democracy.

Bill Hardwig, "Walt Whitman and the Epic Tradition: Political and Poetical Voices in 'Song of Myself,'" *Walt Whitman Quarterly Review*, 17 (Spring 2000): 166–188.
Examines how Whitman manipulates the conventions of ancient epic poetry and challenges its authority as well as conservative political rhetoric of his day.

Donald D. Kummings, ed., *Approaches to Teaching Whitman's* Leaves of Grass (New York: Modern Language Association of America, 1990).
Includes five essays discussing "Song of Myself" from a pedagogical perspective.

Andrew Lawson, "'Song of Myself' and the Class Struggle in Language," *Textual Practice*, 18 (Autumn 2004): 377–394.
Examines the poem's use of language associated with various socioeconomic classes.

Herbert J. Levine, "'Song of Myself' as Whitman's American Bible," *Modern Language Quarterly: A Journal of Literary History*, 48 (June 1987): 145–161.
Examines the poem's use of Biblical genres and its promotion of democratic values.

Levine, "Union and Disunion in 'Song of Myself,'" *American Literature: A Journal of Literary History, Criticism, and Bibliography*, 59 (December 1987): 570–589.
Reads Whitman's poem within the context of political debates over national unity, secession, and slavery.

Edwin Haviland Miller, *Walt Whitman's "Song of Myself": A Mosaic of Interpretations* (Iowa City: University of Iowa Press, 1989).
Includes the 1855 edition of the poem and excerpts from almost three hundred reviews and essays about it.

Dana Phillips, "Whitman and Genre: The Dialogic in 'Song of Myself,'" *Arizona Quarterly: A Journal of American Literature, Culture, and Theory*, 50 (Autumn 1994): 31–58.
Reads Whitman's poem through the lens of Mikhail Bakhtin's theory of "dialogic" literature, which includes interaction among voices representing various social classes.

Gayle L. Smith, "Reading 'Song of Myself': Assuming What Whitman Assumes," *American Transcendental Quarterly*, 6 (September 1992): 151–161.
Discusses the interpretive challenges posed by the poem's grammar and diction.

Daneen Wardrop, "Whitman as Furtive Mother: The Supplementary *Jouissance* of the 'Ambushed Womb' in 'Song of Myself,'" *Texas Studies in Literature and Language*, 40 (Summer 1998): 142–157.
Analyzes images of birth and gestation in the poem and argues that they reveal Whitman's desire for the pleasure of pregnancy.

Part IV
Annotated Bibliography

Eberhard Alsen, ed., *The New Romanticism: A Collection of Critical Essays* (New York: Garland, 2000).
Traces the resurgence of Romanticism in contemporary fiction, with essays by writers such as Saul Bellow, Toni Morrison, and Thomas Pynchon. A valuable introduction summarizes the changing connotations of Romanticism in world literature since the seventeenth century.

The Web of American Transcendentalism <http://www.vcu.edu/engweb/transcendentalism/index.html> [accessed 22 December 2009].
Founded by Professor Ann Woodlief of Virginia Commonwealth University, this site contains links to online information about the Transcendentalists under four main categories: Authors and Texts, Roots and Influences, Ideas and Thought, and Criticism. Includes postings of student work.

William L. Andrews, ed., *Literary Romanticism in America* (Baton Rouge: Louisiana State University Press, 1981).
Includes seven essays focusing on the Romantic elements in the works of Ralph Waldo Emerson and Nathaniel Hawthorne, early African-American fiction, and the concept of the "self-made man" in American autobiography.

Andrews, *To Tell a Free Story: The First Century of Afro-American Autobiography, 1760–1865* (Urbana: University of Illinois Press, 1986).
Analyzes the freedom and constrictions facing authors of slave narratives and other African American autobiographies.

Paula Bernat Bennett, *Poets in the Public Sphere: The Emancipatory Project of American Women's Poetry, 1800–1900* (Princeton: Princeton University Press, 2003).
Examines how women writers explored and debated the issues of women's rights in the poetry they published in American magazines and newspapers.

R. J. M. Blackett, *Building an Antislavery Wall: Black Americans in the Atlantic Abolitionist Movement, 1830–1860* (Baton Rouge: Louisiana State University Press, 1983).
Examines the roles of African-American abolitionists in the transatlantic abolitionist movement.

Walter Blair, *Native American Humor* (New York: American Book Company, 1937).
An anthology with critical introductions.

Paul F. Boller Jr., *American Transcendentalism, 1830–1860: An Intellectual Inquiry* (New York: Putnam, 1974).
Traces the development of American Transcendentalism and its religious, philosophical, and social origins.

Lawrence Buell, *Literary Transcendentalism: Style and Vision in the American Renaissance* (Ithaca, N.Y. & London: Cornell University Press, 1973).

A landmark study of Transcendentalist literary achievement in nonfiction prose, "through a combination of intellectual history, critical explication, and genre study."

Buell, *New England Literary Culture from Revolution through Renaissance* (New York & Cambridge, England: Cambridge University Press, 1986).
Examines the development of literary institutions and their effects on authors such as Emerson, Henry David Thoreau, Hawthorne, Harriet Beecher Stowe, and Emily Dickinson.

Scott E. Casper et al., eds., *The Industrial Book, 1840–1880*, volume 3 of *A History of the Book in America* (Chapel Hill: University of North Carolina Press, 2007).
Authoritative essays on various topics in book history, including discussions of manufacturing, publishing, authorship, copyright, and reading patterns.

Phyllis Cole, *Mary Moody Emerson and the Origins of Transcendentalism: A Family History* (New York: Oxford University Press, 1998).
Analyzes the foundational contribution of Ralph Waldo Emerson's aunt to his thinking and to the development of Transcendentalism in New England.

Leslie Fiedler, *Love and Death in the American Novel*, 1960; revised edition (New York: Stein & Day, 1966).
A groundbreaking study premised on "the failure of the American fictionist to deal with adult heterosexual love and his consequent obsession with death, incest and innocent homosexuality," with important discussions of James Fenimore Cooper and Edgar Allan Poe.

Michael T. Gilmore, *American Romanticism and the Marketplace* (Chicago & London: University of Chicago Press, 1985).
An economic approach to the work of Emerson, Thoreau, Hawthorne, and Herman Melville, arguing that the antebellum shift from an agrarian to a market economy resulted in ambivalence of authors to the commodification of literature, as well as their complicity with market forces.

Paul Gilmore, *The Genuine Article: Race, Mass Culture, and American Literary Manhood* (Durham, N.C.: Duke University Press, 2001).
Examines the relationships between antebellum American literature and mass culture, and examines how ideologies of race and class helped shape how male authors constructed identities of literary masculinity.

Len Gougeon, *Virtue's Hero: Emerson, Antislavery, and Reform* (Athens & London: University of Georgia Press, 1990).
A convincing study of Emerson's activism, and by implication the ways Transcendentalism encouraged abolitionist reform.

Bruce Greenfield, *Narrating Discovery: The Romantic Explorer in Literature, 1790–1855* (New York: Columbia University Press, 1992).
Considers the effect of Manifest Destiny on the writing of Washington Irving, Poe, and Thoreau, among others.

Philip F. Gura, *American Transcendentalism: A History* (New York: Hill & Wang, 2007).
An essential introduction to the movement as a conscious redirection of the American democratic experiment, placing authority in the human heart. Detailed and grounded in individual thinkers and their lives.

Robert D. Habich, *Transcendentalism and the* Western Messenger: *A History of the Magazine and its Contributors, 1835–1841* (Rutherford, N.J.: Fairleigh Dickinson University Press, 1985).
Examines the magazine as a seriatim definition of Transcendentalism and a barometer of the changing responses to it.

Daniel Walker Howe, *What Hath God Wrought: The Transformation of America, 1815–1848* (New York: Oxford University Press, 2007).
A comprehensive social history of the United States between the War of 1812 and the Mexican-American War, emphasizing developments in literature, industry, technology, reform, religion, and politics.

Jennifer A. Hurley, *American Romanticism* (Chicago: Greenhaven, 2000).
A collection of articles that places Romanticism within social, political, literary, and philosophical contexts.

Aaron Kramer, *The Prophetic Tradition in American Poetry, 1835–1900* (Rutherford, N.J.: Fairleigh Dickinson University Press, 1968).
Examines the role of major Romantic poets in addressing key social issues, including the war with Mexico, the Fugitive Slave Law of 1850, and the mistreatment of Native Americans.

A. Robert Lee, ed., *Nineteenth-Century American Poetry* (Totowa, N.J.: Barnes & Noble / London: Vision Press, 1985).
An important collection of essays focused on Romantic verse.

Maurice S. Lee, *Slavery, Philosophy, and American Literature, 1830–1860* (Cambridge, England: Cambridge University Press, 2005).
Analyzes the impact of the slavery controversy on mid-nineteenth-century American literature and argues that those texts tried and failed to resolve that conflict.

David Leverenz, *Manhood and the American Renaissance* (Ithaca, N.Y.: Cornell University Press, 1989).
Examines the development of masculine literary identities by several American Renaissance authors.

R. W. B. Lewis, *The American Adam: Innocence, Tragedy, and Tradition in the Nineteenth Century* (Chicago & London: University of Chicago Press, 1955).
Traces the development of a mythic figure that directed and embodied nineteenth-century American culture, "a figure of heroic innocence and vast potentialities," with attention to Romantic writers such as Emerson, Thoreau, and Hawthorne. Includes his famous distinctions among the parties of Hope, Memory, and Irony.

Jerome Loving, *Lost in the Customhouse: Authorship in American Literature* (Iowa City: University of Iowa Press, 1993).
Argues for the thematic connections among twelve canonical authors and their representative texts, grouped roughly into earlier writers who explored themes of innocence, purity, and individualism and later writers who explored the individual's immersion in social circumstances. Extends Romanticism to such authors as Henry James, Mark Twain, Kate Chopin, and Theodore Dreiser.

Leo Marx, *The Machine in the Garden: Technology and the Pastoral Ideal in America* 1964; Thirty-Fifth Anniversary Edition (New York: Oxford University Press, 2000).
Examines the contradictory attitudes expressed in nineteenth-century American writing toward pastoralism and mechanization, with special reference to Romantic authors.

F. O. Matthiessen, *American Renaissance: Art and Expression in the Age of Emerson and Whitman* (London: Oxford University Press, 1941).
A key text in the scholarship of American literature that defines the American Renaissance as a coherent literary period and examines the connections among the period's canonical texts.

Walter Benn Michaels and Donald E. Pease, eds., *The American Renaissance Reconsidered* (Baltimore: Johns Hopkins University Press, 1985).
A collection of seven essays that examine the American Renaissance from a revisionist perspective.

Perry Miller, *Errand into the Wilderness* (Cambridge, Mass. & London: Belknap Press of Harvard University Press, 1956).
Includes Miller's famous essay "From Edwards to Emerson," which traces the line of descent from eighteenth-century mysticism to the Transcendentalists.

Miller, *Nature's Nation* (Cambridge, Mass.: Belknap Press of Harvard University Press, 1967).
Includes essays on Romanticism and Transcendentalism by one of the premier intellectual historians of the mid twentieth century, including "Emersonisan Genius and the American Democracy," "Melville and Transcendentalism," and "The Romantic Dilemma in American Nationalism and the Concept of Nature."

Barbara Packer, *The Transcendentalists* (Athens: University of Georgia Press, 2007).
A thoughtful and gracefully written introduction, focusing on social and religious reform. Originally published in *The Cambridge History of American Literature*, volume 2, edited by Sacvan Bercovitch (New York: Cambridge University Press, 1995).

Donald E. Pease, *Visionary Compacts: American Renaissance Writings in Cultural Context* (Madison: University of Wisconsin Press, 1987).
Reads the canonical texts of the American Renaissance within the cultural context of the nineteenth century and traces how critical analyses of these texts during the mid twentieth century reversed nineteenth-century readings of these works.

Timothy B. Powell, *Ruthless Democracy: A Multicultural Interpretation of the American Renaissance* (Princeton: Princeton University Press, 2000).
Examines the competing forms of nationalism (expansionist and nativist) in mid-nineteenth-century history and literature with special focus on the works of Stowe, William Wells Brown, and John Rollin Ridge as well as Hawthorne, Thoreau, and Melville.

Angela G. Ray, *The Lyceum and Public Culture in the Nineteenth-Century United States* (East Lansing: Michigan State University Press, 2005).
Argues for the increasing commercialization of the lyceum movement.

David S. Reynolds, *Beneath the American Renaissance: The Subversive Imagination in the Age of Emerson and Melville* (New York: Knopf, 1988).
Explores the connections between popular nonliterary texts and the canonical works of the American Renaissance.

Anne C. Rose, *Transcendentalism as a Social Movement, 1830–1850* (New Haven, Conn. & London: Yale University Press, 1981).
Considers the public and private reformist activities of Bronson Alcott, Orestes Brownson, George Ripley, Margaret Fuller, and Elizabeth Peabody, whose social experiments were an outgrowth of their liberal Unitarianism. Especially good on Brook Farm, the Fruitlands community, economic reform, and changing domestic relationships.

Constance Rourke, *American Humor: A Study of the National Character* (New York: Harcourt, Brace, 1931).
An influential argument that humor's function is to create social cohesion among a disunited people by depicting American types. Includes discussions of the Southwestern humorists.

Joan Shelley Rubin, *Songs of Ourselves: The Uses of Poetry in America* (Cambridge, Mass. & London: Belknap Press of Harvard University Press, 2007).
Situates poetry in the emotional and social lives of Americans, largely from 1880 to the 1950s but with intriguing implications for the lasting influence of Romantic poetry.

Jeffrey Steele, *The Representation of the Self in the American Renaissance* (Chapel Hill: University of North Carolina Press, 1986).
Examines the rhetorical strategies used by Emerson, Thoreau, Fuller, and Walt Whitman to depict the self, with a discussion of the reaction by Poe, Hawthorne, and Melville.

Helen Thomas, *Romanticism and Slave Narratives: Transatlantic Testimonies* (Cambridge, England: Cambridge University Press, 2000).
Explores connections between Romantic literature and antislavery discourse, including early slave narratives.

Jane Tompkins, *Sensational Designs: The Cultural Work of American Fiction 1790–1860* (New York & Oxford, England: Oxford University Press, 1985).

Examines canonized and noncanonical literature as "agents of cultural transformation rather than as objects of interpretation and appraisal" to show how Romantic fiction appealed to readers' needs to understand and cope with their times.

Joseph Urgo, "Capitalism, Nationalism, and the American Short Story," *Studies in Short Fiction*, 35, 4 (Fall 1998): 339–353.
Argues that the American short story is a capitalist art form.

Arthur Voss, *The American Short Story: A Critical Survey* (Norman: University of Oklahoma Press, 1973).
Traces the development of the short story in America through its major nineteenth-century subgenres—folktale, allegory, romance, horror, mystery, regional humor, and local color—as embodied in the work of Irving, Hawthorne, Melville, Poe, Twain, Bret Harte, and other prominent authors.

Robert Weisbuch, *Atlantic Double-Cross: American Literature and British Influence in the Age of Emerson* (Chicago & London: University of Chicago Press, 1986.)
Examines American redefinition of the relationship with British culture during the Romantic period, which results in an "aggressive, parodic response" to British writers.

René Wellek, "The Concept of 'Romanticism' in Literary History: The Term 'Romantic' and Its Derivatives," *Comparative Literature*, 1, 1 (Winter 1949): 1–23.
An important essay that explores the history of the term "Romanticism" in European literature and defines Romanticism as reactive, "a movement which rejected the critical concepts and poetic practice of the eighteenth century."

Edmund Wilson, *Patriotic Gore: Studies in the Literature of the American Civil War* (New York: Oxford University Press, 1962).
A classic history of literary activity in the 1850s and 1860s, with useful commentary on Harriet Beecher Stowe and George Washington Harris.

R. Jackson Wilson, *Figures of Speech: American Writers and the Literary Marketplace, from Benjamin Franklin to Emily Dickinson* (New York: Knopf, 1989).
Examines how five American authors worked out their relationship to the literary marketplace by defining what it meant to be a writer; includes chapters on Garrison, Emerson, and Dickinson.

Ronald J. Zboray, *A Fictive People: Antebellum Economic Development and the American Reading Public* (New York: Oxford University Press, 1993).
Traces patterns in publication, taste, reading habits, and book distribution.

Part V
Glossary

Cult of True Womanhood: A term used by historian Barbara Welter in 1966 to describe the main characteristics attributed to "true" women in America from roughly 1820 to 1860: piety, purity, submissiveness, and domesticity.

Daguerreotype: An early type of photography developed in France in 1839, in which an image was exposed directly onto a polished silver surface.

Didacticism: In literature, the use of texts to teach moral lessons. Edgar Allan Poe famously criticized "the heresy of the Didactic" in his essay "The Poetic Principle," where he claimed that the worth of a literature text should be measured by beauty, not truth.

Domestic fiction: One of the most popular literary genres of the day, domestic fiction was sentimental and moralistic, often depicted young women facing and overcoming obstacles, and was written primarily for young female readers. Many authors of such fiction were women.

Doppelgänger: A character that strongly resembles another character in a literary text; a common feature of Gothic literature.

Framed tale: A story within a story reported by an outside narrator, in which the differences between the two narrators are revealed. Especially prevalent in works by the Southwestern humorists, who used it to highlight the different sensibilities of urban and rural Americans.

Higher criticism: A method of biblical analysis, developed in Germany but prevalent in the United States after the 1820s, which treated the Bible as a historical document whose stories were open to human interpretation. Higher Criticism was favored among the Transcendentalists, who found it congenial to the idea of the individualistic search for truth.

Literary nationalism: The promotion of a literature written by Americans, using American themes, language, and settings. Though the movement dates to the 1780s, it endured into the Romantic era, finding expression in Emerson's "Phi Beta Kappa" address of 1837.

Lyceum movement: Developed in the 1830s as a form of adult education, in which local lyceum societies would sponsor the discussion and debating of current issues and ideas. By mid century the local lyceums had become venues for traveling lecturers such as Ralph Waldo Emerson and Frederick Douglass.

Lyric poetry: The most common poetic form in Romanticism, expressing the perspectives, moods, and emotions of a single narrator (often love or grief) and stressing the interplay of sound and meter.

Manifest Destiny: A term that gained currency in the 1840s to describe the perceived right of Anglo-Americans to expand their political and cultural control across the North American continent.

Noble savage: The concept that Native Americans and other nonwhite people possessed an inherent goodness despite their lack of education or familiarity with white civilization and institutions. James Fenimore Cooper's heroic Chingachgook is perhaps the most famous expression of the noble savage in American Romantic literature.

Popular sovereignty: A policy regarding the question of whether slavery would be permitted in the Kansas-Nebraska territory during the mid 1850s. Under popular sovereignty, settlers would decide the slavery question by majority rule.

Reason: Often used by Romantics to designate the higher faculty of intuition, as opposed to Understanding, which was associated with the lower faculty of sensory perception and logical connection. The distinction was famously developed by the British poet Samuel Taylor Coleridge but adopted by writers such as Ralph Waldo Emerson.

Romance: As a genre, often distinguished from the more realistic and "middle class" novel by its emphasis on mystery (especially hidden identities), exotic settings, extremism in plot and character, the impingement of the supernatural, and a fascination with the struggle of evil and good. The Romancer, Hawthorne asserted in the Custom House introduction to *The Scarlet Letter*, requires a "neutral territory, somewhere between the real world and fairyland, where the Actual and the Imaginary may meet."

Romantic racialism: A phrase coined by George Fredrickson to describe a set of racial stereotypes and condescending attitudes regarding persons of African descent that was popular among Northern whites in nineteenth-century America. Most commonly, Romantic racialism portrayed black people as naturally musical, good-natured, religious, superstitious, simple, loyal, or docile.

Scottish "common sense" philosophy: An important influence on nineteenth-century American literary criticism. Eighteenth-century Scottish philosophers such as Thomas Reid believed that objects exist in reality and that humans perceive them directly, in contrast to idealists, who argued that nothing exists outside of the human mind. This pragmatic philosophy led many American literary critics to value simplicity, plausibility, and intelligibility in literary works.

Separate spheres: A widespread belief in nineteenth-century America that women belonged to the domestic sphere while men belonged in the public sphere, and that women should not try to step beyond their proper place. This idea was paralleled by a belief that men and women were fundamentally different in terms of behavior and temperament.

Transcendental controversy: A debate, crystallized in the reaction to Emerson's 1838 "Divinity School Address," over the importance of miracles to validate Christianity. More traditional Unitarians believed that biblical miracles were necessary to prove the divinity of Jesus; Transcendentalists tended to see the miraculous in everyday life, not in the historical past, and to locate the authority of religion in the individual conscience, not in scripture.

Trickster figure: A magical character in Native American oral tales, where he may be comic or serious, mischievous or avenging, human or divine or shape-shifting. The term is also sometimes applied to certain characters in the Southwestern humor tradition, such as George Washington Harris's Sut Lovingood.

Unitarianism: A liberalizing of traditional Calvinist doctrines, especially of original sin and the divinity of Jesus. Unitarianism developed in the late eighteenth century and was valued by the Transcendentalists for its belief in human beings' "likeness to God," in the benevolence of the divine, and in the view that Jesus was a moral example. Eventually, many Transcendentalists came to disagree with what they considered Unitarianism's rationalism and emphasis on scripture.

Index